Reshaping Beloved Community

THE AFRICANA EXPERIENCE AND CRITICAL LEADERSHIP STUDIES

Series Editors: Abul Pitre, PhD, North Carolina A&T State University; Comfort Okpala, PhD, North Carolina A&T State University

Through interdisciplinary scholarship, this book series explores the experiences of people of African descent in the United States and abroad. This series covers a wide range of areas that include but are not limited to the following: history, political science, education, science, health care, sociology, cultural studies, religious studies, psychology, hip-hop, anthropology, literature, and leadership studies. With the addition of leadership studies, this series breaks new ground, as there is a dearth of scholarship in leadership studies as it relates to the Africana experience. The critical leadership studies component of this series allows for interdisciplinary, critical leadership discourse in the Africana experience, offering scholars an outlet to produce new scholarship that is engaging, innovative, and transformative. Scholars across disciplines are invited to submit their manuscripts for review in this timely series, which seeks to provide cutting edge knowledge that can address the societal challenges facing Africana communities.

Titles in this Series

Survival of the Historically Black Colleges and Universities: Making it Happen
Edited by Edward Fort
Engaging the Diaspora: Migration and African Families
Edited by Pauline Ada Uwakweh, Jerono P. Rotich, and Comfort O. Okpala
Africana Islamic Studies
Edited by James L. Conyers and Abul Pitre
Improving the Perception and Viability of HBCUs: A 360 Degree Perspective
Edited by Kimberly Y. Walker and Comfort O. Okpala
Reshaping Beloved Community: The Experiences of Black Male Felons and Their Impact on Black Radical Traditions
By Marlon A. Smith

Reshaping Beloved Community

The Experiences of Black Male Felons and Their Impact on Black Radical Traditions

Marlon A. Smith

LEXINGTON BOOKS
Lanham • Boulder • New York • London

Published by Lexington Books
An imprint of The Rowman & Littlefield Publishing Group, Inc.
4501 Forbes Boulevard, Suite 200, Lanham, Maryland 20706
www.rowman.com

6 Tinworth Street, London SE11 5AL, United Kingdom

British Library Cataloguing in Publication Information Available

Library of Congress Cataloging-in-Publication Data
Names: Smith, Marlon A., 1972- author.
Title: Reshaping beloved community : the experiences of Black male felons and their impact on Black radical traditions / Marlon A. Smith.
Description: Lanham, Maryland : Lexington Books, 2018. | Includes bibliographical references and index.
Identifiers: LCCN 2018036975 (print) | LCCN 2018039026 (ebook) | ISBN 9781498569347 (electronic) | ISBN 9781498569330 (cloth : alk. paper)
Subjects: LCSH: Prisons and race relations—United States. | African American men—Effect of imprisonment on. | African American prisoners—Social conditions. | African American radicals. | Imprisonment—Social aspects—United States. | Criminal justice, Administration of—Social aspects—United States.
Classification: LCC HV6197.U5 (ebook) | LCC HV6197.U5 S65 2018 (print) | DDC 365.608996073—dc23
LC record available at https://lccn.loc.gov/2018036975

™ The paper used in this publication meets the minimum requirements of American National Standard for Information Sciences—Permanence of Paper for Printed Library Materials, ANSI/NISO Z39.48-1992.

Printed in the United States of America

Contents

Introduction

> When the high priest and his associates arrived, they called together the Sanhedrin—the full assembly of the elders of Israel—and sent to the jail for the apostles. But on arriving at the jail, the officers did not find them there. So they went back and reported, "we found the jail securely locked, with the guards standing at the doors; but when we opened them, we found no one inside." On hearing this report, the captain of the temple guard and the chief priests were puzzled, wondering what would come of this. Then someone came and said, "Look! The men you put in jail are standing in the temple courts teaching the people."
>
> —Acts 5:21b–26, New International Version

This project does not emerge from a book on incarceration or a theory about incarceration; rather, it emerges from my experience as a practitioner in the field of prisoner reentry for a faith based pre-release prison reentry program.[1] Indeed, while working as a theologian in the area of social and restorative justice for over fifteen years with over seven years directly in the area of prison reentry, I had become increasingly concerned about the lack of attention paid to those labeled felon in both sacred and secular communities of the United States. In my years as a prison reentry professional I continually encountered resistance from black community and civic leaders, historically black institutions, and various individuals in the black community when it came to addressing the problems faced by black felons in particular.

I found relatively few people and organizations willing to invest in helping ex-offenders find jobs, housing, education, counseling and other resources. For instance historically black colleges and universities in the area hesitated to extend college classes and admission opportunities to the men in our prison. Moreover, many of these HBCUs invested little effort in helping ex-offenders attend their schools post-incarceration. In addition, the decrease in federal funding for college education for offenders both inside and outside of prison helped to solidify their station in society as second-class citizens.

Even more disturbing to me was the difficulty and often times unwillingness of black churches and their members to address the structural problems that African Americans with felony convictions face in society. Often times their engagement with incarcerated men in my prison was restricted to prison worship services or bible studies. Admittedly, some churches participated in buying Christmas toys for children whose parents were incarcerated. Yet rarely did any of these churches or community members work to address the structural impediments that limit felon opportunities post-incarceration. Even less had ministries, programs, or outreach efforts that welcomed felons back into the community.

Therefore, as a practitioner of this work I wanted to find ways to show the value black felons offer to black communities in particular and the United States society in general. Ultimately, my concern for the men, women, and children impacted by incarceration led me to investigate not simply the causes of incarceration but also why the problems that black felons faced were not being significantly addressed by institutions in the black community. In addition, I wanted to know why the ideas and practices that black people have traditionally held within community under the principles of Beloved Community as offered by Howard Thurman and Martin Luther King Jr. were not being applied when black bodies are labeled felon.

For this project, my definition of Beloved Community does not begin with King or Thurman, but rather extends further back to a form of engagement within black resistance movements that serves as the foundation of black radical thought, which undergirded King and Thurman's belief of community. This definition explains why the ideal of Beloved Community seeks to advance the radical and complete equality of all human beings.

This radical idea of complete equality is not despite our cultural and racial differences but rather illuminated by those differences, especially as it relates to race. Thus the historical and contemporary black radicals I incorporate in this book all share the idea that black culture offers a progressive representation of inclusivity and human dignity that refuses to be tainted by slavery or white supremacy—or in its now contemporary form of penal captivity. That radical thought is and has always been the Beloved Community, a transformative radical project.

However, to be fair to the contributions of King and Thurman, both men added much of the spiritual aspects specific to their own time as did Frederick Douglass, John Marrant, Prince Hall, and others. For example, King's concept of Beloved Community was influenced by Gandhi, who was also influenced by Tolstoy's *The Kingdom of God Is Within Us*. For this reason the ongoing thinking and reshaping of Beloved Community has continually reimagined radical equality to include women, poor people, and others.

I mention the historical legacy of this radical thought to point out early in this work that Beloved Community is neither a new idea nor is it static. Rather, the radical project that we know as Beloved Community grew from something specific to Black radical culture that we have seen in the work of black radicals as early as Marrant and Hall. For this reason, what we know of Beloved Community now will not and should not be what we will know of it in the future.

Ultimately, I wanted to show the great contributions that men labeled felons have offered society, as one who spent years working with men and women in prisons across Texas. Therefore, this book seeks to position black felons, particularly black male felons, and the history of black male incarceration squarely within black radical traditions in order to show how black felons in general, and black male felons in particular have been excluded from both the American political landscape and marginalized within black communal spaces.

By black radical I mean those thoughts, philosophies, and practices that articulate and advocate for deep levels of social transformation in the lives of black people. For many black radicals, particularly those I highlight in this book, such transformation only occurs through the dismantling of systems and structures. Often times these systems and structures have been used to capture black people into various institutional structures of slavery or captivity.

I explore Black radical traditions because it offers a distinct conception of being, and ultimately revolution, that is free from white Marxist analysis that tends to presume European models of history and experiences. This is crucial because European models substantively and materially downplay African American history and experiences. This is most certainly true of Black felons. Thus, as Cedric J. Robinson point out in *Black Marxism: The Making of the Black Radical Traditions*, any conversation about African American history and culture must acknowledge that black radicalism is linked to Africa and the experiences of blacks on western continents.

Therefore, I focus on black radical intellectual traditions because they house the critical thought on black people's political, religious, social, cultural, and historical experience in the United States. For instance, in "Black Studies and the Racial Mountain" Manning Marable argues that the black intellectual tradition is "the critical thought and perspectives of intellectuals of African descent and scholars of black America and Africa and the black diaspora."[2] For Marable the black intellectual tradition is characterized by: (1) its ability to describe black life by articulating black experience from black people's point-of-view, (2) its ability to correct false and racist ideas and stereotypes that devalue the full range of black humanity in society-at-large, and (3) its ability to prescribe pragmatic solutions that empower black people.

However, the material work on incarcerated black bodies is mainly absent from much of the work produced within these intellectual traditions, particularly the ability to articulate black experience from black felons' points-of-view. As such, this book builds on attorney and activist Michelle Alexander by introducing the value of black male felons' cultural production to the American political and social landscape. In *The New Jim Crow: Mass Incarceration in the Age of Colorblindness* Alexander expresses the concerns of many of us who work in the area of incarceration and reentry. She outlines the hardships that felons face post-incarceration and lays the foundation for the development of a much needed and broader conversation that targets the end of mass incarceration.

Alexander supports this goal by: 1) detailing the history, culture, and political atmosphere that gave birth to an American caste system; 2) articulating the contradictions in the war on crime, particularly drug crimes, as presented by politicians; 3) outlining how incarceration expands the disenfranchisement of felons and the disproportional impact it has on historically marginalized groups, particularly African American and communities of color. She goes on to contend that mass incarceration is "metaphorically the New Jim Crow and . . . all those who care about social justice should fully commit themselves to dismantling this new racial caste system."[3]

In the end, Alexander charges those of us concerned with this issue to do an even deeper investigation of black incarceration in order to bring greater public awareness to the problem. This book answers Alexander's charge by using the cultural production of black male felons to challenge society at large to redefine the category of felon. This redefinition process begins by inserting the felon into the black radical traditions in order to show the long-standing tradition that felons bring to black radical projects.

Therefore, in response to Alexander's challenge and in an attempt to resolve the issues I faced as a practitioner in the field, I explore the history of black male incarceration in the United States beginning in the nineteenth century. In the process of my research I realized that many black radical scholars conflate the subjective experiences of black male felons with the communal experiences of black people. In other words, many black radical scholars overlook how individual black felons' experience the world differently from black people without felonies.

This conflation of black experience is a problem because it not only denies the unique experiences of black felons in the United States, but it also marginalizes the roles black felons have played in the history of black people in the United States. Moreover, to reject the participation of black felons or to exclude black felons' unique experiences in the black community in particular and the larger society in general subverts the ideal of inclusivity that both Thurman and King envisioned for the society.

As previously stated, both Thurman and King's vision for society was encompassed in the radical theory of Beloved Community. Here again, when I speak of the Beloved Community throughout this book, I am speaking to the place where theories on human fulfillment become recognizable in the lives of people through concrete structures, institutions, and symbols. In other words, Beloved Community is a black radical product that is manifested within concrete structures, symbols, and institutions that are erected specifically to allow human beings the opportunity to flourish in life.

An example of the erection of concrete structures and symbols for the manifestation of Beloved Community can be seen in James Cone's book *The Cross and the Lynching Tree*. According to Cone, the cross and the lynching tree are examples of two concrete symbols that enable people to break their silence on race and Christianity in American history. In *The Cross and the Lynching Tree* Cone contends that "the cross placed alongside the lynching tree can help us to see Jesus in America in a new light, and thereby empower people who claim to follow him to take a stand against white supremacy and every kind of injustice."[4] For Cone, the lynching tree is a metaphor for race in America. Although, the lynching tree is a symbol of America's crucifixion of black people, it also enables a transcendent perspective to emerge that empowers people to resist oppression and affirm their humanity.

Moreover, in a conversation with Bill Moyer, Cone says that the presence of crucifixion and lynching today, is in the United States prison system. He contends that "crucifixion and lynching are symbols . . . of the power of domination . . . with black people being twelve percent of the US population and nearly 50 percent of the prison population. That is lynching."[5] In this way the prison becomes another type of deep symbol for the lynching of black bodies, and the response by black bodies to that lynching are depictions of the grotesque. They are depictions of the grotesque because they reveal both the light and the dark sides of American politics and culture.

By highlighting the cross and the lynching tree Cone also shows how the grotesque initiates deeper conversations about life and culture in United States. In *Beyond Ontological Blackness: An Essay on African American Religious and Cultural Criticism*, Victor Anderson juxtaposes the Nietzschean grotesque aesthetic to heroic racial aesthetics in Western thought in order to press beyond representations of blackness that become ontological in function. Anderson argues that "the grotesque aesthetic holds in tension the ambiguities between attraction and repulsion, and exposes both the light and dark sides of culture."[6] In other words, the grotesque aesthetic forces the viewer to recognize that a casual glance at certain depictions, actions, and representations may not be useful in helping individuals understand what is really taking place in the work of the artist.

However, unlike Anderson, I press beyond mere aesthetic features of the grotesque within cultural criticism in order to talk about the grotesque as also actions, movements, ideas, and practices that are responding to injustice and oppression. This alternate examination of the grotesque reveals a new lineage within black radical traditions, as well as the function of the prison as a key to the construction of the black male felon.

Thus, my concept of the grotesque, particularly as it will relate to Nat Turner's rebellion, is to show how the grotesque is a set of principles that underline and guide the work of certain black radicals, particularly black male felons, and their revolutionary movements. These guiding principles not only require a sustained engagement with these actions and practices in order to ensure a more profound critique of culture and politics, but also to think more critically about the principles of Beloved Community in popular social justice movements.

Ultimately, the deep symbols that emerge from Beloved Community, as a result of the grotesque, highlight the overarching political work at play in the black community's search to obtain human fulfillment. Thus, Beloved Community as a black radical product is inherently a political project because it places black cultural production in an exchange with black social and political life in order to manifest a more just society.

This type of "creative exchange" helps us see other places of human suffering and despair. Indeed, Cone uses the symbols of the cross and the lynching tree to institute a practice of creative exchange with the grotesque in his interview with Bill Moyer. In other words, creative exchange becomes the practice of taking both good and bad experiences in life and placing them in dialogue with the values, theories, hopes, and ideas that undergird how societies and cultures think about themselves as believers and purveyors of democracy and justice. These types of creative exchanges have occurred in other aspects of United States political life. For instance, the drafting and adoption of the US Constitution was a creative exchange between white land-owning men.

Yet, as Cone points out in his conversation with Moyer, often times the creative exchange among the drafters of the US Constitution was to affirm the domination and control of white people. It lacked an exchange with the grotesque. For instance, it lacked hearing the experiences of women, slaves, and indigent people. Indeed, this affirmation among white land-owning men occurs because often the creative exchange with the "cross and the lynching tree" are left out of the exchange. Cone contends that "people don't like to talk about things that is really deep and ugly."[7] However, when both the ideal symbols and the horrific symbols are placed in exchange with the theories and practices that inform a society or culture then Beloved Community is concretely manifested.

Certainly, one way the ideal of Beloved Community has exceeded its spiritual underpinnings that King, Thurman, and Cone speak to is in the way men who have been labeled felon, such as George Jackson and Lyfe Jennings, have used nonreligious strategies to further the project by striving to eradicate racism and other forms of injustice. Their writing or performance, as a form of cultural work, aspires to the goals of Beloved Community but does not enter through the churchyard or a racial apologetic identity narrative. Rather they enter through the prison yard and grotesque representations of murderers, conmen, and thugs.

The black male felon reminds us that black cultural production has historically revealed the complex experiences of black people in the United States. Thus paying greater attention to the experiences and perspectives of felons is an important project if we are to attain meaningfully inclusive goals and even expand the accepted meanings of African American culture beyond the limits by King's connection to the black church. In other words, many of the cultural products we encounter from black people in United States inevitably are tied to political dimensions that made blackness a social category in the nation—both the good and the not-so-good ones. Yet without the black felon as part of that community of exchange, we limit a political dimension within black experience.

We encounter many of these artifacts through music, books, testimonies, revolutions, churches, and other cultural artifacts. Black radical scholars such as Alain Locke, W. E. B. Du Bois, Anthony Bogues, Cornel West, and others have spoken to the historical function and importance of black cultural production in revealing the political and social theories by black radicals. Yet only when these theories are placed in an exchange with other ideas and institutions for the development of concrete structures are they made real in the lives of people. In other words, Beloved Community is manifested only when these theories are made concrete through symbols, structures, and institutions that impact the everyday lives of people—whether they convene to share ideas in the prison yard or the churchyard.

Ultimately my desire to find archival examples of intellectual work that addressed the lived experiences of black felons triggered my investigation of black radical history. I soon realized that although scholars such as Du Bois, West, Bogues, and others spoke to black experience they failed to distinguish black felons' experiences from the communal experiences of black people. The failure to differentiate the experiences of black felons has caused many scholars to overlook the contributions that black felons offer to the black community in particular and the larger community in general. In particular, they failed to investigate how black felons' cultural production such as their writings, music, resistance movements, and more articulate the black felon's experience in society, and how that is integral, in many ways, to African American experience as a whole.

This oversight of black felons' cultural production occurs in part because black life, particularly black religion, black activism, and black popular culture is largely isolated to restrictive areas of interest and academic study. In other words, the marginalization of black felons' experiences happens in large part due to a subsuming discussion on race, poverty, and gender. Although these categories give significant attention to issues of racial injustice, gender discrimination, and economic disparity they fail to provide the same level of interrogation, compassion, and care to the injustices that emerge when racial bodies are labeled felon.

To emphasize my point, here I will reiterate that cultural productions emanating from carceral space are distinct from, but in many ways mirror, the history of slavery and other forms of oppression. Later in the book, I discuss the ways that carceral space in particular can be reconfigured as a significant and creative space of production that we must not ignore if we are to fully understand the meanings of blackness in American culture. This is also vital if we are to ever move beyond some of our racist baggage to enact real creative exchange and work toward Beloved Community.

Felons are the invisible in society, including many black communities. This often occurs because within African American studies, the black church, black activism, and black popular culture, certain black figures are given greater prominence and importance. For instance, In *The New Jim Crow*, Alexander outlines the problems of black representation that arose within activist culture because of the limited work of civil rights organizations to advocate for persons labeled felon or criminals. She argues that "even at the height of Jim Crow segregation—when black men were more likely to be lynched than to receive a fair trial in the South—NAACP lawyers were reluctant to advocate on behalf of blacks accused of crimes unless the lawyers were convinced of the men's innocence."[8]

Indeed, the depiction and representation of certain black figures throughout US history belies a more subtle problem for black people that are labeled felon. With rare exceptions, it has been much more difficult to reconfigure the images of black felons to make them comfortable within a white hegemonic structure. As a result of this, it becomes necessary to fully engage black felons' writings, sermons, music, art, and other cultural production in order to understand the diverse and complex ways blackness exists in society, particularly when it juxtaposes with Black Christian iconography.

THE BLACK CHURCH AS A SITE FOR CULTURAL PRODUCTION AND BLACK REPRESENTATION

This book argues that the cultural production of black male felons is source material for black radical thought because they differentiate the experiences of black felons from the experiences of black people. Indeed, as source material for black radical history, we can better understand how black male felons addressed violence, social oppression, and other forms of discrimination in light of their incarceration and penal captivity. Ultimately, an examination of the cultural production of black male felons expands black radical scholars' notions of black radical thought and intellectual history. Moreover, by inserting the experiences and ideas of black male felons as expressed in their cultural production I am able to expand the representation within black radical history.

The expansion of black radical history occurs specifically because I place black felons in the timeline on African Americans' quest for freedom and dignity. Furthermore by placing the work of black felons in a creative exchange with American political ideas and practices I am able to include other deep symbols, such as prisons, that allow for the expansion of Beloved Community.

Thus, by including the ideas and experiences of black male felons, which are often diminished within black radical traditions, I reshape the types of representation we have available for Beloved Community. For example, by offering a reflexive look at the work of Nat Turner, it becomes clear how Turner as felon shows us the role the prison plays in the criminalization of black male bodies and the impact it has had on black radical praxis. In other words, putting Turner's rebellion in creative exchange with the prison ensures society's ability to rethink not only Turner's work, but also the role and the function of the prison in the lives of black people in the United States.

My rationale regarding Turner and other black male felons is based on the premise that a conflation of the experiences of black male felons with the more general social experiences of black people marginalizes black male felons within black life, history, and culture. Furthermore, this marginalization of the individual is antithetical to the principles of Beloved Community because it denies the inclusion of a certain experience in seeking individual human fulfillment. Moreover, the exclusion of the individual human fulfillment denies the role that experience has on the social identity of people.

Thus, it is of central importance in this book to highlight the cultural products that African American felons produce. In particular, this book looks at their prison writings, music, sermons, and more. Highlighting these cultural products within the frame of black radicalism in particular and American radicalism in general reframes black radical history to include the black felon as subject within black experience and culture.

Furthermore, by placing the cultural production of black male felons at the center of this conversation I show that Black Studies is more than merely a subcategory of some race-based ideology, but rather a critical body of scholarship that seeks to dismantle powerful racist intellectual categories and white supremacy itself. In other words, by including black male felons at the center of black radical traditions I advance the notion that Black Studies is a subversive form of inquiry into the political and social life of the United States.

Indeed, a study of cultural products by black male felons within Black studies, African American studies, Africana studies, black religious studies, black liberation theology, etc., builds on black radical intellectual work by denoting another site for its intellectual inquiry. For example, by engaging the work of black male felons, black radical scholars can see how the development of the prison industrial complex and the experiences of black people within those spaces limited black radical intellectuals' investigation of the various political and social techniques used to capture and ultimately erase certain black bodies from the American political landscape.

Ultimately, the Beloved Community as a black radical product expands as other forms of cultural production inform its history. However, the expansion of that history and American political thought that composes black radicals' notion of Beloved Community has been limited because black theologians and religious scholars in particular, and black radical scholars in general, very often don't include black felons in the tradition. In other words, the notion of Beloved Community expands when the cultural production of black male felons is placed in an exchange with other radical theory and praxis for the construction of concrete structures, symbols, and institutions.

These new structures, symbols, and institutions help manifest supportive communal interaction and individual human fulfillment to include black felons. For example, within some restorative justice communities felon paintings and stories have been used to show the impact incarceration has had on the relationship between felons and their children. As a result, programs for children and felons have been created and supported such as Angel Tree and Storybook Dad reading programs.

Although we know that Beloved Community occurs when certain radical thoughts and praxis come together in political concert to make manifest the hopes of oppressed people in society, we are still falling short. Once, again it is based largely on the way we value certain people over others. The inability to actualize concrete structures, institutions, and symbols for black felons within Beloved Community occurs because of the way many black radical intellectuals view and read black felon's cultural production. In *Black Heretics, Black Prophets: Radical Political Intellectuals*, Anthony

Bogues argues that "when we deploy the traditional method of studying ideas which searches for links, coherence and integration, regularity and linearity, it excludes from our horizon that which is different, and forces us into a false canonization process."[9]

In this same way, the current reading of black cultural production ignores the complex ways black felons work helps to shed light on the social erasure of their individual identity. It also distorts the various ways they seek to strengthen their social connectivity in the world over and against systems and structures that operate to deny their value. Felons are erased because they exist and operate under a biased intellectual canonization process.

Ultimately the canonization process within black intellectual traditions hinders opportunities for black felons to include their unique experiences within the community of voices on issues of social and political justice. As a consequence, black felons are hindered from both achieving individual fulfillment and supportive community interaction because of the ways they are currently marginalized within Beloved Community. In this way, the black felon exists in another form of isolation from black people and the broader society.

Eventually, the complex ways black felons are isolated in society led me to expand my research deeper into black life. In doing this, I soon discovered that black liberation theologians, black religious scholars, and many black radical political scholars failed to bridge the gap between black intellectual life and the work of social and restorative justice advocates to address the impact incarceration has on black felons in communities of color, particularly black male felons. Ultimately, this deeper investigation of black incarcerated males' experiences revealed that black male felons provide an alternate trajectory of thought that extends the experiences of black people past simply the discourse on racial slavery in the United States. However, like many other black radicals in history, much of the fundamental concepts that informed this thinking began with ideas about the role and the function of religion in the black religious cosmos.

Therefore, discovering that black religious thought informed these black radicals, I specifically began my quest with the black church and black religious scholars on issues of incarceration. This start was also prompted by the idea that the black church has historically been the primary tool resourced to make manifest Beloved Community. Moreover, this was important in order for me to better understand why the black church was not more engaged in the public policy and social justice conversation around incarceration.

Du Bois, West, and other black radical scholars speak to how the black church crafted and housed many of the tools used to challenge systemic injustices against black bodies throughout the history of black people in the United States. For example, in *Prophesy Deliverance!: An Afro-American*

Revolutionary Christianity, Cornel West argues that the black church "came into being when slaves decided, often at the risk of life and limb, to 'make Jesus their choice' and to share with one another their common Christian sense of purpose and Christian understanding of their circumstances."[10] Indeed, black sermons are one of many cultural products found in black churches that helped to catalyze black social justice movements and black political engagement.

The cultural products housed within black churches allowed the institution to become the arbiter for Beloved Community. It stood as the epicenter for the deployment of theories and resources for the bringing forth of Beloved Community. For these reasons, the black church stood as the leading cultural artifact for Beloved Community. Therefore, I ventured to find other cultural artifacts within black religion that might speak to the history of black incarceration. In doing this I discovered the work of Rima Vesley-Flad. She argues that "reformed theology provided justification for antebellum, postbellum, and post-Civil Rights civic leaders to implement and sustain punitive institutions of punishment that disproportionately penalized people of African descent."[11] In other words, the appropriation of Christianity by African Americans made it difficult for black churches and black religious leaders in particular to adequately address the emergence of penal institutions. This inability of the black church to construct creative ways to redress the emergence of prisons in the United States helped to reify the justification for the deployment of prisons and penal institutions.

Therefore, in spite of the growing penalization of African people through punitive institutions, the black church as a social justice agent for black people failed to produce cultural artifacts, such as sermons and songs, which clearly articulated the impact incarceration was having on the identity, voice, and personhood of those labeled felon in the United States. This prompted me to ponder if black theology, which is the systematic thinking about the liberative expression of the black church in society, was sufficiently equipped with the tools necessary to address the sustained punitive institutions that disproportionately penalized African people.

Indeed, the lack of cultural products within the black church to address the problems of incarceration inspired me to investigate how the tools produced by black male felons could influence the discourse within black religion concerning black incarceration. Vesley-Flad argues that "an alternative discourse on crime and punishment, rooted in liberal and liberation theology, has been largely absent from the public domain."[12] In other words, a theological hermeneutic that centralized the experiences of black incarcerated men and women was needed in order to expand our understanding of the role and value black felons and the cultural artifacts they produced have played in black history and culture.

BEYOND THE VEIL: A LOOK AT BLACK PRINCE HALL MASONS AND BLACK MASONIC LODGES

Ultimately, I surmised that if I could expand the cultural artifacts utilized within black religious discourse then I could begin to reframe notions within black radical intellectual traditions and advance the public discourse on penal captivity. I reasoned that this approach would more effectively speak to the challenges and experiences of black incarcerated people. In addition, I realized that the appropriation of reformed theology not only influenced the work of early black preachers within black churches, it also influenced the way black radical intellectuals engaged issues on criminal and restorative justice. For instance, the theological writings from black religious leaders in black churches took on a more apologetic function. This apologetic function helped to construct apologetic black religious figures. These apologetic figures intentionally or coincidentally worked to hide the black felon more deeply within the core of black religious institutions.

Consequently, the lack of cultural products by black felons and the growing apologetic figures within black churches made my search twofold. First it was vital to find cultural products from black felons that would expand black religious discourse. Second it was necessary to expand the types of representation available within black religion.

Burdened with this task, I began to search out other black spaces within the black religious cosmos that might more accurately represent black male felons within black radical traditions. This search led me to black masonic lodges. In *"Face Zion Forward": First Writers of the Black Atlantic, 1785–1798*, Joanna Brooks and John Saillant argue that "these lodges, like the black churches emergent in the same era, provided important resources for black political and cultural development."[13] While reading the work of black Prince Hall Masons such as Prince Hall, John Marrant, David Walker, Richard Allen, Absalon Jones, Martin Delany, and others I discovered that the black religious writings within these spaces offered a more radical idea of Christianity and black representation from those deployed within black churches.

Although, Marrant, Allen, and Jones were ministers, their work as ministers was the influence of black masonic teachings by Prince Hall. For example, on June 24, 1789, Marrant preached a sermon using Romans 12:10 as his text for the Festival of St. John the Baptist. In the heading of the sermon Marrant writes "at the request of the Right Worshipful the Grand Master Prince Hall, and the Rest of the Brethren of the African Lodge of the Honorable Society of Free and Accepted Masons in Boston."[14] Indeed, throughout the sermon Marrant makes specific claims to how his identity as a Prince Hall mason informed his thinking as a Christian minister. For instance, Marrant writes:

> These and many other duties are required of us as Christians, every one of which are like so many links of a chain, which when joined together make one complete member of Christ; this we profess to believe as Christians and as Masons.—I shall stop here with the introduction, which brings me to the points I shall endeavor to prove.—
>
> First, the anciency of Masonry, that being done, will endeavor to prove all other titles we have a just right as Masons to claim—namely, honourable, free and accepted.[15]

I soon came to understand that the cultural products produced in black churches, compared to black masonic lodges, impacted the relationship between black theological and religious discourse. This impact could be seen most sharply when I compared black human rights ideas within black churches and black radical praxis by early black radical intellectuals in black masonic lodges. Some of the differences in ideas between these two institutional spaces centered around notions of reform versus revolution, inclusion versus separation, and nonviolent resistance versus violent resistance.

Since black masonic lodges and black masons articulated a more confrontational engagement with American political structures than those publicly expressed in black churches they were often times victims of attack by white racist institutions and subject to greater forms of erasure. Brooks and Salient contend that "Prince Hall and his lodge members were lampooned in newspaper reports and caricatured in cartoons well in the nineteenth century."[16] Moreover, these same white racist institutions began to highlight black churches and promote black religious figures in order to limit black radical activities.

Yet, in spite of this, many black radical scholars overlooked the growing correlation between black criminalization and incarceration and black radicals who held to black masonic traditions and beliefs. As a result, the impact prisons and jails had on social justice work by certain black people went largely unrecognized by black radical scholars. This inevitably overshadowed how the deployment of the United States prison began to construct the identity of black males as felons in order to limit black radical agendas.

I came to realize that too often black church, black radical scholars, and many black social justice organizations and advocates marginalized the historical function of incarceration. For instance, many scholars within the black radical intellectual tradition and activists alike overlooked the relationship between the emergence of black radical protest within alternate spaces such as black freemasonry and the emergence of penal institutions. In doing this they minimized the work of black felons in early nineteenth century liberation efforts such as engaging racial conversations because they did not thoroughly investigate prisons and jails. In other words, many of these groups failed to connect how early black radicals were quickly criminalized and disposed of through penal institutions.

Although there is much discussion on the lynching of black males, often these radical intellectual scholars failed to show how the prison and criminal courts helped to advance the criminality of black people, particularly black males. This happened in part because of the moral apologetic function that the church played in American society. Indeed, the criminalization of early black radicals allowed for the deployment of false narratives about certain black bodies labeled felon because they were largely viewed as antithetical to the moral ideas and practices of black churches.

Therefore, it is not surprising that rarely do we speak to ways black felons and black people accused of crimes utilize biblical writing to inform their unique social justice projects. However, many of these persons such as Nat Turner, David Walker, Martin Delany, and others used biblical scripture to justify their protest and rebellions even in light of the real threat of prison and penal captivity. Yet, too often, narrative experiences of black incarcerated activist and felons is overlooked as a resource for shaping our understanding of black religious thinking and black radical movements, with the notable exception of King's letter from the Birmingham jail, though neither King nor the charge was for a felony conviction.

AN EXCHANGE WITH THE GROTESQUE: MOVING BEYOND THE BLACK CHURCH AND BLACK HEROIC FIGURES

Ultimately, the exclusions of these early black radicals and their use of scripture to inform their radical work reengaged my concern about the contemporary black church's seemingly inconsistent political engagement on issues of incarceration. My concern regarding the contemporary black church was threefold. First, I was concerned that the principles of Beloved Community would be pragmatically restricted to a privileged minority group if the lived experiences of black felons in the United States were not addressed. When I speak of Beloved Community as it relates to the contemporary black church in this way I mean to suggest that I was concerned that the black church would not adequately develop a theoretical set of ideas regarding human interaction and exchange that are recognizable through concrete structures and systems that would guide individuals, communities, and groups in society toward greater human fulfillment, particularly as it relates to black male felons.

I reasoned to myself that a void would exist within the black community if the contemporary black church did not function as an institutional body for extending Beloved Community to black felons. Thurman argues that "whenever the individual is cut off from the private and personal nourishment from other individuals or from particular individuals, the result is a wasting away, a starvation, a failure of his life to be sustained and nourished."[17] Moreover, such a void would make it possible to continue to overlook a category of black experience in the United States that has been denied full interaction and exchange in society.

The lack of involvement by the contemporary black church on issues of incarceration also deters the construction and promotion of concrete programs and policies that could allow men and women labeled felon to exercise agency and citizenship in the United States. For that reason, I highlight throughout this book certain actions, movements, ideas, and practices as representations of the grotesque to expose where moral and ethical ideologies of people have yet to construct concrete structures, symbols, or institutions that are available for all people. In this light, the grotesque confronts the black church and its use of racial apologetic images and languages.

Furthermore, the use of racial apologetic images and language within black churches oftentimes masks the harsh realities of many black people, particularly black male felons. Thus, my use of the grotesque exposes many of the underline ideas and practices within some black churches that cut black felons off from the larger community. In this light, the grotesque is the ideas, beliefs, and practices of oppressed people to expose the contradictions that emerge when moral and ethical ideologies fail to construct concrete representations of those ideals.

For certain, the grotesque is the tension that Cone refers to between the cross and the lynching tree. The grotesque illustrates very clearly what the "wasting away" looks like when black felons are cut from the nourishment of others. Moreover, the grotesque, as depicted by black felons, help to challenge the assumptions we hold about certain persons. The challenge to these assumptions leaves Beloved Community open to new forms of black experience that are often the undercurrent of black life.

Although there are numerous propositions within black religion that serve as the foundation for Beloved Community such as nonviolent resistance in social justice action, this book rests most prominently on the idea that the cultural production of black male felons would ensure that social structures would be put in place to secure the value and dignity of the private individual. In other words, for Beloved Community to become concretized in the lives of black felons there must be an intentional interworking of human actions to address the ambiguities or grotesqueries of life that exists because human beings are both individual and social agents. Thurman makes the point that society must wrestle with the ambiguity that arises because of this "paradox of conscious life."[18] This paradox is the understanding that one is both free and bond, individual and social, living and dying.

Therefore, by including the writings and experiences of black male felons, I build on Howard Thurman and Martin Luther King's notion that society must be a search for common ground that deals with both the uniqueness of one's private agency as well as strengthening the interconnectivity between the individual to the larger society.

Second, I was concerned that a lack of attention to felons would advance a false notion of Beloved Community as merely a utopian idea that lacked substantive social and political engagement. For while the term "Beloved Community" was coined in the early twentieth-century by philosopher Josiah Royce, it was popularized in several of Dr. King's writings and civil rights activism. King states in several of his writings "that the aftermath of nonviolence is the creation of the beloved community."[19] However, King's notion of nonviolent resistance did not deny the harsh reality in the struggle for freedom and liberty. In other words, Beloved Community does not erase what Victor Anderson terms the grotesque or ambiguous experiences of people. According to Anderson "the creative exchange between racial identity and social reality makes the meaning of race ambiguous and not absolute, relative and not simple, open to difference and particularity and not closed, and cognizant of both the light and dark potentials of race in our social experience."[20]

The grotesque has traditionally been used since the Renaissance in art or literature. Most popularly, the term has been used to describe anything from the fantastic to the monstrous. It has been associated with many artistic genres, from the Gothic to the danse macabre. For instance, in *Rethinking the Concept of the Grotesque: Crashaw, Baudelaire, Magritte*, Shun-Liang Chao adopts a rigorous approach to the study of the grotesque and establishes contradictory physicality and the notion of metaphor as two keys to the construction of a clear identity of the grotesque. Ultimately Chao is able to suggest a lineage of the grotesque aesthetic and to cast light on the functions of the visual and of the verbal when evoking it.

However, in this book I extend the idea of the grotesque past Anderson and Chao in order to think of the grotesque as also actions and movements. These actions and movements as representations of the grotesque also help to establish contradictory physicality and explore metaphor as keys to understanding the work of black male felons. In addition, these representations of the grotesque bring to light the function of these actions and movements. Said another way, the cultural production of black felons brings to light this exchange between racial identity and social reality by depicting the more complex ways black people experience the world when branded with the label felon.

As such, the grotesque helps inform our imagination of Beloved Community as an ever-growing and expanding product that makes possible creative ways of seeing and viewing objects as subjects. Indeed, without this form of exchange black male bodies are left to the imagination of white racist structures such as prisons and penal institutions. However, the path toward establishing Beloved Community is also "answerable to the exclusionary practices of white racism."[21] Indeed, as Anderson suggests, the impact of white racism, in many cases including but not limited to radical activism, limited black self-representation to productive practices of black heroism.

Within literal, historical, and religious work blackness is equated unfortunately to a form of black heroic performance. Anderson argues that, "Black heroic genius provided twentieth century African Americans cultural philosophy with stable rhetorical categories for construing the historical significance of African American presence in American culture."[22] This meant that black representation embodied racial images such as Martin Luther King, Jr. and Sojourner Truth and denied black images such as Nat Turner. For Anderson, "pressing beyond ontological blackness requires African American religious [and cultural] critics to subvert racial discourse . . . that would bind black subjectivity to the totality of racial identity."[23] This means that wherein black heroism uplifts blackness, it prescribes a particularly type of blackness that excludes the felon.[24]

This absence in part explains why the fetishizing of the black male body in white imagination has allowed the deployment of a black heroic apologetic figure to come forth in ways that deny ideas of the grotesque, particularly as depicted in the ways black male felons' struggle to attain civil and human rights. Moreover, the absence of cultural products by black male felons situates the black heroic figure in opposition to more diverse representation of black males.

Furthermore, the absence of black cultural production by black male felons limits the array of black cultural production that black radical intellectuals utilize within black radical intellectual traditions. For the above reasons, I illustrate throughout this book how the grotesque as presented by black male felons forces society to continually reevaluate its definitions and concepts of Beloved Community in order to address the disharmony in life.

An examination of the grotesque in this way show us how love is not merely a sentiment but rather a measurable result of human interaction and mobility that wrestles for meaning in the midst of violence and other injustices. Indeed, King argues that "nonviolence does call for love, but it is not a sentimental love. It is a very stern love that would organize itself into collective action to right a wrong by taking on itself suffering."[25] In doing this, I highlight how the principles of Beloved Community became closed to the grotesque as more creative exchanges with black apologetic heroic narratives and ideas became the central focus of black intellectuals.

Thus, if the contemporary black church, as King illustrates in his civil rights campaigns for black people in the mid-1900s, does not serve as an institutional agent for advancing the principles of Beloved Community in the United States to those labeled felon, then the historical practice of Beloved Community as a tangible goal for contemporary black social justice work cannot be fully actualized for all people. Therefore, in order to ensure Beloved Community is actualized in the lives of black felons I borrow Victor Anderson's idea of creative exchange. Indeed, creative exchange explains how the interchange of ideas and beliefs among people help shape our notions of Beloved Community. However, Anderson and other black religious scholars give little attention to the cultural production of black male felons.

Therefore, I extend Anderson's notion of the grotesque in creative exchange to the cultural production of black male felons to illustrate how black male felons' work is an embodied epistemology that speaks to the ambiguities and hiddenness within black life and culture. I place the experiences, ideas, and concepts that they express through their cultural production in creative exchange with black radical thought in order to reframe black radical intellectual traditions. In doing this I am able to recast black male felons as the authoritative subject of their experience. Ultimately, including black male felons in this type of creative exchange shows how the black male felon as subject expands our understanding of black radicalism in particular and American radicalism in general.

A creative exchange with these black cultural products not only depicts lived and experiential concepts of the grotesque that move beyond the boundaries of religious experience to offer a broader range of experiences, but also encourage scholars to think more profoundly on what it means to speak about Beloved Community. Therefore, unlike Anderson, I move past artistic images of the grotesque to explore in each chapter rebellions, music, books and other black male felons' cultural products to show the complex way black bodies trapped in structures of penal captivity developed a more complex creative exchange for the advancement of Beloved Community. For example, in chapter 2 I place Nat Turner's rebellion in a creative exchange with the principles of Beloved Community to show how the grotesque complicates notions of nonviolent resistance and reimagines the institution of slavery and captivity onto white bodies. Moreover, his rebellion reveals the complex interconnecting workings of socio-political and socio-economic forces both inside and outside of black social spaces to corrupt the message regarding black radical movements. Ultimately, the cultural production of these black male felons challenges us to deepen our understanding of black radicals and literary history and the various spaces wherein black felons are located.

Throughout this book I refer to the spaces wherein scholars might define the cultural production of black male felons as carceral spaces because they hold the ideas, practices, and thoughts of the grotesque over and against the heroic. Indeed, these particular intervening spaces that felons occupy have been virtually overlooked for their intellectual, political, and cultural offerings. Therefore, while it was widely believed that the black heroic image would provide African Americans at-large access to the US democratic project, the cultural production of the black male felons that I highlight show the various ways these figures within the community of blackness helped to marginalize other types of black representation. This marginalization of other forms of black representation ultimately influenced how certain black bodies captured in prisons and jails were viewed both inside and outside of the black community.

Furthermore, the use of the grotesque by black male felons illustrates how principles of Beloved Community came to be restricted to mostly a set of moral ethical ideas. This restriction to moral ethical ideas gave even greater license for black religion and black religious leaders to serve as arbiters of Beloved Community. For example in *Exodus!: Religion, Race, and Nation in Early Nineteenth-Century Black America*, Eddie Glaude, Jr. argues that "by appropriating Exodus, [African Americans] articulated their own sense of peoplehood and secured for themselves a common history and destiny."[26] However, while this common history included slavery, it overlooked the prison as another space for black radical thought and praxis.

In addition, to finding narrative kinship with biblical stories such as the Exodus story or the Pauline Damascus story, black religious leaders became equated with biblical figures such as Moses, Paul, and Jesus. Ultimately, equating black religious leaders to biblical figures such as Moses, Jesus, Paul, and other biblical prophets reified the idea of black heroic imagery as the basis for black leadership and identity. Thus, as leaders became more aligned to black religious figures, the notions of Beloved Community became more squarely rooted within the realm of black religion which as a result allowed black heroic narratives and imagery to become almost inextricably wrapped in biblical heroic figures.

Moreover, the wrapping of black history and black figures in biblical narratives and characters constructed a type of black religious idolatry that caused greater separation among black people inside of the black community. Contemporary scholars Maurice O. Wallace and Victor Anderson show how the construction of black heroic images limited the complex ways black males exists in the world. For instance, in *Beyond Ontological Blackness: An Essay On African American Religious and Cultural Criticism*, Anderson explores the ways that subversive forms of black identity have been subordinated to the totality of limited racial ideology and apologetic black heroic genius. He contends that this racial construction "creates essential criteria for defining insiders and outsiders within the group."[27] Thus the promotion of apologetic black heroic figures as derived in part from religious narrative is in part complicit in the construction of a black cultural and intellectual identity narrative that created greater rifts among elite and non-elite blacks. Moreover, it served as justification for the continual fetishizing of black male bodies that did not ascribe to such categorization.

Although black heroic genius and black religious heroic figures were intended to subvert negative ideas on black worth, they in many ways created additional fetishized forms of representation within black academic, activists, and popular culture. Consequently, many of those racial ideologies and black heroic images are determined by a narrow construction of black masculinity. In *Constructing the Black Masculine: Identity and Ideality in African American Men's Literature and Culture, 1775–1995*, Maurice O. Wallace argues that "while the high profile of race in the West has created out of the black male body a walking palimpsest of the fears and fascinations possessing our cultural imagination, the body of scholarship foregrounding race as a significant text or subtext of masculinity studies remains ironically and inextricably modest."[28] As a result, black cultural production became split between two sectors of blackness—one that tried to sooth white fear of black male bodies and another that tried to stoke that fear.

Indeed, a close inspection of black male felon's cultural production shows how these black males refused to completely conform to apologetic heroic roles and offered more complex ways of performing black masculinity. Yet neither Wallace nor Anderson constructs a historical trajectory of black male felons' cultural production. As a result, they failed to see how aspects of the grotesque by black male felons invigorate a new discussion about black male representation that is not dependent on resolving the fears within white imagination.

Moreover, they overlooked the material consequences that occurred as a result of excluding black male felons' work, particularly as it relates to the notion of Beloved Community. For instance, Wallace explains the pictorial work that hip hop artists and black male felon Tupac Shakur did with fashion and advertising photographer Albert Watson. Wallace offers a critique of the photos that Watson took of Shakur for the 1992 film *Juice*, in which Shakur played a lead role. Wallace states:

> Shakur's counterlook fails. For the veil of the heavy black hood lying sinisterly over Shakur's head diminishes his power to resist the camera's gaze, not least because it villainizes, dresses Shakur in a fiendish garb. His stare threatens, then, with an ocular bravado but never meaningfully challenges the gaze of the white male artist because any significant subversion of it is always already contained—framed—by the subtextual work of black male stereotype. To add insult to pictorial injury, the would-be resistance in Shakur's eyes is mocked, finally, by the signifying phallicism of his short, blunt pistol.Shakur, might just

> as well have been photographed from behind too, since his is a comparably abject pose. (21–22)[29]

Wallace ignores the statement that Tupac as a black male felon makes in this cultural piece. He gives the sole ownership of this cultural work to the photographer, and overlooks what Shakur is saying in the work. Sadly, this is typically the way society has trapped black males into structures of penal captivity and how that is affixed in white imagination. In other words, Wallace dismisses how the black male felon as subject in the art is speaking about his captivity in society. Indeed, had Wallace examined this art with Tupac's own music he might have other ways of thinking about the work and the way Tupac succeeds in presenting the reality of black male felons. As such, Wallace fails to examine how the black male body as felon offers another counter narrative. Thus he marginalizes the role black male felons play in combatting racist assault on black male identity.

Wallace, like Anderson and others, does not illustrate how the cultural production of black males accused and convicted of crimes express their personal agency. By ignoring the black male felon as subject in cultural production they fail to understand how these men fight against racial slavery in the United States, Jim Crow laws, penal captivity, and civil and human rights violations. This again illustrates why an examination of the carceral spaces, wherein black male felons' cultural production largely exists, is important. It is important because it refocuses the examination of the work that black male felons produce from being objects to subjects. Most importantly, in this context it highlights the ambiguities or unresolved tensions imbedded in Beloved Community.

The problem is not just that Anderson, Alexander, or Wallace overlook how the cultural production of black male felons when applied to the principles of Beloved Community highlights the value of black felons to the black intellectual enterprise. They also do not locate a representation of black felons that bridges the work among academic, activist, and popular culture. Therefore, I place the work of Alexander, Anderson, Wallace, and others together in conversation with certain black male felons to construct a black radical intellectual tradition that focuses not on cultural production of black male felons for the exclusion of others, but rather to a radical black intellectual tradition that expands our understanding of these figures for the development of a more inclusive canon itself.

For this reason, I situate this project in the gap between black male felons and black male heroic figures in order to serve as an intervention to the discourse that equates certain black male bodies as criminal and allows certain discursive patterns to go forth that deny the usefulness of black male felons as influential to black radical intellectual projects. I highlight the cultural production of black incarcerated men throughout US history to help better understand how society might enact the principles of Beloved Community more thoroughly in the twenty-first century. In other words, investigating the cultural production of Nat Turner, Huddie Ledbetter, Malcolm X, George Jackson, and other black radical leaders not only confronts us with various cultural products of black male felons, but it also connects the historical trajectory of black male incarceration in the black community to contemporary times. It also highlights how the cultural production of black male felons as grotesque offers us more concrete ways of recognizing Beloved Community throughout various moments in US history and American politics. Ultimately, connecting the cultural production of nineteenth-century black male felons to contemporary forms of black male felon cultural production illustrate how the principles of Beloved Community can remain open to new and diverse forms of black experiences.

Finally, my third concern focuses on the historical legacy of Beloved Community as a black radical product that reveals the exchange between black radical theory and practice. Indeed, the limited investigation of cultural production by black incarcerated men as illustrated in Anderson and Wallace minimizes the influence and significance black felons have had on black radical intellectual traditions. It overlooks the political and social theories that black male felons construct regarding American democracy, penal captivity, black religion, and more. According to Bogues, "to see black radical intellectual tradition as operating wholly inside the Western canon, and then to judge its many contributors solely from that angle, is both to miss the tradition's complexity and to negate the tremendous knowledge that this tradition has postulated about the nature of the West."[30] This is most certainly true of black male felons. In other words, to wholly view the work of black male felons from the narrow lens of race, gender, or other western episteme is to miss the complexity that black male felons offer to the discussion of American politics and black radicalism. Moreover, it erases black imprisoned bodies from the communal discourse on justice.

Ultimately, the lack of attention within black radical intellectual traditions to the cultural production of black male felons diminishes the more complex intellectual history of Beloved Community. For instance, this practice of erasure overlooks the fact that King continues a legacy of Beloved Community that was foregrounded in the work of earlier black radicals such as Nat Turner, Huddie Ledbetter, and Malcolm X. Therefore, if a more thorough intellectual history is not advanced, then we will continue to overlook emerging black radicals that are sitting in our prisons and jails.

For this reason, the particular strain of black intellectual traditions that I will trace in this book has, from its origin, critically addressed and socially combatted the marginalization and dehumanizing effects on black life by

European hegemonic socio-political and socio-economic structures. It will show how the prison and the US criminal justice system has historically attempted to erase certain black bodies from the cultural and political landscape and US political life and the creative ways black felons resisted that erasure.

To show how this erasure happened and the ways black male felons resisted it, I utilize an interdisciplinary approach. I employ the statistical discourse on black incarceration in US history beginning in the late eighteenth century to the present, black urban music, nineteenth- and twentieth-century US literature, and black religion to show how black radical intellectual tradition slowly started to shift. This shift allowed the cultural production of black male felons to be overlooked. Indeed, over time this shift in the historical work and mission within the black intellectual tradition occurred because of a lack of interdisciplinary work that crosses economic, theological, and legal fields.

Therefore, it seemed to me necessary to insert the cultural production of black male felons into the discourse within black intellectual life in order to have a more complete understanding of US history, culture, and politics. Moreover, this intervention would help black radical scholars, particularly within black religion to reimagine the radical political function of Beloved Community for the sake of black felons. In other words, it removes the sole ownership of Beloved Community from the realm of black religion.

Thus this book presents my response to the lack of interdisciplinary research on the cultural production of black male felons in order to raise the level of compassion, care, and concern for those black males trapped in penal captivity in the United States. For instance, little has been done to highlight how these real, imagined, and symbolic social realms of being felon impacts our daily sense of blackness in the world. As a consequence, representation of felons, particularly black male felons, has been deployed without any in depth regard to how black bodies come to be labeled felon and the way the felon label operates in society. This lack of attention concerning the distribution of the label felon onto certain black bodies ultimately leaves a gap in understanding how prison develops a subversive discourse about the US system of justice and democracy.

Therefore, throughout the book I map a black radical intellectual tradition that includes the cultural production of black male felons to show how fetishized black bodies, particularly black males, offer subversive black intellectual male images that depict the hiddenness of black felons. Indeed, the mapping of this black radical intellectual tradition shows how the black radical intellectual canon inadvertently authorized false notions of black intellectual heroism. For instance, one collateral consequence to the black radical canon was a rift in black intellectual life that placed black radical scholars on one side of black experience and black religious scholars on the other. This rift inevitably impacted how the principle of Beloved Community was applied to all of black life in the United States. However, a more complete examination of the cultural production by black male felons helps to reconcile this canonical practice and mend the rift for the whole of black studies.

CHAPTER SUMMARIES: WHERE I ENTER

The introduction to this book lays the foundation for the need to map black male felons' cultural production from early US history to the present to show their influence on black radical projects. In order to interrogate the intersection between the Beloved Community and the experiences of black male felons I first examined the development of institutions and traditions that have historically defined, informed, and contextualized black lives within the United States. In doing this I also reengage African American religious thought and contemporary black liberation theology to Black Radical Traditions, thus connecting the trajectory of black religious intellectual life to a larger historical black intellectual tradition.

This book contains seven chapters beyond the Introduction. Chapter 1 entitled "Slave and Free: The Mapping of Race, Religion, and Punishment in the New World," offers a historical overview of black male incarceration to show how the incarceration of black men in the United States helped to construct false notions about black males beginning in the nineteenth century. I go on to show how that erasure hindered the translation and mission of black radical projects in the nineteenth century. Ultimately, I make claims for an intersectional theory based on Victor Anderson's notion of Creative Exchange and his writings on the Beloved Community in order to place black male felons and the uniqueness of their experience in concert with the principles of Beloved Community. In doing this, I extend Anderson's notion of creative exchange past black religious experience to develop a relational theory of Beloved Community that connects this notion to nineteenth-century black radical writers. I thus link the notion of Beloved Community to a larger historical body of black radical thought.

In linking the notion of Beloved Community to a larger set of historical and contemporary figures, I am able to map a black radical tradition that is composed of both enslaved and free black male felons. This mapping reconnects black religious life to a black radical political tradition that takes seriously the cultural production of black male felons. Moreover, this chapter shows how the repositioning of black religious life calls for a more extensive look into carceral spaces that encapsulated early black male felons' production. Ultimately, this fuller mapping reveals how the quest for black cultural fulfilment intertwined black religious thought, black political radicalism, and black social activism in the face of transforming modern Western notions of punishment in the United States.

In particular, I intersect black religion with black radical political theory and praxis within black freemasonry to not only show the relationship between these two branches of knowledge, but also to highlight the work of the black intellectual enterprise and its ability to more fully address the legacy of black bodily erasure. I track black radical Prince Hall Mason's quest for black cultural advancement and human dignity starting in the late eighteenth and early nineteenth century. I do this in an effort to outline how black freemasonry informed both black radical religious projects as well as positioned black preachers such as John Marrant, Prince Hall, and David Walker as central figures and civil rights catalysts. Most importantly I show how the subversive role of black freemasons as black preachers helped reconstruct the European Christian project and developed counter narratives and ideas for the advancement of Beloved Community—narratives that are similar to those presented by later black radicals such as Nat Turner and other nineteenth- and twentieth-century black male felons.

Indeed, over time Western notions of punishment evolved from plantation culture to prison culture. Therefore, in chapter 2, "The Construction of Nineteenth Century Black Prison Radicals: An Address to Nonreflexive Interpretations," I offer a reflexive interpretation and archival material to show how nineteenth-century black male felons were structurally erased from black radical intellectual life because of the inability of black radical scholars to link the cultural production of Nat Turner to the emerging prison industrial complex. Specifically, I show how Nat Turner's rebellion signals to the early prison practices to reimagine the black male body as criminal.

Thus, I insert Nat Turner into this discursive rupture to show how their radical activity impacts the discursive landscape within black radical traditions. I also insert black male felons and the cultural products they produced into the discursive rupture developed in chapter 1 to construct a creative exchange that outline the ways both sought to promote greater human fulfillment for black people. I also show how the use of juridical discursive practices and the construction of the prison industrial complex transitioned the discourse on race and morality. This transition within the discourse redefined black radical activity and reshaped the social perception of nineteenth-century black male radicals such as Nat Turner. Therefore, by inserting early black male felons and their cultural products into this rupture I begin to offer a link between the mission of nineteenth-century black radicals to the work of twentieth- and twenty-first century black imprisoned intellectuals. Ultimately this redefinition and reshaping of black radical activity impacts the way black academic and activists might interpret nineteenth century imprisoned intellectuals as source for black radical intellectual traditions.

Chapter 3, "A Challenge to Black Heroic Images: Huddie Ledbetter and the Politics of a Black Male Felon," explores the black male felon Huddie Ledbetter. Ledbetter shows how black radical praxis and black cultural production gradually began to shift as prison and incarceration became a sustained threat to black males. I particularly use Ledbetter to show how black males in the turn of the twentieth century used music, wit, and force to develop a type of creative exchange that not only subverted the mission of prison as a destabilizing force in black male achievement, but also ensured relative forms of freedom and independence for himself. In this light I show the creative ways twentieth century black imprisoned men continued to resists captivity and social immobilization. Although these ways were often more subtle, they were no less subversive—particularly the music. The mapping of this tradition also illustrates how black imprisoned men helped shape new ideas about subjectivity, personhood, and citizenship in the United States.

In addition, I illustrate how the current use of apologetic language masks the work of the black male felon's cultural production in many of the same ways that it masked the radical activity of black freemasons of the nineteenth century. I also show how the cultural products produced by these black imprisoned intellectuals have been marginalized because of the way carceral spaces have been ignored. However, by highlighting the cultural products within these carceral spaces I spotlight how many black imprisoned males point us to new locations for research and investigation. In doing this, I show that black male felons actually alter the way we think of apologetic language and black heroic imagery as tools for black liberation and as tools for the construction of Beloved Community.

Indeed, these black imprisoned men illustrate how the masking of their work diminishes the complexity of black agency. It also subsumes the discourse on black value with black apologetic figures. Ultimately these black apologetic figures and their work are often deemed as antithetical to black imprisoned intellectuals and the cultural products black felons produce.

In chapter 4, "Twentieth Century Black Radical Prison Intellectuals: Malcolm X, George Jackson, and the Expansion of Nineteenth Century Black Prison Praxis," I continue to insert black male felons into this discursive rupture by examining the work of twentieth-century black male felons, Malcolm X, and George Jackson. In particular, I highlight how their incarceration influenced their cultural products, their books, marches, and rebellions and more. Indeed, their cultural products illustrate how the prison constructed their language and their activity as black radicals. I also outline how Malcolm X and Jackson's work unites academic, activist, and popular culture in order to expand the terrain within black radical traditions.

Ultimately, this chapter illustrates how these black male felons shaped political and social discourse in activist and popular culture in the twentieth century, particularly the influence they had on the emergence of hip hop culture in the late 1970s and early 1980s. Thus in this chapter, I make clear how these twentieth century black imprisoned intellectuals made way for a twenty-first century black radical imprisoned intellectual engagement model. Yet I show how their work continues to struggle to reveal new modes of thinking about black masculinity, US democracy, and justice.

In chapters 5 and 6, I explore the cultural production by twenty-first century black male felons to highlight the contemporary conditions of black incarcerated bodies. In chapter 5, "Prison Prophets: Twenty-First Century Black Male Felons on Race, Religion, and Mass Incarceration," I link the challenges and possibilities of hip hop to longer standing black cultural products such as blues and gospel to show the value hip hop provides for understanding the impact of black male felons to black intellectual life. I show how the early ideas of black cultural production hindered a fuller investigation of hip hop as a valuable form of intellectual inquiry.

Lastly, I continue this investigation in chapter 6, "Expanding the Beloved Community: Black Church, Black Felons and Mass Incarceration," exploring more deeply the work of two-time convicted felon and hip hop artist Lyfe Jennings's music from his first CD. Again I use black music by black male felons to narrate black experience. I insert Jennings into the discourse on black religion, justice, and politics by offering a critical narrative analysis of his CD *Lyfe 268-192* which details his journey to prison and his life post incarceration. I show through Jennings' CD how hip hop music serves as a pragmatic philosophy that is informed by an embodied epistemology. Not only does Jennings's CD call into question the discourse within black religion, black feminism, and black incarceration, but also I utilize his writing and music to construct a theory of black male suffering that is not often explored in order to reconstruct the black male felon in the social imagination.

I conclude this book by offering a series of next steps in the research on imprisoned intellectuals for academic, activists, and popular culture. This includes addressing the diversity of black incarcerated men by age, class, and sexual orientation. I also outline the need for black radical intellectuals to explore the impact that the incarceration of black men has on black female incarceration and juvenile incarceration in the United States. Thus the full work of this project is to reveal how the work of black male felons might serve as source material for the construction of a Beloved Community that is ever changing and expanding to include the fullness of black experience in the world.

NOTES

1. I worked for seven years as the Texas State Reentry Manager for Innerchange Freedom Initiative (IFI). IFI is a pre-release prisoner reentry program under Prison Fellowship Ministries. The Texas IFI program is located at the Carol Vance Prison Unit in Sugar Land, Texas. All the men in the 365-bed unit participated in an 18-month in-prison program and were case managed for two years post-release in IFI Texas's four-city reentry zones to include Houston city and surrounding counties, Dallas/Fort Worth and their surrounding counties, and San Antonio.

2. Manning Marable, "Black Studies and the Racial Mountain," *Souls: A Critical Journal of Black Politics, Culture, and Society* 2, no. 3 (Summer 2000): 17–36. http://www.columbia.edu/cu/ccbh/souls/vol2no3/vol2num3art2.pdf.

3. Michelle Alexander, *The New Jim Crow: Mass Incarceration in the Age of Colorblindness* (New York: The New Press, 2010), 11.

4. James Cone, *The Cross and the Lynching Tree* (Ossining, NY: Orbis Books, 2011), xix.

5. James Cone, *The Cross and the Lynching Tree*, interview by Bill Moyers, YouTube. Published on January 26, 2014, video, 26:11–26:48, https://www.youtube.com/watch?v=BVyo5dzYs44&t=2s.

6. Victor Anderson, *Beyond Ontological Blackness: An Essay on African American Religious and Cultural Criticism* (New York: Continuum Publishing Company, 1995), 17.

7. Cone, Interview 11:54–11:56.

8. Alexander, *The New Jim Crow*, 214.

9. Anthony Bogues, *Black Heretics Black Prophets: Radical Political Intellectuals* (New York: Routledge, 2003), 3.

10. Cornel West, *Prophesy Deliverance!: An Afro-American Revolutionary Christianity* (Louisville: Westminster John Knox Press, 2002), 15.

11. Rima Vesley-Flad, "The Social Covenant and Mass Incarceration: Theologies of Race and Punishment," *Anglican Theological Review* 93, no. 4 (2011): 541.

12. Rima Vesley-Flad, "The Social Covenant," 559.

13. Joanna Brooks and John Saillant, *"Face Zion Forward": First Writers of the Black Atlantic, 1785–1798* (Boston: Northeastern University Press, 2002), 15.

14. Joanna Brooks and John Sailant, "*Face Zion Forward*," 77

15. Joanna Brooks and John Sailant, "*Face Zion Forward*," 79.

16. Joanna Brooks and John Sailant, "*Face Zion Forward*," 16.

17. Howard Thurman, *The Search for Common Ground* (Richmond, IN: Friends United Press, 1986), 3.

18. This term comes from Howard Thurman's book *The Search for Common Ground* (Richmond, IN: Friends United Press, 1986).

19. This quote comes from "In Love" An Experiment in *A Testament of Hope: The Essential Writings and Speeches of Martin Luther King Jr.* However, King also records similar statements of beloved community being the aftermath of nonviolent resistance in his 1957 speech *Birth of a New Nation* and his 1959 speech *Sermon on*

Ghandi. King's philosophy of Beloved Community can also be found at http://www.thekingcenter.org/king-philosophy.

20. Victor Anderson, *Creative Exchange: A Constructive Theology of African American Religious Experience* (Minneapolis: Fortress Press, 2008), 40.

21. Victor Anderson, *Beyond Ontological Blackness*, 62.

22. Victor Anderson, *Beyond Ontological Blackness*, 80.

23. Victor Anderson, *Beyond Ontological Blackness*, 85.

24. Victor Anderson explores this entrapment of African American cultural philosophy in depth in his chapter "Categorical Racism and Racial Apologetics" wherein he links the work of black activists, preachers, abolitionists, and scholars to Modern European philosophy. He suggests the duality of Black Intellectual Practice reveals W. E. B. Du Bois's theory on black "double" consciousness, a desire to achieve black excellence within the reality of white oppression.

25. Martin Luther King, Jr., "My Trip to the Land of Gandhi," in *A Testament of Hope: The Essential Writings and Speeches of Martin Luther King, Jr.*, ed. James M. Washington (New York: HarperCollins, 1991), 26.

26. Eddie Glaude, Jr., *Exodus!: Religion, Race, and Nation in Early Nineteenth-Century Black America* (Chicago: The University of Chicago Press, 2000), 9.

27. Victor Anderson, *Beyond Ontological Blackness*, 85.

28. Maurice O. Wallace, *Constructing the Black Masculine: Identity and Ideality in African American Men's Literature and Culture, 1775–1995* (Durham, NC: Duke University Press, 2002), 2.

29. Wallace also critiques photos that Watson took of black male felons Mike Tyson and Bobby Brown. In both pictures he also speaks to the work that Watson is doing and not to how these black felons are engaged in using this medium to speak about their experiences and their ideas as black male felons in society. Like he does with Tupac Shakur, Wallace virtually dismisses how these black male felons utilize this medium and the political and cultural statements they make in the photos.

30. Anthony Bogues, *Black Heretics Black Prophets*, 6.

Chapter 1

Slave and Free

The Mapping of Race, Religion, and Punishment in the New World

In the United States the prison is a concrete cultural and political structure used to trap black male bodies into carceral spaces. Indeed, the prison as a cultural symbol has been depicted in films, movies, and music as a type of rite-of-passage for many black males. These carceral spaces highlight the complex ways mass incarceration structures ideas and practices of punishment onto black male bodies in order to deny many African American men constitutive moral agency. This denial of certain black males' constitutive moral agency is a direct affront to the practice of Beloved Community. In other words, to know that thousands of black males have been stripped of subjectivity, personhood, and citizenship is to realize that the manifestation of Beloved Community is far from concrete in American society for all people.

This means that the very idea of black and male in the United States is perceived to be less than or deficient. For example, these multiple and complex carceral spaces show the various ways black male achievement and social advancement is limited. Not only is black male advancement limited, it is continually being framed through the lens of carceral space. However, this framing of black men and the consequences behind it are never fully addressed because society overlooks the intentional ways prison targets black men. Instead, black inequity and inequality such as poverty, education, and broken families overshadow the discussion around blackness and gender. Thus, these social inequities become the leading issues for examination.

Likewise, the radical concept of Beloved Community became increasingly cut off to ideas, thoughts, and actions that could not be easily framed within a black heroic narrative. For Anderson, "categorical racism and white racial ideology occasioned the preoccupation of African American cultural philosophy with racial apologetics."[1] This increased function brought forth black heroic narratives and images to defend black life and culture against white institutional assault. As a result, Beloved Community became largely viewed through the lens of these black heroic images and narratives. In other words, Beloved Community became largely a product of black intellectual work that was engaged in an exchange with black heroic narratives in order to justify black life and culture against white racist institutional assault.

This shift in Beloved Community left certain black bodies more susceptible to institutional racism and erasure, particularly as the prison regime began to replace racial slavery as a technique for black immobilization. The eventual rise of the prison regime was not only able to fracture the black community in class and gender binaries, but also it was able to disrupt the traditional function of black radical projects. For instance, the subversive work of black churches, black colleges, and other black intellectual products became compromised. Many of these institutions became more concerned with presenting an acceptable form of blackness in public spaces.

Moreover, rarely has an exchange with black male felons and the principles of Beloved Community been initiated to address the role black institutions such as black churches, schools, and black communities play in holding black males captive within these carceral spaces. As a result, many black radical scholars overlook the intentional efforts employed within the United States to incarcerate black male bodies. For instance, rarely is the lack of black male social, political, and economic advancement viewed through the systemic and structural ways black male bodies are situated in these carceral spaces as felons. This not only diminishes an exchange with the grotesque and marginalizes the experiences of black male felons, it reduces concrete moments of Beloved Community in black history and culture.

However, I contend that there exist certain spaces that can actually intervene within black intellectual traditions because they locate the social position of the black felon. I often refer to these spaces as carceral spaces. Ultimately, these carceral spaces highlight black felons' resistance to the conditions that entrap them. In other words, carceral spaces house the ideas, thoughts, and constructs of black imprisoned bodies that continually work to counter the effects that penal captivity has on individuals, groups, and communities in the United States. Therefore, placing these ideas, thoughts, and constructs in dialogue with larger black radical ideas expands the fundamental principles and reshapes commonly-held beliefs of Beloved Community.

Indeed, the marginalization of black male felons is often hidden under the umbrella of blackness, poverty, education, or other more commonly shared racial pathologies. Yet it is through a set of legal discursive and juridical practices that large groups of black men are institutionally marginalized within the society. For instance, in *Punishment and Inequality in America*, Bruce Western points out that by the 1970s "in political campaigns and media portrayals, criminal offenders were regularly personified by poor young black men."[2] He also highlights and differentiates the life conditions of black men with and without a felony conviction to show why the idea of poverty as the entrapment for black male bodies is not fully true for the conditions of incarceration. In other words, the structure of incarceration targets black male bodies more so than it targets income inequality.

However, when addressing the issue of incarceration, poverty becomes the leading conversation for talking about blackness. Incarceration naively and wrongly is thus thought of as the result of the inability to fully address poverty. Ultimately, the safety of black male bodies becomes systemically marginalized as other racial pathologies come to the center. As this phenomenon of black male incarceration increased, the pictorial landscape no longer needed the use of racial language to reshape communities of color because blackness alone became the sole basis for understanding incarceration. Western contends that, like the statistical data used in the nineteenth century, the current "scientific evidence for intractable criminality and the political association of race with crime undercut the basic assumption of rehabilitative outlook—that criminal offenders could change their behavior and be like the rest of us."[3] In other words, society grew to believe that it could not change crime because it could not change blackness. Consequently, this notion polarized society both inside and outside of black communities into law-abiding citizens versus the criminal class.

The entrapment of poor black and undereducated black males into structures of penal captivity grew as the relocation of jobs in urban cities deteriorated. Thus the gap that existed between certain black men and every other group within the United States widened because poverty became overwhelmingly apparent in black communities. Indeed, the interchange of events between racialized political forces and the collapse of urban markets can be tracked back to the nineteenth century migration of blacks to the urban cities in the North. However, the entrapment of blackness by economic class cannot tell the full story of hyper incarceration on black male bodies. In *The Condemnation of Blackness: Race, Crime and the Making of Modern Urban America*, Khalil Gibran Muhammad highlights the emergence of black people, particularly black men, as synonymous with criminality starting with the publication of the 1890 US census.

Both the lived experiences and statistical discourse for many black male felons shows how the Beloved Community became ever more closed to an exchange with the grotesque. Like Michelle Alexander, Muhammad designates the late nineteenth century as the start for modern racial criminalization in the United States. He employs the social science work of Thorsten Sellin, W. E. B. Du Bois, and Ida B. Wells in an attempt to "deracialize" black criminality and build on whiteness and critical race scholarship to investigate the genealogy of racial discourse on crime statistics. In particular, he shows how prison statistics became the basis of a national discussion about black males as a dangerous and criminal population.

Ultimately, the statistical discourse beginning in the nineteenth century shaped the perception on black communities, which in turn shaped how certain communities were resourced and supported. According to Muhammad "new sources of statistical data were joined to ongoing debates about the future place of African Americans in modern urban America."[4] Indeed, exploring the genealogy of racial crime statistics not only illustrates how both the US rural south and urban north used crime statistics to frame black males in particular as criminal, but also it signals to why black communities began to fracture into subgroups. For instance, Muhammad contends that "postbellum southern black out-migration to the urban north . . . fueled an invidious black migration narrative framed by crime statistics and reshaped broader racial discourses on immigration and urbanization during Progressive era."[5] This migration also impacted how black communities understood and talked about themselves as both a religious, political, and economic body.

The fracture within black communities by religion and class has held firm for over two centuries. Moreover, the same statistical discursive pattern utilized in the South to unjustly entrap black men during the era of Jim Crow in the nineteenth century and to the fracturing of black communities is still utilized today. For instance, the Sentencing Project's 2013 publication entitled "Trends in U.S. Corrections" not only shows that an increase in prison populations is most pronounced in Southern states such as Louisiana, Mississippi, Alabama, Oklahoma, and Texas, but also it shows that at 36 percent, black people represent the largest racial and ethnic group in state and federal prisons. According to the report, one in ten black men in their thirties is in prison or jail on any given day.[6] This ongoing statistical discourse has allowed an underclass group to exist within black communities. Yet the mere tolerance of an underclass group challenges the way the black community, particularly black religion within black communities, thinks about itself as arbiters of Beloved Community.

Indeed, the same statistical discourse that lends to the criminalization of black male bodies in the current age was also used in the early nineteenth century to say that black men in general were lazy, dangerous, and irresponsible. In addition to the overcrowding of black males bodies in prison, the statistical discourse shows the influence incarceration has in the employment rate of black men in the United States from the nineteenth century to the present. In *Marked: Race, Crime, and Finding Work in the Era of Mass Incarceration*, Devah Pager explores how much of a barrier criminal records represent in trying to find low wage jobs. Her study reveals that not only do black men with felony convictions have an almost zero chance of finding employment but black male applicants with no history of a criminal background fared no better in finding employment than a white applicant who just got out of prison. In a CNN video series entitled "Black in America" Pager states that the "findings suggest that being black in America today is basically equivalent to having a felony conviction."[7] Yet, the criminalization of black male bodies and the impact it has on black masculinity is rooted in a longer history in the United States than offered in Pager's investigation.

Indeed, the statistical discourse shows that since the inception of prisons in the United States, black male incarceration has grown continuously over the last two centuries. However, the fundamental problem is not just that these statistics create a social perception about blackness, particularly black males, but that the statistical discourse goes forth largely with no real examination of the institutions, structures, and discursive practices that lend to the construction of the black male felon. Instead, it reifies the notion of black male bodies as criminal. In other words, the statistical data subtly ignores the history of the South in capturing black bodies for forced service and instead suggest hardened criminal behavior by blacks in those states as the cause for the disproportionate number of black bodies in prisons and jails. This means that the principles used to construct Beloved Community are not being applied to ideas and practices that specifically impact black males.

Admittedly, the exact numbers of black men incarcerated in prisons and jails in the late nineteenth and early twentieth centuries are shaky at best. The insufficient data on early black male incarceration is largely because of the insufficient record keeping in early jails and prisons. It is also because of the social idea about black bodies as disposable. For example, a report by Patrick Langham for the Bureau of Prisons provides differing numbers from the history noted on the Bureau of Prisons website. Yet Langham's numbers and the Bureau of Prisons website both show an increasing rate of black male incarceration in disproportion to other groups. Moreover, Langham's research shows that the percentage of white prisoner representation in state and federal penal institutions decreased from 78 percent in 1926 to 55 percent in 1986, while the percentage of blacks represented in prison increased from 21 percent in 1926 to 44 percent in 1986.[8]

Ultimately, the number of black male bodies in prisons suggests that there is more than a strong relationship between black masculine representation and performance with punishment and prison culture. Indeed, when the raw numbers in the late nineteenth- and early twentieth-century are compared to other racial and ethnic groups it is evident that a trend develops which highlights the disparate impact of incarceration and penal captivity on black males. Furthermore, the numbers indicate quite clearly that black males are overrepresented in penal captivity when compared to the overall black male population. This is even more disturbing when evidence shows that the overpopulation of black males in prison continues to grow at exponential rates in the United States. This implies that the principles of Beloved Community have not been applied to all black males equally.

To be clear, this is not to suggest that the statistical discourse only has an impact on Southern incarceration. Indeed, the statistical discourse on race, crime, and punishment places urban cities in the North, such as Philadelphia, Chicago, and New York, in direct relationship with southern cities such as Birmingham, Alabama; Jackson, Mississippi; and Greenville, North Carolina. According to Muhammad, "the statistical discourse on black criminality from the 1890s forward was a modern invention that encapsulated northern and southern ideas about race and crime."[9] Therefore, the notion of criminality as synonymous with black men became a national phenomenon.

The statistical discourse on black male incarceration shows that the principles of Beloved Community cannot just be applied to the prison industrial complex or even the criminal justice system. It also must apply to the cultural value we place on black male bodies. Ultimately, the use of statistical data and prison census reports has been one way to not only entrap black men physically, financially, and socially, but also to deploy a particular way of talking about black masculinity that confines their being to prescriptive discursive spaces. In other words, what society means when it says "black male" has been largely framed in a particular set of ideas and beliefs. This shows that carceral spaces are both physically and discursively structured. Thus black male incarceration is not limited to the prison building.

The statistical discourse shows not only how incarceration rates of black male bodies is disproportionate to the US black male population, it is the central justification for the policing of black male bodies. This has material implications on black males, particularly when the principles of Beloved Community are not applied to the conversation. The felon becomes a symbol for black male bodies and a demarcation for talking about black masculinity. In this way, the statistical discourse helps affix the label felon onto black identity, particularly black men, and marks black male bodies in real, symbolic, and imagined ways. The result of this demarcation is directly related to the statistical discourse concerning black incarceration rates. What is immanently disturbing is the way this demarcation allows for black male bodies to become a justifiable site for punishment and torture.

By the turn of the twentieth century, shifts in the American landscape came to symbolize criminality with blackness, particularly black male bodies. Furthermore, as the correlation between blackness and criminality grew white criminality, particularly among white Irish, Italian, and Polish immigrants lessened. Yet, the marginal investigation by scholars to thoroughly explore the sociological intersection of criminality and blackness left poor urban and rural blacks victim to modern legal discursive practices. This in turn altered the conversation on criminality in profound ways. For instance, these juridical discursive practices not only hindered black people's ability to access education, jobs, and housing benefits, but also blackness "became a more stable racial category in opposition to whiteness through racial criminalization."[10] Consequently, criminality was no longer discussed in plurality and diversity, but rather in singular narrative discourses. This again is illustrative of the ways the principles of Beloved Community are not applied to black male felons because of the ways diversity of experiences has been restricted to singular narrative discourses.

Black male bodies became the isolated image of crime and the site for legalized forms of punishment and torture. Thus, wherein earlier notions and practices of punishment and torture were considered general and nonracially specific, the privatization of discipline transformed punishment and torture into a narrow, racialized system of delimiting acts perpetrated onto the black body by legal discursive practices that were legitimated by nonreflexive statistical discourse. As a result of the emergence and evolution of the statistical discourse on black criminality, the urban North became the production site for modern ideas about race, crime, and punishment.

The criminalization of black bodies was not only the practice of racist southern politicians, criminal justice officials, and white lynch mobs, but also the work of white liberal writers and academics who adopted racist social science data for the justification of punishment of blacks in the North and in the South. According to Muhammad, many white social scientists gave the illusion of presenting objective race blind crime data that ultimately restricted African Americans' ability to access economic and social infrastructures in the United States. Moreover, the joining of race with criminal statistics made way for the emergence of higher police engagement in black populated cities, racialized city laws and codes that regulated blacks' mobility, and public policies that criminalized black people in northern and southern towns and cities.

These current social and cultural practices allow society to continue to advance ideas and practices to justify the criminalization of black bodies as opposed to explaining why the criminalization happens in the first place. Indeed, the rising social science data helped solidify racist cultural notions about the fundamental difference between African American and white Americans. Ultimately, by 1890, twenty-five years after the Civil War, the census served as a metric to both assess blacks' status post slavery while at the same time helping to reshape black identity as criminal. Muhammad contends that "for white Americans of every ideological stripe—from radical southern racists to northern progressives—African American criminality became one of the most widely accepted bases for justifying prejudicial thinking, discriminatory treatment, and/or acceptance of racial violence as an instrument of public safety."[11] This is best illustrated in contemporary times with the ongoing practice of asking persons about their criminal history in school admission processes, employment interviews, housing applications, and insurance forms.

Further, as statistical data becomes more widely resourced, the criminalization of black bodies reifies the beliefs regarding black inferiority and the need to regulate black agency. Despite emerging social science research on the origins of race and crime, the idea of black inferiority and black pathology remains firmly rooted in statistical discourse on black criminality. The incrimination of black culture is ultimately the effect of this discursive practice. According to Muhammad, "beginning in the late nineteenth century, the statistical rhetoric of the 'Negro Criminal' became a proxy for a national discourse on black inferiority."[12] Thus, black crime researchers and reformers, particularly black elites, felt the need to respond to this trend by salvaging black culture from the idea of criminality.

Many black elites began to distinguish themselves from "uncouth" and "criminally inclined" poor blacks as black crime statistics grew. Black colleges, churches, and elite blacks began to embrace Victorian ideals of morality and respectability and saw themselves as the representation for the race's capacity for equal citizenship. Muhammad contends that "black elites often employed the language of racial uplift and the 'politics of respectability' to describe black criminality in terms of class and culture."[13] As a consequence, blacks accused of crimes became isolated in many ways from black communities at large. This real and imagined distinction of black social agency in the early twentieth century not only constructed class biases within black communities, but also often disdain by northern elites for black southern migrants.

This does not mean that certain black elites did not understand or attempt to address the criminalization of blackness in the United States. Many of these black elites addressed the real crime going on in their communities that threatened public safety, as well as the racial double standards in urban crime. Indeed, African American writers and reformers such as James Stemons, a Philadelphia race-relations reformer, along with W. E. B. Du Bois, Ida B. Wells, and others attempted to expose and challenge criminal justice practices that actively suppressed black voices. Muhammad makes the point that "despite their elitism, many black reformers tended to offer 'root-cause solutions' alongside their class-infused cultural critiques of black criminality."[14] This desire to speak to racial double standards in urban crime and uphold black respectability created in Muhammad's account a form of "double-talk."

In the end, the desire to separate black culture from black criminality had lasting effects deep into the twentieth century. For example, not only did the stigma of criminality impact disadvantaged blacks and isolate blacks in the urban north but the stigma of criminality justified much of the punishment and torture that poor blacks faced in the late nineteenth and early twentieth centuries. Muhammad contends that:

> defining black criminality through racial and cultural markers of inferiority was at the heart of post-emancipation race relations. Black Codes, Pig Laws, convict leasing, chain gangs, and lynching were direct consequences of inventing new ways of thinking about blacks and of using criminal laws, criminal justice practices, and violence to target them—all tracked by statistics, reifying racist presumptions that blacks were an exceptional and dangerous criminal population.[15]

Although scholars such as Du Bois would try to explain criminality through the issue of poverty and racial segregation, they failed to disrupt the link between race and crime. Indeed the earlier Du Bois, unlike Ida B. Wells, wanted to deny the central role that race played in the criminalization of black people. Indeed, Muhammad points out that by the 1940s "new knowledge of racial criminalization and a new awareness of the limits of black crime statistics had not guaranteed a New Deal for blacks or a fundamental shift in the scale or intensity of social, economic, or political reform directed toward black communities."[16] In other words, race and punishment in the United States were intentionally made synonymous. It was not haphazard or circumstantial.

Black men are socially targeted and institutionally trapped by mechanisms that limit their personal and social mobility. The consequence of this is the construction of the black male felon. This is a direct result of the principles of Beloved Community not being applied to black male bodies. Moreover, to overlook the lived experiences of black male felons allows black men and as a consequence black masculinity to be falsely aligned with other social pathologies. For instance, to overlook the intentional targeting and institutionalization of black males in society makes room for the false perception that black masculinity benefits from white patriarchy. In other words, to overlook the criminalization of black males allows the false idea that black men are privileged, even marginally, in society because they are biologically gendered as men. When in reality, most of the social science data suggests differently. Indeed it is probably more accurate to state that white patriarchy targets black men, which leaves black men vulnerable to subjugation and assault. Thus the actual working of white patriarchy is to create a system within society that holds power over women and black men. This might also explain the assault of black fatherhood in US society.

Furthermore, the statistical discourse shows that black male incarceration is linked to something akin to race but operates differently when it comes to gender. Indeed, the racial and gender specificity of black male incarceration is isolated in many ways from broader racial and social oppressions. Yet when the call for the study and construction of programs to address gender and racial specificity for black males it is often met with critique. This critique leaves black men in general and black felons in particular vulnerable to ongoing systems of assault.

The moral repudiation of black male felons also created a paradox as it relates to applying the principles of Beloved Community. For example, this statistical discourse appropriated moral and religious language into its legal discursive practices in order to legitimize its legal and juridical biases. The appropriation of moral discursive patterns to justify legal and political policies made it difficult for a moral repudiation of legal and criminal justice practices.

Indeed, the statistical discourse used to advance incarceration speaks to how black criminality not only restructured racial categories in the United States, but also recast birth rights citizenship for African Americans. In other words, the statistical discourse addressed black citizenship by equating it to black behavior. In this light, black radical activity became antithetical to black citizen behavior. Ultimately, criminal courts and public policy officials enacted and adjudicated laws that denied the privilege of citizenship to thousands of African Americans. Often times the denial of black citizenship was based on the most benign socially "deviant" behaviors.

As a consequence, the conversation on black criminality became subject to a black apologetic narrative that sought to legitimate black citizenship as an earned right as opposed to a birth right. In a desire to uphold a standard of black morality within black communities, many black politicians affirmed the development of laws and criminal justice practices that limited basic human equality based on the rights of citizenship. Indeed, Western contends that "we can read the story of mass imprisonment as part of the evolution of African American citizenship."[17] In this way, the effects of imprisonment retracted many of the gains by nineteenth-century black radicals and twentieth-century black reformers to include the reinstitution of legal segregation and a practice of legally denying black felons the right to any social welfare and citizenship. In addition, it legally barred black felons from certain occupations and political disenfranchised them from the vote, thus placing them permanently in a captured space.

Initially, the rise of mass imprisonment and the retraction of citizenship did not affect blacks as a whole. However, as technologies for captivity improved, more black male bodies were captured into prisons and jails. Thus examining the statistical discourse and its larger implications on black communities makes it more apparent why prison is not only a tool for entrapping black male bodies in carceral spaces but also how incarceration is a metaphor for black experience in the United States. Indeed, the US social, political, and cultural systems treats heavily populated black communities as targets for criminality.

Moreover, black men become seen as felons despite their criminal record or lack thereof. Without debate, the effects of mass incarceration is felt most deeply on blacks with little schooling and little economic resources, particularly in the 1980s and 1990s wherein mass imprisonment became common for poor black men. Western contends that "mass imprisonment has institutionalized the marginality of poor blacks, setting them apart from white society and crystallizing social inequality within African American community."[18] This effect is the result of a historic intersection between the political forces of racial conservatism and the collapse of urban labor markets. However, the entrapment of poor black men highlights the sophistication of a penal system that attempts to deny any type of creative exchange to take place between black felons and the larger society. In other words, poverty is not the root issue, but rather the root entrapment comes from the ways penal captivity constructs barriers that deny black male felons from engaging in Beloved Community with others.

THE EXPERIENCES OF FELONS AND THEIR FUNCTION IN THE BELOVED COMMUNITY

In this society, when a person falls under the label "felon," his or her social reality likewise falls incredibly short of the ideals expressed in Martin Luther King, Jr.'s radical conception of a Beloved Community. The various forms of political and social isolation inflicted upon felons in housing, employment, education, civic engagement, and other social access undermines King's notion that society is "tied together in the single garment of destiny, caught in an inescapable network of mutuality."[19] My notion of the Beloved Community, as a black radical product bound to the principles of radical equality, freedom and agency, is based largely on two fundamental tenets. The first is in King's belief that what directly affects one group of people impacts all people. The second is that what constitutes the black intellectual enterprise is the desire to link intellectual exercise with pragmatic structures and movements. These two tenets highlight the fundamental nature of the black radical intellectual traditions.

Admittedly, many of the ideas regarding what constitute black intellectual life are entrenched in a long standing debate. For this reason, black radical scholars such as Manning Marable, Cornel West, Lewis Gordon, Anthony Bogues, and others have attempted to expand the ideas around the function and character of intellectual life. Moreover, these black radical intellectuals have given particular attention to the role of the intellectual as public intellectual. For instance, Gordon asserts that a public intellectual is marked by the nature of their work, "which addresses issues that have an impact on the communities in which they live and condition these intellectuals' roles in such communities."[20] The notion that the work of the public intellectual is inextricable from the communities out of which the intellectual is conditioned explains why the work of Douglass, Du Bois, and King makes possible for certain scholars within the black radical intellectual traditions to continue to examine the cultural life of African Americans. Indeed through this lens one could argue that in many ways, Du Bois, Douglass, and King set the framework for Gordon's concept of the black public intellectual.[21]

However, despite the use of "prison intellectual" within scholarly circles, the exclusion of the felon as a site for black radical traditions and engagement limits the bridging of thought and action for praxis among black radicals. Thus bridging the centuries of black radical traditions and its historic figures with the commonly held narratives about black leaders and intellectuals within the often separate spaces of academic, activists, civil rights communities, and popular culture has become the fundamental work of the black radicals. In this effort, scholars such as Manning Marable, Lewis Gordon, Joy James, and others have attempted to both establish and broaden the scope and significance of the black radical intellectual traditions in which Douglass, Du Bois, King, and others are located. For example, James contends that "since emancipation, black intellectuals have confronted lynching, Jim Crow, electoral and economic disenfranchisement, restrictions to higher education, racist violence, and police brutality."[22]

Indeed, the merging of black intellectual theory with practice has been downplayed in the history of King's legacy. By 1968, King no longer held on to the notion that civil rights alone could solve the problem of black inequality. It is most pronounced in the later part of King's life during his planning for the poor people campaign. This campaign not only bridged the suffering of rural blacks in the South with urban blacks in the North and Midwest, but also sought to challenge concrete structures in the United States concerning employment, income fairness, and housing. For example, to explain the economic disparity between whites and blacks in the United States, King links the broken promises of government to blacks after the civil war to the issuance of land-based grants in the west and Midwest to white peasant and European immigrants. In a speech to a congregation about the poor people's campaign King states that:

> At the very same time that America refused to give the Negro any land, through an act of Congress, our government was giving away millions of acres of land in the West and the Midwest, which meant that it was willing to undergird its white peasants from Europe with an economic floor. But not only did they

> give the land, they built land grant colleges with government money to teach them how to farm . . . they provided county agents to further their expertise in farming . . . they provided low interest rates in order that they could mechanize their farms . . . today many of these people are receiving millions of dollars in federal subsidies not to farm, and they are the very people telling the black man that he ought to lift himself by his own bootstraps . . . now when we come to Washington in this campaign, we are coming to get our check."[23]

In this light, King illustrates how the Beloved Community is the product of a black radical intellectual enterprise that sought to understand, affirm, and promote the human value of individuals by linking intellectual activity and social movement to concrete structures and systems.

However, the same type of political and social engagement by black leaders has been absent when it comes to black incarceration and black male felons. Therefore, black incarceration became more of a conversation about teaching black felons to obey laws as opposed to explaining why and how certain laws were intentionally created to incriminate black people. Indeed, much of the intellectual thinking of Beloved Community and the scholarship around the notion of Beloved Community has overlooked black male incarceration in part because it does not fall neatly within the boundaries of economics, civil rights, and morality. Moreover, ever since Dr. Howard Thurman and Dr. King introduced the concept during the 1950s Civil Rights Movement, their ideas on social ethics which fundamentally constitute the Beloved Community has increasingly been viewed as an idealistic notion to regulate human behavior. This notion is most popularly expressed in King's "I Have a Dream" speech. Ultimately the regulation of moral behavior and beliefs around black Christian intervention is why the Beloved Community has largely been the domain of African American religious scholars and black liberation theologians.

Once again, the statistical discourse on felons highlights these implications and illustrates how incarceration constructs society's ideas specifically about black men. Indeed, the increase in black male incarceration by the 1990s illustrates how the relegation of the Beloved Community to religious domains in American life had political and economic consequences. Not only had the scales not shifted for the better in black communities, but black male incarceration increased exponentially by the 1990s. There is empirical evidence that highlights the collateral effects of black male incarceration on black economic, education, family, and social life. For instance, according to Western's research not only were black men born in the late 1960s more likely to go to prison than to finish a four-year degree or serve in the military, but also by the end of the 1990s one in ten young black children had a father in prison or jail.

Yet, in the 1960s few black intellectuals and civil rights leaders addressed the way the prison was being used to trap black bodies into new structures of captivity. Prisons were not just used as instruments for crime control. They also had social implications. According to Western, it is necessary to show "how the penal system, for a generation of young men, came to reschedule their life course, influence economic opportunity, and shape family life."[24] In this light, it is clear that the imposition and social function of prisons has cultural implications on communities of color. It also shows how it reifies societal claims about black males. Thus by not applying the principles of Beloved Community to black incarceration in the same way that it is applied to poor people explains why mass incarceration has significantly closed the chances for social mobility for many black males. It also has significantly subtracted from the gains that King and other civil rights leaders fought for during the civil rights movement.

King's speech illustrates that the practice of Beloved Community was always intended to be a universal space open to human diversity in all its complexity. Certainly the social ethics that King and Thurman espouse is grounded in black religious language. However, as previously noted, isolating the notions of Beloved Community to the domain of African American religious life inevitably has intellectual, political, and cultural implications that can be witnessed in the way society perceives certain groups of people and sustains certain social and political institutions. Both Thurman and King's hope in human possibility and community advancement is firmly grounded in principles of Beloved Community that were translatable to other public spaces such as politics and economics.

Furthermore, situating the discourse on Beloved Community firmly within African American religious studies and Black Liberation theology has at the very least hindered the intersection of African American religious scholars and Black Liberation theologians with the whole of black intellectual life. In other words, as I have outlined through the statistical discourse, to narrowly define Beloved Community to merely regulative ideas for Christian communities and not a product of a larger black intellectual tradition has impeded scholars from fully exploring Beloved Community for its political, economic, and cultural implications. In *Creative Exchange: A Constructive Theology of African American Religious Experience*, Victor Anderson attempts to disrupt the discursive tendency that binds the idea of Beloved Community to strict ontological discursive categories by exploring complex and diverse religious experiences as a function for understanding Beloved Community. He argues that "Creative Exchange is a philosophical approach in which the constructive, innovative deployment of concepts themselves—such as experience, ambiguity, the grotesque, creative exchange, creative conflict, difference, race, God, world, community, and more—do the work of interpretation; criticism, and directing possibilities toward openness."[25] In doing this Anderson hopes to elevate Thurman and King's notion of Beloved Community past regulative ethical ideals because such ideals are ill-equipped to challenge Western-driven economic globalization—an economic practice that divides communities along socially constructed ontological categories, such as race, nationality, gender, and sexual orientation.

Creative Exchange is a reflexive constructivist theological approach that appropriates pragmatism, particularly the work of Josiah Royce, William James, and John Dewey. For Anderson, the appropriation of early pragmatists allow him to better understand the complexity of religious experience by illustrating how a variety of existing things can be explained in terms of a single reality. He applies *Creative Exchange* to black theology to explore the complex nature of religious experience. By doing this Anderson outlines the necessary shifts that have traditionally informed African American theology in particular and African American religious studies in general. According to Anthony Pinn, Anderson utilizes theology as a "way to interpret the complexities and thickness of religious experience—pointing all the time toward relationality and a longing for a richness of life as the 'Beloved Community.'"[26] Yet, "if experience is a holistic unity of purposes and actions, thought and life, that begs for interpretation," then to relegate the study of experiences to the domain of the religious limits our understanding of Beloved Community.[27] In other words, if scholars are going to expand "beyond near totalizing interpretations," then it is necessary to expand our investigation of experience past the religious in order to better understand how to apply the principles of Beloved Community more fully to the black experience in the United States.

Moreover, for Anderson, race is understood to be a "deep symbol that arises from the interhuman depth structures of human communities and functions as a deeply rooted category in the stock of knowledge that contributes to social meaning in Western culture."[28] As such, this book does not attempt to speak of race as an ontological dimension that is infallible or impervious to historical change and corruptibility. Rather, I seek to speak of race as a social construction that understands itself through a set of historical experiences and practices.

Thus combining the statistical discourse concerning the social, political, economic, and cultural experiences of felons to Anderson's notion of creative exchange allows me to extend the idea of Beloved Community to include the black male felon. More specifically, it expands the interpretative function of Beloved Community past regulative ethical ideals. This not only brings those labeled felon into conversation with African American religious scholars specifically, but also highlights the concrete structures that limit the social and political life of black male felons in the United States.

Anderson admits that neither Thurman nor King intended to limit Beloved Community to simply religious domains. Indeed, he contends that Thurman and King "were very aware that social experiences of white supremacy and Jim Crow segregation, race violence and genocide, and that the rape and torture of black bodies undermine the persuasiveness of their great hope."[29] Thus for King and Thurman the regulative ideals that constitute Beloved Community were always meant to be "concretely actualized wherever genuine creative conflict opens to creative exchange."[30] It is for this reason that Anderson attempts to enlarge "the account of African American religious experience beyond near totalizing interpretations bound by the black church tradition and black liberation theology."[31] However, Anderson does not expand Beloved Community outside of the domain of African American religion or black theology, but rather, further grounds it deeper within the domain of African American religion by utilizing religious experience as the tool for understanding creative exchange.

This is not to assert that Anderson believes that all experience is trapped within the boundaries of the religious. Indeed, he contends that all knowledge claims are fragmented. For Anderson, humans construct their understanding of the world through their engagement with other people. This engagement with others has reciprocal effects. Ultimately, these effects expand the idea of Beloved Community past regulative ethical ideals to "actual events that are concretely manifest in communities of interpretation that are supportive of loyalty to a cause that transcends every particular cause."[32] In other words, engagement with other groups influences every group because of the diverse experiences that any group or individual brings to our collective understanding of any particular phenomena. This leads to the development of a broad collective hermeneutic and the construction of overarching social principles that regulate actual events which emerge as a result of community interaction.

These overarching principles within communities of interpretation transcend any one principle. In this sense, theology becomes an interpretation, through both discursive and nondiscursive practices, of religious experience. For Anderson, "Beloved Community is the concrete actualization of creative exchange with the past, present, and future of Christian faith in community."[33] However, at this place *creative exchange* becomes essentially a theological construction through African American religious experiences. Thus Beloved Community remains simply the domain of African American religious studies and black liberation theology.

Based on Anderson's definition, the actual events that emerge within Beloved Community are subordinated to the particular experiences of the religious, which may or may not fully encompass the way everyone within the community is experiencing certain concrete events. Thus it is important to move beyond discursive and nondiscursive practices of religious experience. Ultimately, this exchange moves black liberation theology and African American religious studies into the larger domain of black radical traditions so that we can have a fuller understanding of black intellectual life.

If African American religious scholars and black liberation theologians are going to fully explore the complexity of Beloved Community, as Anderson desires, then it must expand beyond the exploration of Christian religious experiences. Indeed, if as Anderson suggests that "all theology is interpretation of human experiences and . . . the relevance of theology is in its expressive capacities to take hold of human experience and the world experienced by all" then we must acknowledge that theology is inevitably a political, economic, social, and cultural endeavor as well as a religious one.[34]

This shift in thinking is vital if we are to keep the concept of Beloved Community active, open, and "always forming and anticipated as a concrete event in experience." This necessitates that scholars access more than theology and religious experience as tools for negotiating the notions of Beloved Community. In the end, Beloved Community becomes more than regulative ethical ideas based on metaphysical claims.

Therefore, I broaden the task of theology within this book in order to more broadly interpret human experiences and to discover "creative exchanges" that are better fitting for human flourishing outside of religious experiences. In doing this, "creative exchange" more aptly maximizes the flourishing of human good and highlights the value of those who have been socially dehumanized. As such, the experiences of African American felons must be examined not simply for their religious sensibilities, but rather to better understand the totality of their experiences so that we might concretely manifest communities of interpretation that are supportive of Anderson's notion regarding creative exchange.

Furthermore, the construction of Beloved Community as a black radical endeavor must again represents the tradition of early black radicals who linked theory and practice to form black radical traditions. In order to address these concerns, research within this book builds on the work of Anthony Bogues's mapping of a black radical intellectual tradition to show how black male felons as a site for black radical thought has been ignored by many black radical scholars. Furthermore, it explores how the study of the felon within certain themes of black radical traditions shapes or reshapes the intellectual production that comes forth—particularly as we think of King's Beloved Community as a product of that intellectual exercise.

Consequently, the guiding question to this book is: how might the experiences and social position of those labeled felon influence the intellectual exercise and production of those within black radical intellectual traditions? In *Black Heretics Black Prophets: Radical Political Intellectuals,*

Anthony Bogues illustrates the complexity within black radical intellectual traditions in accomplishing this goal. He outlines the production of knowledge that this tradition has advanced in order to counter the nature of the West and many of the assertions it has made within the Western canon about history, politics, language, and human experience.

Bogues states that "for the last five hundred years or so, the practices of the black radical political intellectual have been in large part a product of modernity."[35] He depicts the ways black radical intellectual traditions have been used as a response to modernity's universalist claims. He highlights how the knowledge produced through black radical practices have from its origins had to produce ideas, thoughts, and constructs within small intervening spaces found within modernity in order to counter much of modernity's dehumanizing effects on black life.

Yet Bogues does not examine carceral spaces as a type of intervening space to capture the thoughts and ideas produced by black felons. To prove his thesis, Bogues highlights several black radicals who have bridged action and thought to produce new ideas that influence black radical intellectual life. Some of these radical intellectuals include such persons as C. L. R. James, Ida B. Wells, W. E. B. Du Bois, and Malcolm X. For instance, he contends that "Malcolm X's political praxis in the 1960s gave new meanings to the notion of human rights and challenged the American liberal theory of rights."[36] Yet, Malcolm's new ideas are not presented as a result of being held in penal captivity, nor are they applied to Beloved Community in ways that give black male felons agency in the world.

Therefore, I investigate these types of intervening spaces in order to fill the gap within black radical traditions. I first show how the prison is a concrete cultural and political structure for trapping black male bodies. Then I go forward to illustrate the complex ways mass incarceration structures the ideas and practices of punishment in order to deny black male felons constitutive moral agency within Beloved Community. Indeed, the concept of Beloved Community is one of many radical ideas that black radicals produced within these small intervening spaces to counter modern conceptions of justice, the value of the individual, and the work of the social. It is within these types of spaces and under these conditions wherein African American religious experience remains open and relational. According to Anderson:

> creative exchange keeps our interpretations and understandings of the meanings and significance of our particular religious experiences open to forms of enlargement that transcend the limits of our particular faith communities and actualizes in the here and now concrete instances, moments, or creative events of what Martin Luther King, Jr. and Howard Thurman called "the Beloved Community."[37]

Ultimately, the emergence of black male felons as a new identity category produces a body of knowledge that creates a new intellectual site on which black radical thinkers might theorize regarding notions of identity, liberation, and social justice. Subsequently, the rise of black incarcerated bodies requires an examination of black radicals' notions about conventional categories regarding black subjectivity, citizenship, and personhood and the radical politics of knowledge they have produced in response to those categories. As Bogues argues, "there is no radical political thought without an accompanying radical politics of knowledge that is able to open up the categories in which we have previously thought about ourselves as humans."[38] In spite of that, most black radical political intellectuals have failed to excavate the emergence of the black male felon as a new identity category and a site for black radical political theory.

In my moment of pondering Bogues models of black cultural production, I realized that the felon, although relational to the Heretic and the Prophet, actually constitutes a third stream of black radical production. For example, unlike the heretic intellectual the felon intellectual is not concentrating his/her efforts on "abandoning white hegemonic educational indoctrination that largely encapsulates the black middle class," rather he/she concentrates on abandoning white hegemonic educational indoctrination that primarily captures poor black men, and restructures black community relations. Furthermore, the felon intellectual is interested in reordering meaning by specifically restructuring the way specific boxes define black male bodies—namely prisons, jails, and other technologies of immobilization.

The value to mine the cultural production of black male felon as a site for black radical political traditions is in part based on the way the tradition has historically constituted black intellectual life. Much of that tradition has been based on black heroic narratives. Put another way, the totality of the black experience has been narrowly constructed and investigated. Ultimately, this type of investigation narrowed the space available for black radicals.

The limited spaces wherein black radical intellectual traditions exist have falsely and narrowly confined much of the work of black radicals to the totality of the "black experience." Bogues notes that the practice of narrowing "the black experience" has developed a habit of studying black thinkers as primarily derivatives of more acclaimed intellectual approaches based on the process of merging five different sources.[39] This influences the ways in which mainstream history of thought negotiates the nature of Africana ideas. For Bogues, these sources present issues for twentieth-century black radical thinkers who are trying to master the protocols, the conventions, and the traditions of the modern Western intellectual tradition—traditions that he claims was constructed on "natural history classifactory schemes of racial order."[40] This scheme situates African people and their descendants as nonhuman.

In an attempt to address the issues that face black intellectual life Bogues explores the meaning and function of the black radical political intellectual. He utilizes Antonio Gramsci, Cornel West, Edward Said, Russell Jacoby, Julien Brenda, and Isaiah Berlin to help define and locate the function and meaning of intellectuals as a social group. Although these theorists are helpful in teasing out aspects of the nature of black radical political intellectuals, they fail to offer for Bogues a viable model for the study of black radical intellectual production. For example, Bogues asserts that while West and Gramsci capture functions of black radical political intellectuals, they fail to define the nature of political engagement and the character of black radical political intellectuals' contributions to radical thought. He argues that neither theorist "spell out the nature and the engagement of the black radical political intellectual in struggles for political and human freedom."[41]

Instead, what arises out of the exploration of these theorists is the idea of the intellectual as either a traditional, organic, or public intellectual. Bogues contends that these "species of intellectual practice" merely help maintain binary opposition in Western thought concerning the nature of the intellectual within mainstream history as either expert or critic. This binary construction of the intellectual fails to provide adequate tools to engage the political intellectual within the black radical intellectual tradition. Thus for Bogues, any attempt to understand radical black intellectuals requires scholars to directly engage the ideas of black radicals in order to discover the questions they raise in their political discourses and practices.

Yet in spite of that assertion, most black radical scholars have failed to excavate the ideas of black male felons as a site for black intellectual life, and to discover the questions black male felons raise in their political discourses and practices. Indeed, ignoring the black male felon as a site for black radical intellectual life provides no real possibility for black Atlantic scholars in general and black radical thinkers in particular to theorize about the discursive practices of black felons on issues of subjectivity, personhood, and citizenship. Moreover, it overlooks the possibility of a new stream of black intellectual production. According to Bogues, there are two major streams of black radical intellectual production—the heretic and the prophetic/redemptive. The heretic is represented by figures such as C. L. R. James, Anna Julia Cooper, W. E. B. Du Bois, Ida B. Wells, and others. The prophetic is composed of "religious" men and women "who developed a set of practices and rationalities that sustained Africans in the diaspora and in continental Africa."[42]

Although both of these streams are commonly linked by the need to merge action and thought together as a form of praxis, they also bring with them specific issues that impact black radical intellectual life. For example, the heretic intellectual finds themselves engrossed in an effort to abandon his/her white hegemonic educational indoctrination that largely encapsulates the black middle class and alienates them from black lower and native class people. Yet, heretic intellectuals within the black radical intellectual tradition have carved out limited discursive space for those native and black bodies labeled felon in the United States.

As a consequence, the heretic intellectual finds himself/herself in a state of "in-betweeness" trapped between colonial powers and the lower class. It is this struggle to return to the lower class that the heretic intellectual begins to speak in a political language that reclaims the agency of black colonized people. For Bogues, the black intellectual becomes radicalized when he/she returns to the native lower orders and begins to carve out the discursive space of the black radical intellectual tradition. He argues that "black radical intellectual production oftentimes began with an engagement and dialogue with Western radical political ideas, and then moved on to a critique of these ideas as their incompleteness is revealed" in order to develop a different set of political and social categories.[43] An example of these heretical ideas can be found in W. E. B. Du Bois's concept of "double consciousness" or C. L. R. James's figure of Caliban, who presents new knowledge after learning the language of his masters.

The redemptive prophetic represents the second stream of black radical intellectual tradition. This stream attempts to break out of the boxes that Western political thought traditionally has confined black middle class heretic intellectuals.[44] Bogues contends that the figures in this stream were involved in localized resistance movements from the eighteenth to the twentieth centuries and composed of four essential elements. The first element of the redemptive stream articulates the political role of the prophetic figure's function as diviner, healer, and prophet.

It is in this space of the prophetic stream wherein I see black male felons as most situated and most overlooked. I find this to be the case because, like the black male felons, "studies of these persons, or the groups they formed and sustained, have yet to be formally recognized as a part of the accepted trajectory of the black radical intellectual tradition."[45] Thus, I attempt to "pause here to reflect for a moment on the matter of insanity, confinement, and subject formation in the colonial context" as Bogues suggests in order to excavate the political trajectory of the black male felon within the black radical intellectual traditions.[46]

Similar to many black male felons, this prophetic stream consists largely of the lower class population and is grounded in a cultural practice and language. Just like Nat Turner and Lyfe Jennings, much of the narrative is embedded in the use of biblical exegesis and the indigenous knowledge systems of colonized natives. The prophetic stream utilizes these linguistic sources to challenge conventional ideas of who and what can be called an intellectual.

The second element of the prophetic is the ability to narrate an alternative story and history of colonialism and redemption. For Bogues, it is not the linear chronology that is important in this element as much as it is the ability to "develop conceptions and historical narratives that collapse past and present."[47] The third element is the creative usage of language to describe social conditions and affirm humanity by reordering meaning to construct an alternative political discourse. Bogues contends that "this discourse refigures political and religious languages, integrating them to create a new political grammar."[48] The fourth element of the prophetic stream is that it creates a symbolic order that counters and overturns the racist hegemonic colonial structure in order to validate black humanity.

Indeed, the current social position of felons within the United States provides unique insight for the intellectual enterprise of black radical traditions, particularly the ways in which their marginal existence challenges the radical notion of Beloved Community as a black radical product. In other words, as Anderson suggests "if the Beloved Community that thinkers such as Howard Thurman and Martin Luther King, Jr. envisioned is concrete and not only a regulative ideal, then our particular families must enlarge themselves in creative exchange with other families and homes in which the filial bonds of kinship increase the plurality of goods connecting all our families."[49] The absence of black male felons from black radical traditions hinders the ability for this increase in plurality.

For sure, the failure to see the kinship of black felons in general, and black male felons in particular, hinders black radical thinkers from maximizing "those goods and desires that make life qualitatively good, fulfilled and flourishing for all its members."[50] Thus Beloved Community is a creative event arising within the creative exchanges of not only home, family, and church as Anderson contends, but also within the creative exchange of prisons, jails, halfway houses and other spaces of penal captivity.

BETWEEN CHURCH AND LODGE: BLACK PREACHERS, BLACK FREEMASONS, AND THE RECONSTRUCTION OF BLACK RADICAL TRADITIONS

There has been much written about the black church in the United States. Yet, little has been said about the role of African American Masonic lodges to bridge the theological praxis among black preachers and churches to larger social justice projects. Therefore, I extend my investigation of US political history beyond Bogues' work. I do this in order to include the development of black secret societies, particularly Prince Hall Masons and the construction of black masonic order on July 3, 1776, to show a "critical point of rupture" in the discourse at the beginning of the US declaration for independence from the British.

This rupture by black radicals in the late eighteenth and early nineteenth century highlight concrete moments in time that influenced nineteenth-, twentieth-, and twenty-first century black radical thinkers, particular black male felons. These earlier black radicals were not only responsible for the radicalization of the black church in the United States prior to the reconstruction church of the twentieth century, but also engaged in an international perspective on liberty and human freedom. Indeed, black secret societies played three fundamental roles in linking US black activism to international freedom movements.

First, black liberation movements through the relationship of black Freemasons in the late eighteenth- and early nineteenth-century created space that would connect blacks in North America to Trans-Atlantic blacks in Canada, the Caribbean, and eventually to Europe and Africa. Indeed, many of these societies sparked the development of later international black fraternal organizations and women's clubs which helped maintain black cultural ideals into the twenty-first century.

Second, the international link upheld by these black secret societies highlight how black intellectual products, such as Beloved Community, have from their origination been concerned with international and multicultural forms of liberation and justice. As such, these societies signal to the international and multicultural ways members perceive and talk about cultural concepts within black radical traditions. Third, these secret societies helped contemporary black radicals not only understand why secrecy and membership was crucial for the work of early black radicals, but also how that secrecy caused certain black intellectuals to both intentionally and accidentally overlook certain black radical political intellectuals.

In order for black secret societies to garner international black support for the liberation of Trans-Atlantic black freedom they had to create and maintain these black secret spaces. Therefore, in order to highlight the spaces wherein black male felons are located and the intellectual offerings that emerge from that space I took care in this project to: 1) investigate where and when new black secret spaces might have developed; 2) examine how these new spaces currently exists in relation to the broader society; 3) determine what new forms of knowledge might they have produced as it relates to black humanity; and 4) expose oppositional structures both inside and outside of these secret spaces that work to marginalize their voices. In doing that I am better able to place those offerings in a creative exchange that allows for a reshaping and more inclusive manifestation of Beloved Community.

Scholars such as Joanna Brooks and John Saillant, C. Eric Lincoln and Lawrence H. Mamiya, Albert J. Raboteau, John Ernest, and Joy James highlight the creation of counterhegemonic texts and ruptures within black radical intellectual traditions. They show how earlier touchstones for plotting the genealogy of a black radical intellectual tradition from black Prince Hall masons to later twentieth-century touchstones such as the emergence of prison industrial complexes better explain how black radicals dealt with the relationship of power, knowledge, and the creation of discursive systems that countermanded the use of black churches as apologetic cultural symbols for Beloved Community. Indeed, the mapping of this black radical intellectual tradition exposes both the intentional and consequential actions of certain black Atlantic intellectual scholars to overlook or minimize the whole of black intellectual life, particularly as it progressed from black sacred spaces such as plantations, masonic lodges and guilds, to secular spaces such as colleges, universities, and prison industrial complexes.

In addition to this significant rupture in 1776, I cite another rupture within Bogues's mapping of a black radical intellectual tradition to include the adoption of the Thirteenth Amendment to the US Constitution at the end of the Civil War in 1865. The adoption of this amendment created an alternative form of forced labor and codified a new system of punishment in the country. In addition, this new amendment, which reunited the northern and southern states again as one republic, allowed penal captivity to become constituted as a new form of punishment. It also allowed for persons, particularly black males, to become socially reconstructed as felons.

The newly constructed black male felon developed into a new identity category that became largely overlooked as black churches became the site for black heroic figures and prisons became the site for black deviants. Ultimately, I cite this concrete moment in time to highlight the rupture that led to the current prison industrial complex which can be seen in convict leasing, peonage systems, share cropping, black codes, and contemporary prison writings. I go on to map a set of imprisoned men that have impacted black radical traditions.

Late eighteenth- and early nineteenth-century black masonic lodges served as production sites for black radical thought and practices. For instance, black masons such as Prince Hall, John Marrant, Absalom Jones, Richard Allen, Martin Delany, David Walker, and others sought to reconnect black thought and identity to Africa in a positive light. In fact, had this reconnection of Africa in a positive light been more advanced, there might be a better way of constructing a positive image of black male felons. Indeed the men and women who made up these black radical religious thinkers not only lead abolitionist and freedom campaigns to combat violence against blacks, but also sparked a radical tradition that impacts black radical agendas to this day.

These black secret societies, particularly African American Masonic lodges, had a large impact in creating space for blacks to engage in complex and opposing viewpoints on issues concerning black life and culture. Similar to black churches, black masonic lodges were an important resource for black political and cultural development. Guided by Prince Hall and his followers, these lodges created space wherein blacks could reinterpret Masonic traditions that more addressed their social position in the Western Atlantic world. In *'Face Zion Forward': First Writers of the Black Atlantic, 1785–1798*, Brooks and Saillant argue that "Prince Hall redeveloped the content of Freemasonry to promote the equality, honor, and dignity of black people."[51] As a result, men within these secret societies helped to lay the foundation for how later black radicals would come to understand and articulate human agency and cultural fulfillment.

Many of the early black churches were founded and directed by black radical masons such as Richard Allen and Absalom Jones of the African Methodist Episcopal Church in Philadelphia. Indeed, many modern era black preachers and abolitionists, including John Marrant, were members of the Prince Hall Masonic Orders. The churches that they founded aided in the development of post-slavery communities that allowed for self-governance, education, and leadership opportunities. These eighteenth- and nineteenth-century black radical masonic leaders helped redefine black identity and agency in the world through their affiliation with this secret black society.

There is little debate that many early enslaved and free African Americans' cultural ideas were informed within a black religious ethos. This black religious ethos was formed out of the racial narrative that is often heard in the accounts of early black preachers and mystics like James Marrant, Harriet Tubman, and Nat Turner. These views were not only emphasized in black churches, but also in other black religious spaces such as black women quilting guilds and black masonic lodges.

However, while the black church existed in the periphery of white Americans these latter black cultural products were often hid in plain view of white eyes. As a result, these differing spaces helped construct different and sometimes opposing narratives and black representations. Brooks and Saillant point out that eventually certain black churches and their leaders, most of whom were not members of black secret societies, "generated competing understandings of black displacement, enslavement, racism, and emancipation, shaped by their differing theological perspectives on the relationship among God, humankind, and history on matters such as predestination, provincialism, free will, and human depravity."[52] This differentiation between black narratives and representation gives insight to how the leading forms of black representation were used to silence black figures such as Nat Turner, Martin Delany, and Ida B. Wells. Indeed, little has been said about how these differing perspectives lent to divergent ideas and practices within the black Atlantic world. Moreover, there has been little work done on how those differing ideas influenced black intellectualism, particularly in regard to black intellectual representation.

Indeed, the differing forms of black representation and the complex function of most black radical and cultural products highlights the difficulty in trying to construct a more positive identity of black male felons. This difficulty increased as the black church became the leading cultural product in African American political and cultural life. What is not often discussed is that the black religious ethos that informed African Americans was substantively different from white Americans, including white abolitionists. C. Eric Lincoln and Lawrence H. Mamiya in *The Black Church in the African American Experience* argue that "while the structure of beliefs for black Christians were the same orthodox beliefs as that of white Christians, there were also different degrees of emphasis and valences given to certain particular theological views."[53]

Ultimately, as black apologetic figures emerged from the black church, black radical figures in others spaces were placed in opposition to them. Therefore, a more complete mapping of a black radical tradition beginning with black religious beliefs and practices of enslaved blacks, such as Nat Turner and Harriet Tubman, and free blacks, such as David Walker and Martin Delany, helps to explain the creative works and practices of enslaved and free blacks to construct meaning within a black sacred cosmos—a construct that existed under the threat of constant terror. Moreover, this mapping also shows the limiting effects on black representation as black churches became the dominant torch bearer for Beloved Community. For this, Bogues reminds us that "the study of black radical intellectual production requires us to be historically concrete not so much in very carefully tracing its original sources as in finding the critical points of rupture and understanding the new categories when they are thrown up."[54]

In many ways, the black church was utilized by white liberals to silence more radical voices that came out of these black sacred spaces. Many black radicals in the United States, including Frederick Douglass and W. E. B. Du Bois, often invoked heroic narratives to justify their public voice and deter white backlash. For example, Brooks and Saillant note that "beginning in the 1790s . . . white men, often in mobs, harassed and attacked blacks who were utilizing public space, effectively denying [African Americans] citizens' rights to act and to express themselves in the public sphere."[55] This attack had profound impact on certain black radical agendas. It inevitably shaped both the perception of black representation and the conception of the Beloved Community, particularly the creative exchange between black heroic and radical figures, as well as between black masonic lodges and black churches.

Consequently, figures such as John Marrant and Nat Turner were challenged to advance a different form of leadership that is often understood as oppositional to black heroic figures. Indeed Marrant's anti-provincial doctrine and Turner's violent resistance to slavery not only illustrates a rejection of Douglass and the early Du Bois, but also shows how these less talked about black radicals orchestrated a form of creative exchange that invokes the grotesque as a means of its work. For instance, black itinerant preachers such as John Marrant presented a perspectives on freedom, faith, and democratic political practices that were revolutionary in thought and controversial for its time. His work was highly controversial within and outside of black social spaces, mainly because he was a loyalist and rejected US provincialism.

Unlike emergent black heroic religious figures, black masonic radicals such as Marrant and Turner appropriated white tools to include Christianity, Western democratic ideologies, and linguistic practices solely for the purpose of subverting white hegemonic systems and combatting the assault of racial slavery and racial oppression on black life. The subversive work by Marrant and other black Freemasons added hidden value to black Atlantic intellectual thought and praxis. For instance, Brooks and Saillant point out that these writings provide a complex and diverse understanding on subjects such as: 1) the role Africa and African religious beliefs had on black liberation; 2) the development of countercultural and emancipationist ideas and movements that where framed by complex Christian theology and Freemasonry value system; and 3) the role and authority given to black political, social, and religious leaders. According to Brooks and Saillant, the "transatlantic perspective allowed black men and black women to analyze the origins and persistence of the slave trade and slavery, to argue against slavery in an idiom comprehensible to both whites and blacks, and to envision a free future for blacks, whether in Africa, Europe, or the Americas."[56]

However, those representatives whose religious perspectives were able to garner greater appeal from white powers within the newly-won US nation, were able to obtain greater economic and political support for their work. Not surprisingly many of the religious perspectives that garnered that support advocated a form of US colonial provincialism. Ultimately, many of these ideologies led to great debate among black leaders and within black communities, especially on issues concerning black migration and resettlement in places such as Canada and Africa as espoused by Marrant and later Martin Delany, but opposed by Frederick Douglass.

While there is adequate evidence to support the role that these churches played in creating space for black political organizations, engaging in unique cultural expressions, and developing a Trans-Atlantic black consciousness, there is less conversation about the growing marginalization of certain identities and voices within these diverging black cultural spaces. As a result, oftentimes black voices that broke from colonial provincialism were marginalized in the broader society while black voices that better articulated white liberal sentiment were advanced in public spaces. This is not to suggest that these perspectives did not challenge certain oppressive practices within the United States, but rather to suggest how more radical voices became marginalized as a consequence of their less provincial views of United States colonialism.

Moreover, conflicting perspectives and understandings of the Old Testament and New Testament impacted ideas of slavery, freedom, love, predestination, and punishment. Theological debates such as those between Calvinism and Arminianism also had influence on the adoption of certain Western religious practices by Africans in the new world.[57] While many of these conflicting perspectives did not deny the religious claim that freedom for Trans-Atlantic blacks was a God-ordained right—a notion that was popularized within Black Masonic teachings—it did impact how certain blacks thought about the methods and tools necessary to obtain that freedom. Consequently, the church, over and above Freemasonry lodges, became the space wherein theological and religious ideologies and methods regarding the means for freedom became clarified. This transition impacted how Beloved Community as a black radical product would be translated and practiced within black sacred spaces.

Ultimately, it is very significant to note black figures who were not members of these secret societies because it signals to the transition in representatives and venues within black communities. In other words, as the principles of Beloved Community began to be translated through non-Masonic black religious figures and institutions certain types of black radical agendas were set aside and certain black radical figures were marginalized.

Indeed, highlighting persons who did not hold membership within these secret societies reveals how certain voices differed in public representation, if not in content, from those who were members of these societies. Most notably, Frederick Douglass was not a member of Princc Hall Freemasons unlike African Methodist Episcopal Church founders Richard Allen and Absalom Jones, Haitian attorney general Prince Saunders, Liberian president Joseph Jenkins Roberts, James Forten, David Walker, Henry Highland Garnet, William Wells Brown, Josiah Henson, and Martin Delany. This subtle difference may explain the very public tension between Douglass and some of his black contemporaries such as Henry Highland Garnet and Martin Delany. It also may explain why Douglass looked to and received more white abolitionists support than his contemporaries and rejected Martin Delany and other's black emigration campaign, including John Marrant.

As such, we cannot ignore the lasting effects black secret societies have had on black radical praxis. Indeed, they have shaped the ideas of black radicals in the minds of black people. Most importantly these black secret societies required black radicals to think about the influence of certain spaces as breeding grounds for black radical agendas and black cultural production. For instance, it should also be noted that black female societies like Eastern Stars, quilting guilds, and the black women's club movement helped to also create black spaces that promoted black human values and cultural norms, particularly along intersectional line of gender and race. In particular, black women's quilts recorded cultural memories and hidden secrets that helped secure freedom for blacks. Furthermore, the emergence of later secret societies, such as black college fraternities and sororities, highlight how black radical intellectual products gradually shifted in form and content. This subtle but influential shift continued to influence aspects of black radial political intellectual production in both its representation and its engagement.

Yet, scholars within black radical traditions failed to challenge the conceptions of felons as outsiders who can be ignored as moral social agents. They have offered few counterhegemonic texts to suggest why black felons have a right to full membership in the American democratic project. Instead, the social position of most black felons highlights a form of social death that subjects them to a nonhuman category that is rarely tracked by black radical thinkers. Although Bogues contends "that there exists a deep political practice in Africana political thought that connects the lived social and political experiences of Africans and the African diaspora to the categories of political thought" there exists little effort among these practices to connect the lived experience of black male felons to these categories.[58]

Ultimately, the inability to connect the experiences of black male felons to the categories of political thought, particularly within black radical traditions, hinders a fuller manifestation of the Beloved Community. However, since the lived social and political experiences of all African people constitute the work of the radical black agenda, then black felons must constitute that work as well. Thus, the question is not whether black felons should be a part of this black radical intellectual tradition, but rather why have they been overlooked by black radical scholars.

Furthermore, by examining their writings and intellectual works what role do black felons play in black intellectual life? In other words, how might the work of black male felons influence the intellectual exercise within the black radical traditions? The answer to these questions begins with a reflexive examination of black male felon, Nat Turner.

NOTES

1. Victor Anderson, *Beyond Ontological Blackness: An Essay on African American Religious and Cultural Criticism* (New York: Continuum Publishing Company, 199), 552.

2. Bruce Western, *Punishment and Inequality in America* (New York: Russell Sage Foundation, 2006), 192.

3. Bruce Western, *Punishment and Inequality in America*, 193.

4. Khalil Gibran Muhammad, *The Condemnation of Blackness: Race, Crime, and the Making of Modern Urban America* (Cambridge, MA: Harvard University Press, 2010), 3.

5. Khalil Gibran Muhammad, *The Condemnation of Blackness*, 6.

6. The Sentencing Project Fact Sheet: Trends in U.S. Corrections, http://sentencingproject.org/doc/publications/inc_Trends_in_Corrections_Fact_sheet.pdf.

7. Devah Pager, "Black in American 2." Interview by Soledad O'Brien. *Soledad O'Brien Presents*, CNN, 2009. DVD, 20:38–20:52.

8. The data for this statistics comes from the US Office of Justice Office of Justice Programs, Bureau of Justice Statistics. The report is entitled *Race of Prisoners Admitted to State and Federal Institutions, 1926–1986* by Patrick A. Langan, PhD (May 1991, NCJ-125618). https://www.ncjrs.gov/pdffiles1/nij/125618.pdf.

9. Khalil Gibran Muhammad, *The Condemnation of Blackness*, 5.

10. Khalil Gibran Muhammad, *The Condemnation of Blackness*, 5.

11. Khalil Gibran Muhammad, *The Condemnation of Blackness*, 4.

12. Khalil Gibran Muhammad, *The Condemnation of Blackness*, 8.

13. Khalil Gibran Muhammad, *The Condemnation of Blackness*, 10.

14. Khalil Gibran Muhammad, *The Condemnation of Blackness*, 10.

15. Khalil Gibran Muhammad, *The Condemnation of Blackness*, 284.

16. Khalil Gibran Muhammad, *The Condemnation of Blackness*, 12.

17. Bruce Western, *Punishment and Inequality in America*, 193.

18. Bruce Western, *Punishment and Inequality in America*, 194.

19. Martin Luther King Jr., "Remaining Awake Through a Great Revolution," in *A Testament of Hope: The Essential Writings and Speeches of Martin Luther King, Jr.*, ed. James M. Washington (New York: HarperCollins, 1991), 269.

20. Lewis Gordon, "Foreword," in *Transcending the Talented Tenth: Black Leaders and American Intellectuals*, ed. Joy James (New York: Routledge, 1997), xiv.

21. Lewis Gordon contends in the foreword to Joy James' *Transcending the Talented Tenth* that towards the end of the twentieth century the public intellectual—one who bridges consensus-building activities with intellectual leadership for the construction of institutions to address social problems—has become overshadowed by the "popular" intellectual. Indeed, the advancement of scholarship by the "popular" intellectual over the public intellectual's work explains in part why scholars have failed to investigate how the transition from slave to felon influenced radical intellectual activities. According to Gordon, "there are many intellectuals who will never find themselves at the center of popular attention because of the unpopularity of their political beliefs" (xiv). I would add this effect is even greater for people whose

political beliefs embody the material evidence regarding their participation or consent to "unlawful" activities and criminal indictments. Most certainly, the emergence of popular intellectual scholarship has had material impact on black radical intellectual traditions. For instance, this form of intellectualism has informed the way many scholars translate Du Bois's 1903 concept of the "Talented Tenth" in *The Souls of Black Folk*. As a result, popular intellectualism within black intellectual life has subordinated more diverse and complex ways of thinking about black intellectual representation in public spaces. From this vantage point, Du Bois's Talented Tenth represents an elite class of black intellectuals who alone were responsible for connecting their educational acumen to the crises of black America.

Furthermore, through popular intellectualism the notion of the "Talented Tenth" established markers and boundaries that not only situated black intellectual traditions from its more radical endeavors, but also created a trajectory of thought that has had lasting impact on how many people see historical black figures. To show the constraints and limitations to this mode of scholarship on historical black radical figures, Joy James reminds us that although the term and the idea of a Talented Tenth was popularized by Du Bois, the concept originated in 1896 among Northern white liberals of the American Baptist Home Missionary Society (ABHMS), which established Southern black colleges such as Morehouse and Spellman College to train Negro elites as a means of race management. From its inception, the idea of a Talented Tenth was designed to shield white America from having to deal with the tragedy of poor blacks. Ultimately, the goal of many liberal whites such as those in ABHMS was to construct a black intellectual that mirrored black life but was loyal to white modern intellectualism. This mirrored form of white modern intellectualism relied less on bridging consensus-building activities to address social problem, and instead developed a racial apologetic that utilized black heroic imagery as its methodology. Thus the role of the black public intellectual was not just to promote black human agency and value, but it also served as social buffer between unprivileged blacks and white society. Consequently, the emergence of these black heroic images largely mirrored white aesthetics, cultural ideas, and intellectual practices. Not only were these characters pervasive within black intellectual life, but also they narrowed the full essence and value of later black radical intellectuals.

Both Anthony Bogues and Joy James point out that the narrowing of black radical intellectual life is evidenced in many of the ways scholars talk about radical figures. For instance, it is often overlooked how Du Bois's personal experience with both black elites and how his intellectual work with poor blacks in cities such as Philadelphia and Atlanta sparked his evolutionary thinking concerning the Talented Tenth. Indeed, Du Bois's radicalization ultimately emerges most clearly as a result of his personal political crises—a crisis that found advocates in working class and poor black communities. Furthermore Du Bois's transforming radicalism regarding the Talented Tenth veered away from an idea that was indebted to a certain white liberal agenda that utilized the advancement of elite blacks to shield white society from the tragedy of black life in the United States to a Pan-African theory that sought political union with indigenous inhabitants of Africa. Du Bois's departure from the notion of the intellectual Talented Tenth within *Souls* to a radical intellectual Pan-African worldview is evidenced in his later work, *Darkwater: Voices from within the Veil*, and highlights a radicalized Du Bois that became more critical of whiteness on black radical projects. Yet this more radical figure is often times overlooked by many scholars who desire to maintain the notion of black intellectual representation as depicted in *Souls*. Therefore, the Talented Tenth is still largely referenced by many scholars as the bedrock theory for black intellectual scholarship. This theoretical position helps sustain this narrow conception of the black heroic intellectual figure. Ultimately, this has allowed for the rise in internal strife within black radical politics, particularly around issues of black representation.

As illustrated through the construction of a Talented Tenth organized around the ideas of white liberals such as ABHMS, black heroic narratives have engaged in a long history of muting radical black voices. Consequently, these shallow narrative representations of black life and culture have marginalized the complex political voices and theories being generated within the black radical intellectual traditions, and in its stead set up binaries between leading black intellectual figures. Furthermore, socio-political and socio-economic forces in many ways impeded black radical scholarship's ability to create a space wherein freedom and independence for the whole of black cultural life could be achieved. The influence of white power on many representations of the black intellectual in social spaces also helped marginalize if not altogether ignore the complex work of persons such as Nat Turner, Malcolm X, George Jackson, Ida B. Wells, Martin Delaney, James McCune Smith, and George Jackson for narrow socially constructed images of black representative figures such as Douglass, Du Bois, and King.

22. Joy James, *Transcending the Talented Tenth: Black Leaders and American Intellectuals* (New York: Routledge, 1997), 3.

23. The excerpt of Martin Luther King giving this speech can be found on YouTube 0:00–1:13, https://www.youtube.com/watch?v=n4vdfugMFbg.

24. Bruce Western, *Punishment and Inequality in America*, xi.

25. Victor Anderson, *Creative Exchange: A Constructive Theology of African American Religious Experience* (New York: Routledge, 1997), 3.

26. Anthony Pinn, "Foreword," in *Creative Exchange*, IX.

27. Victor Anderson, *Creative Exchange*, XII.

28. Victor Anderson, *Creative Exchange*, 4.

29. Victor Anderson, *Creative Exchange*, XIV.

30. Victor Anderson, *Creative Exchange*, XIV.

31. Victor Anderson, *Creative Exchange*, 3.

32. Victor Anderson, *Creative Exchange*, XII.

33. Victor Anderson, *Creative Exchange*, XIII.

34. Victor Anderson, *Creative Exchange*, XIII.

35. Anthony Bogues, *Black Heretics Black Prophets: Radical Political Intellectuals* (New York: Routledge, 2003), 1.

36. Anthony Bogues, *Black Heretics Black Prophets*, 21.

37. Victor Anderson, *Creative Exchange*, 4.

38. Anthony Bogues, *Black Heretics Black Prophets*, 207.

39. For Bogues those sources consist of: 1) the widely held belief that Africana thinkers should be studied primarily for their experiences which as a result rejects any real concern of Africana thought as a political intellectual endeavor; 2) the traditional methods for the study of political ideas and political thought that merely reify discursive practices within Western intellectual traditions; 3) the limitations that arise in plotting the genealogy of black radical intellectual traditions that can be largely surmised from the arguments presented by Michel Foucault concerning the relationship of power, knowledge and the creation of discursive systems as well as Antonio Gramsci's conception of the nature and function of intellectuals; 4) the creation of larger spaces that would allow for the promotion of theories and frameworks by black or anticolonial intellectual traditions that reject the privileged assumptions within Western episteme—an episteme that allows black and other marginal groups to go largely ignored; and 5) "the ways in which Africa is still represented, and its politics and human experiences are portrayed and studied in the so-called serious press, the prestigious organs of the Western intellectual tradition, and the popular mind" (4).

40. Anthony Bogues, *Black Heretics Black Prophets*, 5.

41. Anthony Bogues, *Black Heretics Black Prophets*, 6.

42. Anthony Bogues, *Black Heretics Black Prophets*, 16.

43. Anthony Bogues, *Black Heretics Black Prophets*, 13.

44. It is here that the work of Gramsci and Foucault is most prominent in Bogues's argument. Bogues states that Foucault's work in *Madness and Civilization* "tracks how the emergence of a liberal market economy created a discourse around the treatment and conceptions of the poor population" (17).

45. Anthony Bogues, *Black Heretics Black Prophets*, 16.

46. Anthony Bogues, *Black Heretics Black Prophets*, 17.

47. Anthony Bogues, *Black Heretics Black Prophets*, 19.

48. Anthony Bogues, *Black Heretics Black Prophets*, 20.

49. Victor Anderson, *Creative Exchange*, 23.

50. Victor Anderson, *Creative Exchange*, 23.

51. Brooks and Saillant, *'Face Zion Forward': First Writers of the Black Atlantic, 1785–1798* (Boston: Northeastern University Press, 2002), 17.

52. Brooks and Saillant, *'Face Zion Forward'*, 12.

53. C. Eric Lincoln and Lawrence H. Mamiya, *The Black Church in the African American Experience* (Durham, NC: Duke University Press, 1990), 3.

54. Anthony Bogues, *Black Heretics Black Prophets*, 3.

55. Brooks and Saillant, *'Face Zion Forward'*, 15.

56. Brooks and Saillant, *'Face Zion Forward'*, 3.

57. In addition to the US construction of race, provincial Calvinist religious beliefs largely influenced popular notions that informed patterns of behavior for individuals and groups within the United States' civil society. These religious beliefs too often sanctioned racial injustices. Gradually, many of those religious beliefs were circumscribed and codified into written and/or de facto laws in order to justify various forms of punishment. In *Black Abolitionism: A Quest for Human Dignity*, Beverly Eileen Mitchell argues that "recognition of the power of white supremacy to thwart both the Christian gospel message and democratic ideals, which served as the

foundation for the American experiment, is needed to help clarify the nature of the challenge toward full equality in America for African Americans" (2). In other words, the notion of white supremacy was so ingrained in the cultural psyche of the United States by the late eighteenth century that it was able to negatively impact moral and liberating tenets of Christian and democratic ideals in the United States in order to justify racism, racial slavery, Jim Crow, and penal captivity.

As such, the tragic interplay between democracy and democratic practice propels much of African American critical thought, particularly black intellectual life. John Dewey states in *The Public and its Problems*, "we have had occasion to refer in passing to the distinction between democracy as a social idea and political democracy as a system of government" (325). Black radical thinkers, and black intellectual production as an extension, have continuously had to understand black life within the boundaries of the philosophy of democracy and the practice of democracy in the United States. For this reason Cornel West argues in *Prophesy Deliverance!: An Afro-American Revolutionary Christianity* that "Afro-American thought must take seriously the most influential and enduring intellectual tradition in its experience: evangelical and pietistic Christianity" (15). West defines African American critical thought as the inclusion of prophetic Christian thought and American Pragmatism for the "interpretation of Afro-American history, especially its cultural heritage and political struggles, which provides norms for responding to challenges presently confronting black Americans" (22). For this reason, radical black religious thought has traditionally taken seriously the intersection of theory and praxis in a quest for black cultural fulfillment. This link between theory and experience explains why West tends to lean toward the work of pragmatic philosophers such as Richard Rorty, John Dewey, and W. E. B. Du Bois. African American thought is evangelical and piestic Christianity because it illustrates the intersectionality of theory and praxis as expressed within African American communities. West argues that "this tradition began the moment that African slaves, laboring in sweltering heat on plantations owned and ruled by primarily white American Christians, tried to understand their lives and servitude in the light of biblical texts, Protestant hymns, and Christian testimonies" (15). West borrows from the intellectual work of theologian and religious scholar, Albert J. Raboteau, to highlight how the "black church serves as a rubric to designate Black Christian communities" (15).

Thus, in many ways the black church is the prevailing voice for the articulation of the Beloved Community that Martin Luther King, Jr. would advocate for in the 1960s. However, what is not widely addressed is that the language of the black church is inherently a political discourse as much as it is a theological and religious one. Although West acknowledges that a multiplicity and diverse religious traditions exist within and among black churches—constructing diverse practices and theological and hermeneutical reflections—he also recognizes the overarching socio-cultural environment and political economy out of which these institutions and traditions form. What is certain for West is how and where African American critical thought must provide its greatest attention. For West, the prophetic tradition within the African American church has "been guided by a profound conception of human nature and human history, a persuasive picture of what one is as a person, what one should hope for, and how one ought to act" (16). In other words, the African American church constructed notions of personhood and moral standards to guide individual actions over and against the social and political forces that attempted to deny them such benefit, ultimately producing what we have come to understand as the goal of black radical intellectual life.

58. Anthony Bogues, *Black Heretics Black Prophets*, 20.

Chapter 2

The Construction of Nineteenth-Century Black Prison Radicals

An Address to Non-Reflexive Interpretations

In the aftermath of Nat Turner's insurrection, state authorities in Virginia and North Carolina went to great lengths to preemptively punish free black men and women and many enslaved African Americans because their very existence imposed an implicit threat to racial slavery. A series of musters in the upper South was justified in reaction to Turner, a "self-ordained" preacher who wanted to liberate men and women from the families who kept him and many others in bondage. Turner recruited many slaves to his cause, and believed it was his duty to "arise and prepare myself to slay my enemies with their own weapons."[1] Beginning on August 21, 1831, in just over thirty-six hours, fifty-nine people died. In response, the white people in North Carolina prepared to face the threat of black insurgency by locking down towns, interrogating and, in some instances, torturing slaves.

As news of Turner's rebellion spread from Virginia to North Carolina, volunteer militia units gathered to "protect" whites and their property. In Halifax County, the justices of the peace called on Roanoke Blues to protect the citizens, out of concern that "this spirit of insubordination and insurrection may extend among the larger body of slaves immediately around us."[2] Many Halifax citizens gathered together in order to be protected by the militia and slaves were locked in the county jail and heavily guarded by armed men. Colonel Spier Whitaker wrote the governor of North Carolina relaying how "the alarm cannot subside" within the town.[3]

Further, "Whitaker recounted, the people in the town had seized a free Negro. When they failed to extort a confession from him, they shot him."[4] Men were sent throughout the rural areas of the town to search the homes and gathering places of slaves, while also standing at the entry and exit points of town.[5] In Chowan County, and specifically the town of Edenton which was "a colonial and antebellum trading center" where the leadership of the county resided, patrols were sent in the streets and many men were jailed.[6] In one instance, a group of men was brought to Edenton to be interrogated because of fears they were to be part of a supposed rebellion.[7]

It is very probable that the innocence of these men became irrelevant because Turner posed, in the eyes of white supremacy, a new image of blackness that transcended the limits of slavery. Cast in language similar to the way twenty-first century Americans might imagine "violent felons," Turner's image became, for white supremacist, a vision of blackness that had to be eradicated from the landscape or, if not murdered, secluded to the most minute limits of carceral space.

Black history offers a different view of Turner. If slavery was a perpetual state of war, then Turner's insurrection could have enacted divine justice. To look at Turner as a hero, however, poses a problem, particularly because he was more of a martyr and because his actions had an immediate effect on African Americans in the upper South that looked more like white supremacist terrorism than freedom. Yet, through careful analysis, it is possible to locate a form of black male felon representation that works across academic, activist, and popular culture, one that does not require the advancement of apologetic language or black heroic imagery.

If we contrast Turner's supposed objectives with the way his actions were received by white supremacist, however, we can imagine a retroactive creative exchange that helps us see how he came to symbolize, and even marked a historical transition in white supremacist logic, from the invisibility of the slave as property to the hyper-visibility of the black male felon as public enemy number one. Nat Turner is a seminal example of the black male felon as a nineteenth-century black imprisoned radical whose voice was muted by the US penal system. In this way, he becomes an archetype for the construction of the black male felon.

Turner is not often seen as aligned with ideas and theories of Beloved Community because his insurrection falls far from the pacifist understanding of "turn the other cheek." However, he does confront oppressive institutions of slavery. His confrontation of racial slavery within creative exchange allows us in contemporary times to think about that form of resistance as a means of abolishing racism. Moreover, Turner forces us to wrestle with the grotesquery of slavery in order to manifest Beloved Community. He requires us to ponder the ambiguities of liberty and justice as it relates to dehumanizing racial systems. He also requires us to rethink the notions of guilt and innocence as well as continually reexamine ideas of nonviolence and pacifism as theories for Beloved Community.

To understand Southampton, retrospectively, in the language of creative exchange we must consider the viewpoints and identities that he presumes operate in the institution of slavery. For Turner, the white enslaver represents the institutional structure that needed to be confronted and torn down. In other words, as an antebellum slave and soon-to-be black male felon, Turner projects onto white bodies the institution of racism in the same way the black body represents slavery and later imprisonment. The reimagining of white bodies in the South is a deep religious conviction for Turner as well. He forces us to think creatively about theodicy, redemption, and a theology for oppressed people who exist in the midst of violence and terror.

Ultimately, Turner's revolution symbolizes the voices that were marginalized because of the nature of their engagement and their radical socio-political perspectives. This is in large part because of the growing provincial sentiments in the newly emancipated colonies and the social position in which those colonies place black male bodies.

Furthermore, highlighting Turner as a black male felon illustrates how the prison regime as a structural tool for the state allows a type of disintegration of black prison praxis. In other words, the branding of felon constructs a power and cultural dynamic that overshadows certain work, and allows a type of discourse about black male bodies to go forth with little or no reflexive accountability. For this reason, few have examined how Nat Turner, not solely as a slave, but also as a black male felon influences the US political landscape and how that influence impacts black radical traditions.

Indeed, I am not interested in Nat Turner and other black imprisoned intellectuals as celebrity or pop cultural figures. Rather, I am interested in how inserting these men into the rupture within black radical discourse helps construct a new language for talking about black male felons as sites for black intellectual life. More specifically, I am interested in how certain structures, particularly the prison industrial complex, influence the current discourse around black liberation projects. Thus, offering a reflexive interpretation of that work begins to reveal the constraints in which these bodies exist and operate.

First, I am suggesting that Turner's rebellion and his radical praxis confronts us in creative exchange with the grotesque. His rebellion forces a play on the imagination. As Anderson states, in the grotesque "one is asked to decide either/or, this or that, one way or another."[8] However, Turner's rebellion illustrates that such a reduction in reality is impossible. His rebellion is not reducible to "disjunctive judgments." Instead, Turner's rebellion brings to light the deep social problems that arise when we do not deal with the grotesque. Because of this, it is nearly impossible to quench our desire to make clean and neat the social and private human interactions, conditions, and struggles of Turner's life experiences.

Second, the grotesque forces us to look at the structural causes and implications and not just the effects. Indeed, the grotesque shows us what occurs when we ignore the structural problems in society. In other words, we cannot stop at Turner's killing of men, women, and children, because we will get stuck in an unresolvable binary. Ignoring the grotesque creates binaries that allow society to rest on notions of good and bad, normalcy and estrangement, hope and despair.

This is why the reaction of North Carolina and Virginia militias increased white supremacist terrorism in the aftermath of the insurrection. Yet we must understand that reaction and its causes rather than celebrate Turner as a heroic figure. In a binary of good and bad, we simply cast blame on slavery and white supremacy or make ultimatums about killing innocent people; one group fervently declares that Turner was wrong, and another group justifies his cause. Ultimately, those types of binary constructions close our eyes to the messiness of human interplay and make Beloved Community closed to new ideas, experiences, and beliefs.

Moreover, in an attempt to justify Turner's rebellion individuals feel compelled to construct some type of black heroic narrative and/or image that is not wholly true of the man or his rebellion. However, placing Turner's radical praxis of the grotesque in a creative exchange requires a deeper investigation of what the grotesque is telling us. Anderson makes the point that "the grotesque requires a transvaluation of values whereby the heroic qualities of the Apollonian cult of genius are reoccupied in the grotesque."[9] Turner's radical praxis of the grotesque in a creative exchange puts forward a counter-discourse to romantic tendencies about the horrors of slavery and the responses by those who feel trapped in it.

Turner's representation of the grotesque tells us that the erasure of one's constitutive moral agency—the ability to exist as subject, person, and citizen—brings forth messy and complicated repercussions. Indeed, when we place the grotesque in creative exchange we see that it highlights deeper social and political problems that require deeper investigation and inquiry. For example, Turner's rebellion as a representation of the grotesque shows the difference between the relationship of grotesque with oppression as opposed to the relationship of the grotesque with suffering. In other words, whereas suffering leads us to redemption, Turner shows how the relationship with oppression leads to a different type of political objective. This different political objective not only breaks down the binaries of good and evil, but also forces us to deal with the ambiguities of life. Indeed, it is at those moments wherein society sees deeper more complex social problems that Beloved Community happens.

In addition, Turner's rebellion as a representation of the grotesque shows how the system of racial slavery obliterates the human and places Turner in a type of carceral space. His representation of the grotesque is not a way of suggesting that Turner is evil, but rather, the ways in which the system of racial slavery operates as a system of oppression to erase the humanity of black people. Thus, the carceral space wherein Turner is placed reveals how Turner's activities are the result of a system that limits his choices to only a specific set of actions. For this reason, Turner helps us begin to think about a certain type of connectivity and the ways in which that connectivity results in a redefinition of what human society might be and a desire to struggle for it.

I contend that we get to the deeper point of analyzing Turner's rebellion, which is to force us to see the complexity of the grotesque. The grotesque is not easily dismissed with a quick glance or resolved from a subtle observation. It cannot be understood from the location of one group, but rather calls multiple communities together in conversation for a more nuanced discussion. Lastly, it forces those who hope to make known Beloved Community to stop and engage what we see and hope to accomplish.

Furthermore, if we compare the reactions to Turner's uprising with reactions to other insurgents we can see how the construction of the felon in racialized terms is intrinsic to his story. Turner and other insurgents, say Denmark Vesey, are not the only examples of creative exchange with the grotesque. Indeed, John Brown at Harper's Ferry illustrates a similar type of engagement of the grotesque. His mission at Harper's Ferry is both radical and controversial. However, most do not stop at the point of the killings that took place in Brown's uprising.

Few readers and onlookers, today or in its historical moment, engaged in superficial binary conversations about the right and wrong of Brown's deeds. Instead, many of Brown's contemporaries as well as twenty-first century scholars dig deep into the man. They bring forth his theories on love and freedom. They examine how his ideas of God and Christian beliefs informed his radical praxis. There is an opportunity to see his work as valuable to the discussion on liberty in the United States, particularly when it comes to white males' fight against racial slavery. By no means does an image of whiteness as the key ingredient to the making of a violent felon emanate from the story of Harper's Ferry.

As Cone points out, the grotesque brings together both our symbols and our experiences, such as the cross and the lynching tree, to help us realign our greatest ideals in concrete ways. We also encounter the grotesque in Biblical narratives such as the flood and the plagues in the Genesis and Exodus stories. Certainly, many Christians wrestle with the grotesque in the stories about Jesus on the Cross or the death of Apostles Peter and Paul. Moreover, we allow for nations and states to engage in a creative exchange of the grotesque in order to create just war theories and laws. Individuals fervently debate the various ways that the grotesque is present and useful for domestic and international peace.

However, what is fundamentally different in the creative exchanges with Nat Turner, and most of the other black male felons that I offer in this book, is that they are black male felons. Unlike John Brown, Jesus, or the Apostle Paul, society does not often cloak black male felons in a heroic narrative. We do not assign heroic imagery to their causes. For while these other stories get white-washed through heroic narratives, black male felons are left without cause or justification for their presentation of the grotesque. As a black male felon, Turner does not receive that privilege of heroic idol worship.

Therefore, in a not-so-subtle way, I am trying to illustrate how all of the black male felons in this book force us to deal with the grotesque without heroic narrative and imagery. They challenge us to turn our eyes to the grotesque and examine very closely how it operates in creative exchange. They illustrate that the manifestation of Beloved Community is possible without the use of heroic imagery as vital parts of creative exchange. Indeed, this type of creative exchange is the work that King, particularly in his later years, tried to bring to the understanding of Beloved Community.

Through his poor people's campaign, King attempted to show what Beloved Community looked like when society is not able to cloak the grotesque misery of life in heroic imagery and language. This ability to fully present the grotesque is when the fierce urgency of now becomes crucial to the world. Most certainly, none of these black men seem to have time nor are they inclined to wait for the world to figure out how to "pretty" up what they are doing. Huddie Ledbetter, Malcom X (we have been trying to make Malcolm prettier for years), George Jackson, Tupac Shakur, and Lyfe Jennings all point us to the grotesque and force us to ask: now that we see it what are we going to do about it?

Certainly, contemporary scholars have made strides in recognizing prison intellectuals in the twentieth century and the work that they have done. The rethinking of the image of felon, to generate the very term "prison intellectual," signals a creative exchange between preconceived ideas about incarcerated men and women and what they might contribute to ideas of freedom and agency. For instance, Dylan Rodriguez and Joy James help expand the idea of the public and radical intellectual to include imprisoned men and women. In particular, they explore the writings of state and federally convicted men and women to highlight the impact felons have on knowledge production.

We might consider the radical work of nineteenth-century figures like Turner as a precursor to the exchange that takes place when Rodriquez or James reconsiders modern prison intellectuals. Certainly, by including imprisoned men and women into the category of intellectual, Rodriguez and James help expand the character and function of the intellectual. For instance, in *Forced Passages: Imprisoned Radical Intellectuals and the U.S. Prison Regime*, Rodríguez argues that "imprisoned radical intellectuals construct a critical political practice that cannot be easily situated within the disciplinary conventions of civil society or the academy."[10]

For Rodríguez, the structural and systemic ways that convicted men and women are institutionally denied access to national public life creates the need amidst this caste group to build a collective cognitive praxis. Furthermore, effectively exploring this collective cognitive praxis serves as the material evidence for an emerging imprisoned radical intellectual that introduces new "vernacular forms, including the construction of new languages of agency, politics, freedom, identity, community, sovereignty, and struggle."[11] This imprisoned praxis and new language is often indicative of the grotesque. The language that comes forth is not often wrapped in black heroic narrative, but rather communicates through harsh, confrontational, and profane language.

The negative idea of blackness that white supremacists constructed around Turner carries through in the rise of the prison industrial complex. It is, in many ways, the monolith of racist power. As such, contemporary prison intellectuals must confront, undo, and create moments of creative exchange with an order to construct a new identity and understanding of blackness that builds upon the bare roots of human existence. This bare root is found in the isolated space that is most often occupied by the felon.

Ultimately, this collective cognitive praxis is crucial in large part because it reveals the character of imprisoned intellectuals whose existence is largely foreign to people living in the "free world." In other words, those labeled "felon" in society often are forced to reflect through radical means of the grotesque nature of their existence. For this reason, Rodriguez gives significant thought to a radical philosophical praxis that follows a line of structured opposition by a radical captive intellectual class. He argues that "none are more alienated from prevailing political systems than those who have been stripped of their civic status as citizen subjects, rendered out of the formal polity, and bodily subjected to the prison's regime of immobilization and disintegration."[12] This immobilization and disintegration largely occurs because the horrifying structure of imprisonment is founded on an interconnection between the way society understands and utilizes displacement and degradation as a means of social death.

In order to understand this particular form of social death, Rodriguez critically departs from the work of Orlando Patterson's notion of social death and Michel Foucault's notion of state punishment at the place of imprisoned intellectual praxis to highlight the uniqueness of incarceration as a form of bondage in the United States. By highlighting imprisoned intellectual praxis, Rodriguez illustrates how the state's particular use of power to capture men and women through what he terms a "prison regime" becomes the site for a new way of interpreting the world. As such, Rodriguez examines political theoretical notions and struggles that are generated by imprisoned radicals to confront the material and conceptual notions of freedom and liberty in the United States.

Often, these political theories and struggles confront more passive theories of resistance. We can thus see the genesis of the prison regime's logic in the reaction to Turner and the social and political white supremacist construction of him as a felon—a violent madman with no empathy for even women or children. However, through a reflexive interpretation and creative exchange with the grotesque, we can also see the genesis of the felon's logic particularly when we consider the dehumanizing and perpetual state of war that Turner wanted to end.

Rodriguez structures much of his theoretical investigation concerning the configuration and political life of contemporary US prisons around the work of post-1970s imprisoned radical intellectuals, but his concepts also apply to the Turner case if we reconfigure its history in the process of creative exchange. He calls the political work of these post-1970s imprison intellectuals "radical prison praxis" in order to frame the institutional and discursive oppositional critique that emerges as a result of imprisoning men and women. These imprisoned bodies have been both constituted and delimited by the prison regime. According to Rodriguez, this regime relegates certain men and women to an imprisoned category through legitimated state violence.

In addition, the power of this prison regime is mobilized by a complex set of systems and discursive practices that rely on a particular reified institutional structure. This institutional structure ultimately constitutes the complexity and fullness of what we understand as the prison industrial complex. In other words, the prison industrial complex creates an intricate web of technological devices that captures imprisoned men and women in much more than the mere confines of prison buildings. Rodriguez argues that to mobilize state power the prison must generate a "technology of domination" that "exceeds the narrow boundaries" of prison walls. In outlining prison regime technology of domination, Rodriguez helps to clarify how the prison system forms spaces of control outside the licensed political domain of civil society. This new form of technological captivity creates a new form of social death that Patterson and Foucault help initiate a discussion of but do not fully advance to articulate its twenty-first century effects.

As such, radical prison praxis pushes back against conventional interpretations and theories of freedom and liberty that have traditionally utilized US liberty documents as the basis of understanding the US institutional ideas of justice, liberty, and freedom. In other words, radical prison praxis offers an oppositional critique to the notion that the foundation of the US ideas on justice and democracy are grounded primarily in its Bill of Rights, Constitution, and Constitutional Amendments. Indeed, the term radical prison praxis provides a way for scholars to better understand the relationship between the intellectual work of imprisoned intellectuals and the various structural systems that impact the daily lives of imprisoned men and women. It highlights how the structure of the prison regime becomes an alternate site for defining the US ideas of liberty and democratic practice. This alternative space is not ruled by civility but rather degradation. Thus in revealing the more brutal nature of this space, radical prison praxis more aptly reflects the degradation and violence hidden within US society.

Rodriguez illustrates how carceral punishment is utilized by state powers to construct a form of social death that goes virtually undetected by the larger society. However, there are moments of creative resistance, such as the Southampton insurrection, that at pivotal moments gave glimpses of this construction even in the nineteenth century.[13]

Consequently, radical prison praxis at various points in history have been able to reveal the tension between US claims of freedom and democracy and the prison as a source of social death. Indeed, by highlighting the critique that emerges from radical prison praxis Rodriguez is able to both posit and site the emergence of imprisonment as a central "constitutive logic" of American social/racial formation. He argues that "this political lineage refutes and displaces, confuses, and short-circuits the coherent and durable sets of political assumptions that define the commonly enforced limits of public discourse and social intercourse in the United States."[14]

Indeed, the insertion of the imprisoned radical intellectual and the conditions that allow for his/her emergence challenges commonly held notions about justice in US politics—which upholds democratic values of equality and access as the basis for its political work. Rodriquez illustrates the ways the ideas produced by the felon as an intellectual is often dismissed because of the lens through which most approach their work. Therefore, he attempts to structure the imprisoned intellectual within a frame that allows for scholars to view not only the felon, but also the structure in which the felon comes into existence. This gives greater legitimacy to the category of radical imprisoned intellectual. Indeed at this moment of legitimacy we are able to perceive where and how instances of creative exchange happens.

However, Rodriquez also overlooks moments of creative exchange within earlier carceral spaces and the way those concrete moments impacted US political society and black imprisoned radicals. Many of these voices date as far back as Nat Turner and other black slave insurrectionists. As a result, Rodriguez constructs a framework for defining political engagement and constructing an archetype for an imprisoned intellectual that is limited both in its history and its archetypical makeup. Thus, his engagement on imprisoned radical intellectuals is mobilized through specific modes of operation and excludes the radical prison praxis of former slave felons and nineteenth- and early twentieth-century felons, particularly those men and women held captive under the convict leasing system.

Joy James attempts to address the narrowness of Rodriquez's use of imprisoned intellectuals by acknowledging the multiple publics and varied civil societies that shape public spheres. In other words, she acknowledges that unexplored public spheres might locate unacknowledged and unrecognized public intellectuals. In *Imprisoned Intellectuals: America's Political Prisoners Write on Life, Liberation, and Rebellion*, she states that "despite shared antiracist and anti-imperialist politics, US political prisoners differ in identity, ideology, and strategy."[15, 16] Yet James, like Rodríguez, highlights representatives of the tradition through the written work and activity of imprisoned radical intellectuals largely through "traditional" political prisoners such as Martin Luther King, Jr., Mamiya Abu-Jamal, Angela Davis, and the like. She narrows the field of political prisoners and ultimately the possibility of creative exchange with other black imprisoned men and women.

A REFLEXIVE LOOK INTO NINETEENTH-CENTURY BLACK IMPRISONED INTELLECTUALS

Certain black male figures, namely Nat Turner and nineteenth-century black male Texas inmates, illustrate the real, imagined, and symbolic ways black male felon representation influences black radical projects. The insertion of these black male felons highlights how the construction of black heroic images and the advancement of black heroic narratives within black intellectual life slowly started to shift from its original meanings and belongings. For example, a gradual shift toward black exceptionalism lent to the exclusion of other black identity categories such as black felons. Thus, the very same black intellectual enterprise that was initially constituted to affirm black subjectivity, personhood, and citizenship began to overlook the conditions of subversive black identity groups like black felons as constricted black heroic images and shallow black heroic narratives became the dominant ideal for black liberation, particularly within academic and activist culture.

In truth, very little is known about Nat Turner the man and many of these early imprisoned radicals. For instance, the only genuine description that historians have to give face and identity to Turner is described in the warrant for his arrest by then Virginia governor, John Floyd. In a documentary, Henry Louis Gates contends that we "have to recreate Nat Turner . . . [because] we have a very fragmented disjointed narrative which purports to be the confessions."[17] Therefore, Turner not only highlights a way in which felons are constructed through social imbalances and injustices but he also symbolizes how the work and meaning of the black male felon is erased and re-characterized to such the extent that it draws attention away from the social inequities that worked to construct the felon in the first place.

This fragmentation happens in part because the site wherein the *Confession* is recorded operates within a type of power relations that allows Thomas R. Gray, the attorney who interviewed Turner, to control the translation of Turner's narrative. This is significant because it illustrates how the voice of the felon is continuously mediated by the state and state-appointed actors. Gray not only frames the rebellion for the listener by categorizing the actions as atrocious and cruel, but also he later defines the actors in the rebellion as "diabolical."

The biased nature of Gray's writing provides warranted suspicion that he is not an objective interviewer. For instance, he states in the beginning of Turner's *Confession* that:

> in the first instance in our history of an open rebellion of the slaves, and attended with such atrocious circumstances of cruelty and destruction, as could not fail to leave a deep impression, not only upon the minds of the community where the fearful tragedy was wrought, but throughout every portion of our country, in which this population is to be found.[18]

Furthermore, Gray's narrative account illustrates how the discursive space about the black male felon is limited and restricted to a certain set of conditions. For example, Gray constructs a type of universality for black criminal behavior. In the end, this highlights the need for the black felon to construct alternative discursive terrains.

Moreover, Gray is able to advance the idea for a new form of state immobilization technology. Indeed, his written introduction justifies both the actions by the criminal court in South Hampton and later courts across the South. He insinuates that the activity of black bodies is inherently threatening and that this particular population's defiant behavior is not isolated to the state of Virginia. Furthermore, Gray sets the stage for a type of interpretation of black male bodies in particular, when he states that society should be fearful throughout the country "in which this population is to be found."

Ultimately, the prison regime gets legitimized for its control over immoral and socially deviant people. Consequently, any resistance that seeks to overcome violent racial practices against black people is thought of as a threat to civil society and the prison regime is considered the tool for controlling that threat. This explains why Turner's arrest overshadows a broader national discussion on justice and policy. For instance, the language that we now hear Turner use to tell his story about his resistance to racist practices becomes the property of the state, which can be used for anti-black resistance. Indeed, his private words, social actions, and personal beliefs are all shaped by an agent of the state.

Turner's life illustrates how the structure of the prison regulates the discussion of morality and justice in the United States. Often that discussion is positioned in favor of the state. We see this in the way Turner's public identity is filtered through the state's criminal apparatus. Yet there has been little discussion about Turner's actual arrest and incarceration and the ways the state created a racialized system of criminal justice that has influenced how society would come to talk about black civil disobedience and nonviolent resistance. As a result, his leadership in the South Hampton slave insurrection is largely debated on moral and ethical grounds. There is little conversation how the prison regime was constructed to interrupt nineteenth-century black radical activity. Even less is stated about how the prison and Turner's eventual incarceration and execution legitimized new forms of racial control.

Not only does the prison regime diminish Turner's radical praxis, it also nurtures white fear. The nurturing of white fear allowed many to argue in favor of southern slave-holding states. It also equated Turner's rebellion and other nineteenth century black radical praxis as the threat to a peaceful communal life. Indeed, that fear became the central focus for the advancement of penal forms of captivity. Through a reflexive examination of Turner, we can see how the advancement of the prison erases Turner's voice and replaces it with the state's agenda. This erasure of black prison praxis illustrates how an exchange with the grotesque began to decrease and the discourse on Beloved Community struggled to remain open to diverse forms of black identity.

Indeed, Nat Turner's attack on the white slave-holding systems in South Hampton, Virginia, in 1831 probably best dramatizes how state power in the South fortified a new form of punishment as a means of both protecting a white privileged class and erasing black radical praxis. The mobilization of state power to entrap men and women, particularly black men, within the confines of a penal system dates as far back as the founding of the United States. James argues that "the United States has a long and terrible history of confinement and disappearance of those it racially and politically targets."[19]

A steady increase in the mobilization of state power through racialized criminal justice systems began to expand more rapidly as antislavery revolts in the South started to escalate and radical abolitionist agendas started to take hold. This enhanced mobilization slowly began to transform the political tools in the South. For instance, enhanced penal codes and judicial courts found extreme ways to criminalize black behavior through minor and suspicious offenses.

Ultimately, the advancement of this prison regime became the redress to a radical black slave abolitionist class that was starting to impact the social and cultural life of white slave-holding citizens in the South. As James points out "the 'abolitionist' assertion is further complicated if we consider how contemporary racism and penal captivity likely evolved from within a historical colonial-settler state built upon, and enriched by, anti-Indigenous genocide and African enslavement."[20] Eventually, southern states such as Virginia, Alabama, Georgia, and Texas not only resisted the encroachment of abolition by introducing new technologies to incarcerate black bodies, but also states like Virginia and Texas began to interconnect race, crime, and politics to such an extent that a punitive revolution began.

Turner's rebellion and ultimate death highlight some of the earliest instances of confrontation with state-sanctioned domestic warfare—namely slavery and incarceration. Indeed, it is within this context that the prison regime became a new technological site for control and domination. This evolutionary practice is revealed through a reflexive look at Turner's words and work. For instance, Turner's *Confession* highlights a new vernacular for talking about justice in society, as well as reveals a form of black radical imprisoned praxis that changed the political landscape throughout the South. According to Rodriguez, radical prison praxis is "an active current of political-intellectual work shaped by a condition of direct and unmediated confrontation with technologies of state and state-sanctioned (domestic) warfare."[21] Not only did Turner's rebellion spark fear in the hearts of many slave-owning whites, but also it emboldened radical abolitionists across the country. The growing fear among whites in the South and the inspired zeal of black and white abolitionists in the North helped to construct state police agents in the South that were authorized and empowered to mobilize state power through criminal justice laws and punitive punishment.

Furthermore, the *Confession* illustrates how Turner's work as radical insurrectionist can be seen as a precedent in the later radical work of Martin Delaney, Frederick Douglass, and W. E. B. Du Bois. It can also be traced to the twentieth-century radical prison praxis of Malcolm X, George Jackson, and even twenty-first century black radical imprisoned intellectuals. For while other nineteenth century radicals such as Denmark Vesey were executed for similar radical praxis, Turner's radical praxis is not only well documented but also has a direct connection to the prison regime. In other words, whereas Vesey was accused and hanged in 1822 for rumors of being a leader of a slave insurrection in Charleston, South Carolina, Turner's insurrection is without question.

Turner's conviction and ultimate death as a black male felon in the South exposes both the power and growth of the prison regime as an emerging system for bodily immobilization and as an effective tool in erasing black radical praxis. His rebellion highlights more than simply a resistance by slave insurrectionists to a slave state. Indeed, it signals the sophisticated and transformative response of the white slave-holding states to mute a growing black radical movement. In other words, Nat Turner's rebellion illustrates how the use of the prison regime in the nineteenth century created a cautionary tale for black radical voices. This regime literally helped to erase a class of black people from the landscape of black radical life in ways white militia and white vigil anti-units could not. For instance, white militias and vigil anti groups where continuously criticized by southern and northern white Christians, irrespective of their position on slavery.

NAT TURNER AND THE DEVELOPMENT OF NINETEENTH-CENTURY RADICAL PRISON PRAXIS

Turner's sixty-to-eighty-person slave rebellion triggered a massive mobilization of nearly three thousand armed white militia and vigil anti-units in Virginia and North Carolina. In the film documentary *Nat Turner: A Troublesome Property*, historian Eric Foner contends that "the balance of sheer military power was weighted tremendously against the slaves in this country."[22] For Foner, the inability of slaves to effectively organize, gain access to arms, and structure their fight within a military tradition made it impossible for them to mobilize a successful slave insurrection. He argues that the "violent brutal reaction to [Nat Turner's rebellion] was meant as a warning. It was meant to frighten those who might be contemplating acts like this in the future. It was meant to demonstrate the power of white society."[23]

The power that Foner mentions was in large part transferred from slave plantations to criminal courts and penal institutions. In doing this, the courts and penal institutions gave the veneer of civil redress to corrupt state actors irrespective of bondage or race. Thus, the introduction of the prison regime served to erase black radical voices as effectively, if not more so, than violent white militia groups. It also gave the appearance of what justice should look like in a civil society.

Increasingly, the brutal acts by these white militias were not only considered uncivil and inhumane, but it also motivated white citizens, particularly in the North, to the cause of abolition. According to historian Peter Wood, "there is no doubt that there is a cult of violence that surrounds the tension between black and whites during slavery times and after."[24] This cult of violence became subject to a growing criticism. As Wood states in the documentary, it is difficult in contemporary times to "fathom cutting of people's heads and putting them on poles, parading them around, hanging bodies up in chains, dismembering the body [and] taking them home as souvenirs."[25] This difficulty was mitigated through a prison regime that slowly started to legitimize a type of violence against black bodies in ways white militia groups could not.

The prison served as a structure for regulating both illegal and immoral behavior. As a result, it informed how Turner's life would for centuries be documented, particularly in history and dramatic writings. Indeed, Turner's incarceration is instructive to the way conversations on civil disobedience and nonviolent resistance leads the national discussion on justice and policy. For instance, the vernacular that Turner uses to tell his story about forms of resistance to racist practices gets overshadowed by white fear to black radical praxis. Furthermore, the prison regime gets legitimized as a structure for bodily immobilization by presenting itself as a way of containing immoral and socially deviant behavior. Therefore, black resistance becomes recast as a threat to civil society and the prison regime lacks any formal critique for the way it operates as a racialized institution used to immobilize black bodies.

However, a reflexive look at the insurrection helps cast a new narrative. As a black male felon, Turner's *Confession* links captivity and incarceration in a way that common slave narratives fail to do. For instance, the work of the prison regime gives us a means of examining the methods of silencing slave activity and replacing it with propaganda materials and narratives. Turner's *Confession* shows the complex ways incarceration and the prison regime has long-controlled and corrupted the personal and social narratives of black imprisoned men and women.

In the end, Turner is killed under the label felon. The injustice to the slave is erased. Instead, we are left with the corrupt nature of the black male. Yet, Turner still leaves us with a glimpse into the idea of white supremacy. As a black male felon, Turner is linked to a longer historical narrative of black male punishment and resistance. This longer historical narrative suggests that the attempt to corrupt black radical praxis was not met without some resistance.

Turner shows the effects that black resistance to white systems of oppression and erasure has on black subjectivity, personhood, and citizenship. This ancestral line of resistance includes not only Nat Turner, but also Denmark Vesey and Harriet Tubman, among others. Thus, it should not be overlooked that we encounter Turner's story within a structure that legally, socially, and morally reshapes how we might otherwise think of the moral dilemmas of slavery. This is why Nat Turner's physical location is valuable in understanding his work and his words.

It is significant to also point out that Turner's *Confession* directs our attention to the grotesque in a way that captures the actual words of black males held in penal captivity. The Confession becomes an invitation for an engagement with the grotesque as presented by a black male felon. Although, we cannot fully legitimize Turner's confession as offered by Gray, we can see how the central place of the *Confession* becomes valuable for our understanding of black prison praxis. In other words, by delegitimizing the

Confession, we encourage an investigation of that space wherein the black male body is held captive.

Indeed, the prison as the location of Turner's *Confession* reveals how the structure of the prison regime has long since been the site for erasing and delimiting radical activity and shaping later black radical projects. The erasure of that history has lasting material effects. Much of the loss that we incur happens because of the actual space wherein we formally encounter Nat Turner—the prison cell. Traditionally, the prison has lead scholars to ignore the way we come to understand, evaluate, and measure the success and failure of black radical activity such as Turner's rebellion.

Instead of revealing the insightful work of those held in this space, the prison shapes a social perception and idea that nothing good can come from the prison and that the bodies held there only serve to corrupt civil society. For this reason, Turner's conviction and murder by the state has allowed some to believe that his form of resistance was a failure. This in some ways lent to a growing narrative that nonviolent, peaceful resistance movements have not only been more effective in the fight for justice, but also are considered more justifiable forms of resistance to state oppressive systems in a civil society. It also has made way for the heroic to gain greater appeal than the grotesque.

Furthermore, the formation of the prison creates a type of discursive practice that ignores the ways nineteenth-century prisons and the criminal justice system appropriated and legitimized certain white racial mob characteristics and white vigil anti-activities. It also allowed for the transference of power into the hands of police and other state-appointed actors to increase as federal manumission and emancipation laws started to sweep across the South. Inevitably, this allowed black radical scholars to ignore how Turner's language of agency, politics, freedom, identity, community, sovereignty, and struggle is embedded in his political praxis as a black male felon and not solely as a rebellious slave.

In the end, Turner's *Confession* illustrates how the black male felon becomes distinctively a political agent. For instance, Turner's trial and conviction reveals the contradiction regarding the idea of the slave as non-human. In other words, at the moment Turner is found guilty of a crime against the state, notions that black slaves are not human is invalidated. It is important to make this distinction because it shows the persistent need for a social reassignment of black identity by the state. This reassignment offers another mode of understanding the social construction of identity in society.

The rejection of the black male felon as valuable resource to civil discourse helps to explain why few have explored how the capture, conviction, and criminalization of Nat Turner as a black male felon changed both abolitionism and the criminal justice landscape across the South. For instance, through criminal court records Turner's conviction provides a means of engaging state ideals and practices that are not often available in slave records and documents. Refocusing the gaze on Turner from black male slave to black male felon allows us to see the effectiveness of the prison regime to erase black bodies from the social, cultural, and political landscape.

The transformation of the black slave to the black felon explain in part why contemporary black radical intellectual scholars have allowed nineteenth-century radical prison praxis to go virtually unnoticed. As Foner points out in the documentary, "we know all about the victims, the white victims, of Turner's rebellion—who they were, where they were killed, what their names were . . . nobody knows the names of even the innocent blacks who were killed or imprisoned or beaten afterwards."[26] Yet the names of the black victims are not a part of society's official historical memory.

This effectiveness of this transformation also impacted abolitionism. For instance, abolitionists and their work became framed as not just a threat to plantation owners and southern racism, but also a threat to civil society and safety. Yet, articulating the experiences of those early black felons and how their new social identity shaped the way they experienced and lived in the world still remained hidden. All of this resulted in the label "felon" becoming another means for rejecting or subverting one's full human agency.

However, a reflexive look at Nat Turner allows us to map another type of black radical tradition. This tradition holds the memory of forgotten slaves who eventually became black felons. This mode of investigation can also bridge gaps within black radical intellectual life to a history of radical praxis that is not often examined. Certainly, filling this gap will help reveal why the history of black people in the nineteenth century has traditionally been disjointed and misunderstood. Thus, to not focus on Turner as a black male felon ignores the numerous ways that black male felons starting in the nineteenth century may be utilized as a site for understanding the conditions, circumstances, and ideas of black slaves that might—as a consequence of their status—not otherwise be heard.

Seen from this perspective shows how Turner's conviction shines a light on the inner values and concerns that mobilize black insurrection—namely, violence against black bodies. Ultimately, a nonreflexive look at Gray's recording of Turner's rebellion and disjointed confession legitimizes whiteness and seeks to cast Turner's rebellion as unjustified and inhumane. For instance, in the documentary, Kitty Futrell, of the Southhampton County Historical Society, says that "when people bring that argument to me that [in] war . . . you kill people . . . but that's declared. This is my position . . . that's declared, you give people the chance to know that I am going to fight you, or that I might kill you, these people were not given that opportunity."[27] Futrell illustrates how casting the label of felon onto Turner provides a means for critiquing black violence against white people, while ignoring how that violence is merely the response to white violence against black people.

Whiteness is also legitimated as a type of compromise with black humanity. For instance, in another part of the documentary Rick Frances, a descendant of one of the white families killed in Turner's rebellion, states that "the killing of the women and children sticks in [his] craw more than anything else. [Turner] would certainly be remembered better by history if he had limited the killing to adult males or just all white adults."[28] As a type of compromise to whiteness, Frances dismisses the fact that Turner was the property of a white child at the time of his rebellion. In doing this, he legitimizes the structure of slavery as an institution by making the central focus of his argument about Turner and not the slave state and those who practiced slavery.

In addition to legitimizing whiteness and dismissing the impact of slavery as an institution on black life, Frances does not consider the response of white mobs and their killing of innocent black people in South Hampton. White consent to the terror of racial slavery legitimizes the criminalization of black men. It also ignores the institutional structure that repositions Turner into the category of felon.

Black people have longed wrestled with the dilemma that Frances presents. For instance, Bruce Turner, a descendent of Nat Turner, argues in the documentary that, "the evil that [Turner] saw was what was needed to be destroyed, and the only way to force the destruction of that evil was to make the price so high that those who was practicing slavery would eventually sue for peace and say we cannot keep slavery because it will cost us too much."[29] However, as a felon, Turner radical praxis is neutralized. It gives the appearance that the state has taken back any power that insurrection might have offered. In other words, the mark of felon delegitimize black radical praxis.

William Styron, the author of the controversial 1960s fictional novel *The Confessions of Nat Turner*, exemplifies in the documentary the sophisticated ways that black radical praxis is delegitimized. The conviction and labeling of Turner to the caste of felon is utilized as a tool to invalidate his claims for justice while at the same time validating the ideas around black radical praxis as absurd. Styron contends that "any intelligent reader coming on the confessions, the original confessions of Nat Turner, and then reflects on those confessions for a while would have to say to himself [that] this guy is a crazy lunatic. There's something really strange. . . . The moment he says to Mr. Gray 'was not Christ crucified.'"[30] Similar to the depiction in Styron's novel, Turner as a black male felon in much of white society is characterized as a subversive to civil society as opposed to a subversive to a slave-holding state.

However, the recorded information from Turner's *Confession* shows a distinct mode of thought that reveals more than just the ramblings of a deluded crazy person. Indeed, there is much to be said about the fact that Turner was killed as a felon and outlaw and not simply a slave. For instance, Nat Turner as felon and the prison as a structure for bodily immobilization offer a critique on the discourse on justice and the US political ideology. Also, using Gray's record of Turner's *Confession* illustrates how the prison reinstalls a new type of overseer for black people.

Within the interview, Gray suggests a failure in the structure of the slave system to adequately control black bodies. For example, Gray's account reminds us that Turner's father lived and died as a runaway slave, showing the flaw in the slave state. He uses Turner's *Confession* to highlight to a white supremacist South the activity and danger of escaped slaves. However, the prison regime becomes a protector of whiteness. He offers reasons for mobilizing new ways of controlling back activity. This activity moves from slave plantations with overseers to prison units with guards.

In many ways, the idea and value of the overseer in the slave system becomes enhanced in the prison regime. First, wherein the slave overseer is solely the employee of a slave owner, the introduction of the prison regime transforms the overseer into an agent of the state. The power of the state to employ overseers helps to construct a system that reauthorizes the white male gaze on black radical activity. Ultimately, this authority becomes another type of state-sanctioned form of control onto black bodies.

Second, the use of the prison regime impedes the possibility for escape. It fortifies a structure of control that gives the illusion of safety by implying that escape is more difficult in a prison system. Unlike the slave plantation, the state is able to create a system to recapture black bodies as felons more effectively than fugitive slave laws could capture runaway slaves. This is largely because felons are equated as being subversives of civil society whereas slaves are merely thought of as loss of property. In doing this, the state is able to brand the felon as property in ways that the slave system could not.

Both the fragmentation within Turner's *Confession* and the delegitimizing of black imprisoned praxis allows for broad and diverse interpretations of Turner and his rebellion. As a consequence, authors have been able to transform both Turner's identity and the meaning of his rebellion. The ability to transform Turner's identity has caused many to struggle with determining whose voice is actually coming through in the *Confession*.

Scholars such as Henry Louis Gates, Mary Kemp Davis, and Vincent Harding question the authenticity of the *Confession*. Sentences ascribed to Turner within the *Confession*, such as when he says "now finding I had arrived to man's estate, and was a slave, and these revelations being made known to me, I began to direct my attention to this great object, to fulfill the purpose for which, by time, I felt assured I was intended," do not easily comport to the vernacular of most unlearned slaves in the mid-nineteenth century. Yet, the words still help us to understand how the cultural ideas of certain states lent to the development of certain institutions. According to Harding, "it is very clear by now that we cannot take Nat Turner's *Confession* at face value, but it is also very clear that we cannot cast it aside."[31] The vitality of Turner's *Confession* hinges in large part on the location wherein we first encounter the man.

Surely the inability to ignore Turner's *Confession* makes the examination of the prison a vital part of our interpretation of his words and deeds. For instance, Gray records Turner saying "I now began to prepare [the slaves] for my purpose, by telling them something was about to happen that would terminate in fulfilling the great promise that had been made to me—About this time I was placed under an overseer, from whom I ranaway—and after remaining in the woods thirty days, I returned, to the astonishment of the negroes on the plantation, who thought I had made my escape to some other part of the country, as my father had done before."[32] The prison structure becomes the ultimate space for black radical political praxis. It also becomes the location for the transformation or death of blackness.

But even as it relates to Beloved Community, Turner illustrates how the prison becomes a type of ecclesiastical structure for the development and exposition of the black prophetic. Certainly it is important not to ignore the prophetic language that Turner ascribes to his work. It is particularly noteworthy to point out that Turner extends the discourse on justice beyond the boundaries of civil society in order to construct a new discourse on justice that precedes William H. Seward's notion of Higher Law Theory.[33]

In the end, Turner suggests that appeals to the US justice system and its founding documents alone will not liberate slaves. In doing this, the narrative critiques foundational documents such as the US Constitution and its claim to liberatory ideals. It reveals that the primary source for understanding freedom and justice in US society is dependent on an alternate discursive terrain that arises out of an oppressive space.

In this way, Turner articulates a type of transference of power from the slave plantation system to the penal system. This transference has not traditionally been examined through the words of nineteenth-century black felons. However, by examining Turner as black male felon shows how the black prophetic tradition can be located in spaces outside of the black church. Harding contends that "Nat Turner must have eaten up the Christian and Hebrew scriptures, and must have begun to feel and see and sense himself as the embodiment of these."[34] This is also crucial in understanding how identity is shaped within certain structures.

In this light, Nat Turner's *Confession* as a nineteenth-century black radical becomes an archetype to better understand the lasting effects of the criminal justice system on black life and culture. Turner's work helps black male felons become a part of a historical register that allows for a certain remembrance about US society that is not often captured through the narrative of runaway or escaped slaves. Furthermore, the location of the *Confession* informs how we hear Turner, not as simply property of an individual, but also as property of the state.

Turner's *Confession* become a valuable resource for black radical intellectual traditions and begins to map black radical imprisoned intellectual praxis. It allows contemporary scholars to more readily access the function and role of the prison in the nineteenth century as a system of control. Also, the bodies within the prison become a site to understand a particular type of historical, cultural, and political perspectives, particularly the nature of United States criminal justice system. Ultimately, we gain greater insight on the role of the prison regime by examining the impact and transformation of the prison to silence black voices and erase black radical bodies from memory.

NOTES

1. Charles Edward Morris, "Panic and Reprisal: Reaction in North Carolina to the Nat Turner Insurrection, 1831," in *The North Carolina Historical Review* 62, no. 1 (North Carolina Office of Archives and History, 1985): 29–52, http://www.jstor.org/stable/23518997.
2. Charles Edward Morris, "Panis and Reprisal," 34.
3. Charles Edward Morris, "Panic and Reprisal," 35.
4. Charles Edward Morris, "Panic and Reprisal," 35.
5. Charles Edward Morris, "Panic and Reprisal," 35.
6. Charles Edward Morris, "Panic and Reprisal," 35.
7. Charles Edward Morris, "Panic and Reprisal," 35.
8. Victor Anderson, *Creative Exchange: A Constructive Theology of African American Religious Experience* (Minneapolis: Fortress Press, 2008), 10.
9. Victor Anderson, *Creative Exchange*, 131.
10. Dylan Rodriguez, *Forced Passages: Imprisoned Radical Intellectuals and the U.S. Prison Regime* (Minneapolis: University of Minneapolis Press, 2006), 108.
11. Dylan Rodriguez, *Forced Passages*, 75.
12. Dylan Rodriguez, *Forced Passages*, 110.
13. To ensure that this intellectual work is placed within its proper context, Rodriguez foregrounds important historical and political conditions of the post-1970s US prison industrial complex. He contends that radical prison praxis critique: 1) explains how we regard the context, possibilities, and historicity of political subjectivity specific to the formation of the prison as a regime of power; 2) forms an idea of praxis by the use of terms that are linked historically to a lineage of imprisoned radical intellectuals; and 3) examines the formation of praxis at the site of imprisonment in order to shift the presumptive political geography of praxis from the juridical and cultural domains of civil society.
14. Dylan Rodriguez, *Forced Passages*, 2.

15. Joy James, *Imprisoned Intellectuals: America's Political Prisoners Write on Life, Liberation, and Rebellion* (Lanham, MD: Rowman & Littlefield Publishers, 2003), 7.

16. Furthermore, James points out that there are other ways of thinking about prison political praxis that is more extensive and inclusive of radical imprisoned intellectuals. For example, she uses Antonio Gramsci's argument in his *Prison Notebook* to argue that "every group has an 'organic' intellectual caste, one that functions as a vehicle to articulate, shape, and further the aspirations of its constituency" (3). Unlike Rodriguez, James makes room within a stratified culture that includes the possibility for men or women within the caste of felons to engage in critical and philosophical thought even when such thought is not legitimated by the state or society. For this reason, she argues that "the imprisoned intellectual is a public intellectual who, like his other highly visible and celebrated counterparts, reflects upon social meaning, discord, development, ethics and justice" (3–4).

17. *Nat Turner A Troublesome Property*, directed by Charles Burnett (2003; Los Angeles, CA: California Newsreel, 200e), DVD (11:27).

18. Nat Turner, *The Confessions of Nat Turner* (Baltimore: Thomas R. Gray, 1831), 3.

19. Joy James, *Imprisoned Intellectuals*, 9.

20. Joy James, *Imprisoned Intellectual*, 7.

21. Dylan Rodriguez, *Forced Passages*, 2.

22. *Nat Turner: A Troublesome Property*, DVD (3:15–3:22).

23. *Nat Turner: A Troublesome Property*, DVD (4:44–4:54).

24. *Nat Turner: A Troublesome Property*, DVD (4:44–4:54).

25. *Nat Turner: A Troublesome Property*, DVD (4:55–5:07).

26. *Nat Turner: A Troublesome Property*, DVD (4:55–5:05).

27. *Nat Turner: A Troublesome Property*, DVD (16:39–17:01).

28. *Nat Turner: A Troublesome Property*, DVD (18:11–18:26).

29. *Nat Turner: A Troublesome Property*, DVD (18:28–18:47).

30. *Nat Turner: A Troublesome Property*, DVD (15:48–16:08).

31. *Nat Turner: A Troublesome Property*, DVD (11:56–12:15).

32. Nat Turner, *The Confessions of Nat Turner*, 9.

33. William Seward was a US senator, state governor, and secretary of state for the United States between 1861 and 1869. He began his political career in 1831, one year after the death of Nat Turner. A staunch opponent to the spread of slavery and through ongoing debates with slave holding state representatives, Seward was a leading promoter of Higher Law Theory's notion that the Christian law of love superseded constitutional law. Indeed, Seward, along with other white radical abolitionist such as John Brown, vigorously upheld the idea that no written law should be enforced if it didn't ascribe to certain unwritten principles of morality, fairness, and justice. In *Race, Citizenship, and Law in American Literature*, Gregg D. Crane contends that "the higher law tradition invoked by Seward to read slavery out of the Constitution is complex and includes a wide range of formulations, but the core idea is constant and may be expressed (if not implemented) simply: to be legitimate, law must be just" (13). However, Seward, who was raised in a slave-holding family, along with staunch

abolitionist such as William Lloyd Garrison appropriated and advanced a notion of higher law theory that emerges from black churches and black religious figures. Black nineteenth-century radicals such as James McCune Smith and Frederick Douglass were among the leading black radical intellectuals that adopted and advanced a Higher Law Theory that, while debated in the walls of Congress, was well settled in black religious spaces.

Indeed, the condition of black lives was never fully stable because much of the actions and agreements that came about were the result of democratic compromises. These compromises yielded less than radical results. It is within these volatile conditions that much of the foundation for black radical intellectuals in the United States was situated. Black eighteenth- and nineteenth-century radical intellectuals were compelled to construct an alternative archetype to European-centered radicalism that would articulate the hopes and dreams for free and enslaved blacks in the United States on a more consistent basis. For this reason, Frederick Douglass would often have to forsake or cautiously navigate their relationships with white abolitionists and their movements for black radical abolitionist agendas that more directly called for an address to the urgency of enslaved blacks in the United States. Crane argues that, unlike many white abolitionists' beliefs, "Douglass's higher law conception emphasizes the personal and political transformation entailed in moving from private moral inspiration to dialogue and action" (113). For Douglass, the notion of higher law extends from a radical Christian religious belief that was shared by persons such as Ralph Waldo Emerson, Charles Sumner, William H. Seward, John Brown, and other radical abolitionists who argued that certain values and practices are universal in their truth. These universal truths for certain radical thinkers formed notions of justice and also influenced how radicals of the eighteenth- and nineteenth-century understood the authority of written laws and social practices. As such, the argument regarding higher law was pivotal in the debates over the justification of slavery in the United States.

Indeed, Douglass's belief in higher law theory became the basis of how he perceived black sovereignty and agency, particularly the expression of agency through social and political action. The urgency to engage belief with direct action defines much of the work of black radicals. In spite of the fact that "for almost two hundred years all kinds of American radicals [including black slaves to 1960s black militants alike] have traced their intellectual origins to the Declaration of Independence and to the Revolution it justified" the black radical intellectual often inserted a moral cry for independence and liberty that called for an immediate reimagining of freedom, nation and law (7). As such, the reality of black life for black radical intellectuals in the United States brought with it different motivations and experiences that informed both their theory and praxis. The black radical agenda developed more personalized perspectives of American radicalism that radicalized existing sacred and secular institutions in order to address many of the realities of black life in the United States.

34. *Nat Turner: A Troublesome Property*, DVD (12:51–13:09).

Chapter 3

A Challenge to Black Heroic Images

Huddie Ledbetter and the Politics of a Black Male Felon

Few men born in the nineteenth century better represent the complex identity of black male felons in the late nineteenth and early twentieth century than Huddie Ledbetter. Ledbetter intentionally subverted US ideals of justice and liberty. In addition, his life and songs unmasked the complex identity of late nineteenth- and early twentieth-century black male felons by offering a contrast to the conventional use of black heroic narrative within history. He forces black radical scholars to reimagine alternative black representation as sites for black radical work. Most apropos to this chapter is the creative ways Ledbetter as a black male felon utilized carceral spaces to intervene in larger cultural, political, and economic spheres. This intervention becomes a type of creative exchange that is useful in the construction of Beloved Community.

While Turner's rebellion is probably the most radical response to white slave-holding systems in the United States, Ledbetter's prison praxis highlights how black felons responded to southern states such as Texas and Louisiana's attempt to reinvent human bondage. In the years leading up to the Civil War, the Lone Star State continually voted and approved the building of a penitentiary in 1842, 1845, and 1846. However, it was not until 1848 that an actual prison got past the initial construction stage. At that moment, the institution of black bondage through prisons and the Texas criminal justice system became solidified in the political, economic, and social culture of the state.

In light of encroaching emancipation, Texas more so than any other prison state all but effectively foreclosed the possibility for black radical prison praxis. The Lone Star State's use of the prison regime to transform technologies of immobilization and erase black radical praxis served as a pivotal moment in both US penal and political history. In *Texas Tough: The Rise of America's Prison Empire*, James Perkinson points out that Texas became the epicenter for the growing use of carceral punishment in the South and built one of the roughest penal regimes in American history.

While exposing the subtle ways Texas entrapped black men into various forms of penal captivity including chain gangs, cotton and sugar plantations, and convict leasing, Ledbetter depicts the creative ways that black male felons intervened in the erasure of black life. Indeed, Ledbetter's greatest offering to black history comes in his ability to resist social and cultural erasure by southern prison institutions. Furthermore, Ledbetter demonstrates that not all black Texas penal captives were without agency and voice.

Although the agency and voice of many black Texas penal captives was limited and largely mediated through white counterparts, it was not completely erased. Through Ledbetter we are able to see the subversive role of black music. Black music has always been a tool for black liberation. Black music helped slaves navigate the Underground Railroad. It served as a battle cry for freedom demonstrations. Indeed, Ledbetter gives a glimpse into the subversive ways some black felons used music to disrupt the structural erasure of their freedom.

I contend that much of this structural form of bondage in Texas has persevered into the twenty-first century in large part because the notion of creative exchange that Ledbetter utilized has not been accessed as a tool for prison reform. His prison praxis reveals how black felons utilized the wit of a people who survived slavery to combat racial violence. He also calls attention to innovative ways of creating Beloved Community in political and criminal justices spaces in Texas.

It is not an overstatement to suggest that Ledbetter provides new ways of thinking about black radical political engagement. However, placing Ledbetter within the lexicon of the black radical tradition is not to suggest that he is above critique or that he is not a "bad guy." Similar to Nat Turner's Rebellion, it is hard to overlook the violent narrative of Ledbetter's life, his continual circle of violence, and his ongoing challenge with substance abuse.

Those that study the life of Huddie Ledbetter would certainly not label him a saint. In truth, he spent much of his life in and out of prisons and jails. Even before he was initially convicted in 1915 at the age of 26 (circa) and sentenced to the Harrison County Chain Gang, he had spent his youth and teenage years in and out of unsavory environments, to say the least.

As a black male felon, he refused to yield his own personal agency and subjectivity. After his official adult arrest in 1915 in Harrison County, he escaped and lived under the pseudonym Walter Boyd. If it had not been for him living under an alias, he would have probably served a longer sentence when he was convicted again in 1918. Even on his second conviction when he was sentenced to Imperial Farm in Sugar Land, Texas, he attempted a second escape with another inmate on August 15, 1919. His second escape attempt proved unsuccessful. He was recaptured by officials and forced to serve the remainder of his sentence. Yet, we cannot ignore how Ledbetter continued to disrupt efforts of entrapment in both physical and discursive spaces.

Ledbetter places many of his experiences and feelings of prison in his music. He exposes the agenda of the prison regime through his lyrical expression. Consequently, it is Ledbetter's music that allows for a form of creative exchange that makes Beloved Community concrete. For instance, through a creative exchange with his music it is possible to see the various ways black male bodies are targeted for labor by former slave plantation owners. This new form of forced labor allowed southern plantation owners to maintain their wealth far past the abolition of slavery.

In addition, Ledbetter's music reveals the prison world, while at the same time allowing a platform for those in carceral spaces to be both seen and heard by those outside of prison. Indeed, his music provides a way for incarcerated and free people to engage in a creative exchange that opens prison life and culture to a larger audience. This exchange between free and imprisoned black bodies help to construct a concrete event that actualizes Beloved Community. It is at the moment Beloved Community is manifested that the institutional structures in society that limit black felons are revealed.

Ledbetter's work and life permits his audience to move beyond the mere experience of incarceration and forced labor into a creative exchange that enlarges the filial bonds of kinship with non-felons in ways that maximize social desires for justice and freedom. For instance, this filial kinship became actualized in his relationship with Texas governor Pat Neff. This inevitably led Governor Neff to pardon Ledbetter's sentence. Although, Governor Neff believed that releasing Ledbetter was akin to releasing a tamed animal. This wasn't a concern for Ledbetter. Freedom was freedom!

This filial bond would be recreated later in Ledbetter's relationship with John Lomax and his son. Through Ledbetter, we can see how at the moment of creative exchange society is able to actualize Beloved Community beyond a mere regulative ideal by pointing out delimiting political and economic structures that hold black felons captive. These delimiting structures can be seen in the actual captivity of black felons and the ways black felons are viewed in the white imagination. This explains why the conversation about black incarceration is not really about accountability or personal agency; instead, it is about what it means to be a black person in Texas at the time.

Certainly, the way Ledbetter engaged in his creative exchange might be uncomfortable for some people, especially for those that hold to a black heroic standard. Ledbetter's creative exchange gives off the appearance of minstrelsy more so than any type of black heroic image. His critics forthrightly argue that he helps to reinforce the ideas that many white racists held about black people. However, Ledbetter passivity within white spaces does not just reinforce negatives ideas of blackness in the white imagination. Indeed, he does not even care if it did. So if we can move past that notion, we can see that Ledbetter's performativity also shows the way incarcerated and captured men and women negotiated freedom and expressed their agency.

Ledbetter shows how black male bodies garnered a type of restricted freedom within white institutional arrangements that were literally meant to kill them. When he capitulates to the white patriarchal structure within prison he does so as a means of subverting it. In truth, this form of black masculinity is merely a subversive way to distort those institutional arrangements for black agency. Ledbetter knew that his black radical praxis took on a type of minstrel performance—a performance that eventually led to his release after seven years on a thirty-five-year sentence.[1]

Lastly, Ledbetter shows the unique ways that incarcerated people directed attention to the impact imprisonment had on families and communities. Through his creative exchange he reorients the way society engages black felons by demonstrating their value. In Ledbetter's case it was his ability to creatively narrate the culture of black life to white people. An example of this can be heard in his song *Midnight Special*. Ledbetter uses the song as a means of reorienting society's perception of black incarcerated men, and he does it without them being conscious of it.

Also, Ledbetter's music reveals the way black imprisoned men constructed a new language for talking about freedom and justice. For instance, *Midnight Special* illustrates Ledbetter's use of a double entendre to shed light on the prison culture in Texas. The Midnight Special actually refers to the train that would pass through the prison farm. The late-night train delivered verdicts concerning prison releases by the governor. It also delivered news from loved ones. This explains why Ledbetter asks in the refrain to "let the midnight special shine a light on me" because the light represents the train that brought news (and sometimes escape).

The midnight train was a symbol of hope for felons. By utilizing this imagery, Ledbetter reveals the way incarceration informs the lyrical content, imagination, and expressions in his music. The molding of his thought as constructed by the experience of prison into lyric and music becomes another form of prison praxis.[2] In doing this, Ledbetter creatively gives a "freeworld" audience a glimpse into a world that is often hidden.

Furthermore, Ledbetter's prison praxis is a creative exchange between carceral spaces and black cultural production.[3] In other words, Ledbetter's interaction with Governor Neff, the Lomaxes, and later the world of folk music represents the way a certain group of men and women in prisons and jails are able to construct a set of practices and rationalities that are informed by imprisonment and incarceration. These practices and rationalities allowed these men and women to sustain themselves through structures of bondage, both inside and outside of prison.

Huddie's release from prison in Texas, and subsequent release in Louisiana, shows how he entered into a space of creative exchange with not only Governor Neff in Texas but also Lomax in Louisiana. This creative exchange did not require the use of religious narratives or imagery. Rather, Ledbetter's creative exchange entailed the tools of carceral spaces that are largely experienced in penal captivity. These tools ultimately led to his early prison release not only in Texas, but also became part of his identity after his release from prison in Louisiana.

Bringing the experience of incarceration into the light of day in conversations in many ways constitutes a creative exchange with people living "in the free world" who would otherwise forget those who are in prison. In some rare cases, convicts in Texas prisons managed to write letters to family members, church leaders, and even elected officials articulating their harsh experiences in prison. For example, Perkinson cites from a more graphic prison investigation report wherein one black Texas inmate describes being forced by a guard to lick the human excrement off another prison inmate. Letters such as this provided some limited insight into the structure and treatment of the prison system in Texas.

In addition penitentiary records, lease payments, demographic indicators and even death tallies give us some insight into the culture of incarceration in Texas. As Perkinson points out "from the end of slavery forward, Texas's prisons have predominately and disproportionately disciplined the same sort of people: poor black men living on the margins of society."[4] These black men were often illiterate as well.

Since many of the black inmates were illiterate, is it not surprising that much of the early part of Texas prison history required historians to rely heavily on Anglo-Americans, particularly literate white convicts, for an understanding of the treatment and conditions within Texas prisons. According to Perkinson, "state and university archives contain hundreds of records written by white convicts at Huntsville and Rusk; by contrast, prisoners of color concentrated on the farms—and women prisoners generally—are poorly represented."[5] Consequently, not until the Civil Rights era did any women or persons of color publish any in-depth exposé on life in Texas prisons, with the exception of Huddie Ledbetter, most commonly known to his fans as Lead Belly.

Huddie William Ledbetter not only used his musical talent and cunning personality to negotiate his freedom, but the legendary bluesman also used his musical career to give light to the social injustices in Texas prisons. According to Perkinson, Ledbetter is "Texas's first black convict to record his experiences in the sort of rich detail previously found only in white prisoner memoirs."[6] His stories gave insight into the treatment of black Texas inmates as well as depicted the limited space wherein black prison praxis engaged in moments of creative exchange with elected officials, prison officials, and white businessmen.

Ledbetter's ability to intervene in those spaces is significant because most of the close political and economic relationships after the Civil War were forged between former Texas slave owners and Texas politicians. Indeed, many of these former slave owners became the first to operate Texas's successful convict lease system. Because of the importance of black labor to the economic and political power structure in antebellum Texas, black slave owners in local, state, and federal offices rose from 58 percent in 1850 to 68 percent ten years later.

In the aftermath of slavery, cheap black labor had to be marshaled in a new way. Perkinson contends that, "by 1890, Texas was imprisoning more African Americans than any other state in the Union."[7] Archival and ethnographic research details how the historical struggle of Texas conservative and liberal politics constructed not only a uniquely harsh model of criminal justice for the country, but also a regime of state-sanctioned punishment based on mob style justice, similar to lynch laws.

Ultimately, nineteenth- and early twentieth-century historical corrections statistics in the United States shows how the history of punishment became far more of a southern story than has generally been realized. Yet, while these statistics show how the history of punishment became largely a southern story, it does not fully explain how this form of punishment went so long without much repercussion from federal government or black civil rights organizations. Indeed, much of those answers lie in southern stories held in the folk culture of those Texas inmates during that time.

Ledbetter was born in 1889, a little over forty years after Texas had established its first prison unit. The season in which he is born aptly situates him within a space and time in Texas wherein the state's free labor market was being substantially reorganized. In fact, by the time of Ledbetter's birth, Texas had fortified new techniques of immobilization for black people. Even though Texas was the last southern state to introduce the penitentiary before the Civil War, by 1848 the state had enacted a penitentiary statute that resulted in an established prison unit. Moreover, it developed the framework for the entire state's prison industrial complex.

The daily rhythms of the contemporary prisons in Texas—such as the legendary Eastham unit, the site of a bloody breakout by the Bonnie and Clyde gang—was built in the nineteenth century and has scarcely changed since. Like many other prisons in the South, racialized imprisonment in Texas arose from white supremacy, combined with peonage, convict leasing, and lynching. The interworking relationship of all these elements of torture delayed emancipation's promise to thousands of African Americans for a century.

Yet Texas, unlike many other Confederate states, not only delayed emancipation, they also created an entire profit center that aided in that delay. Perkinson contends that "a half century ago—before the Montgomery bus boycott, before the War on Poverty, and before the conservative reaction against the social experimentation of the 1960s—blacks in the United States were imprisoned at roughly four times the rate of whites."[8] This drastic rate of incarceration was a result of both racism and the profiteering of labor by prison farms and factories.

Ledbetter's life and work makes clear two distinct phenomena. First, he represents the carceral state of black males born in the nineteenth century. Second, he highlights how nineteenth-century prison structures gradually became the leading form of social control over black male bodies going into the twentieth century. Both his music and life signals to the complex relationship between black masculinity and white patriarchy, particularly the dynamic ways white patriarchy entraps black masculinity within carceral spaces.

Consequently, Ledbetter's music highlights the various creative strategies that black felons employed to better their conditions in life while at the same time resisting the marginalization by black elitists. Indeed, through Negro blues and folk music, Ledbetter was able to communicate with diverse groups that garnered some degree of compassion for the bodies that lived under penal control. Using the power of black creative genius, he was able to use his music as a tool for subverting the penal system.

Although it is not often addressed in black radical traditions, Ledbetter's folk music created space for openness to talk about the criminal justice system in the South in ways that Du Bois and Ida B. Wells could not. Moreover, his engagement in this type of creative exchange not only influenced politicians to release him from prison but also helped to establish him as a Rock and Roll Hall of Fame blues and black folk singer.

Furthermore, for Ledbetter to avoid being killed during his incarceration is witness to his ability to endure Texas's prison regime tactics. Perkinson contends that "untold thousands of African American men living on the borderlands of freedom suffered similar fates in the first decades of the twentieth century; they did their time, either survived or didn't, and faded from the historical record."[9] In the Texas Prison Biennial Reports, Perkinson points out that overall African American convicts in Texas died at nearly twice the rate of white Texas convicts. This imprisoned population boom and reconstruction increasingly impacted more black men as Texas added a convict lease program to its prison structure.

Arguably, the number of blacks imprisoned in Texas's convict leasing system had a larger toll than southern lynching. For while research and advocacy efforts brought attention to the 3,220 African Americans that were lynched in the South between 1880 and 1930, little light has been shined on the over thirty thousand deaths associated with convict leasing across the South in the span of five decades. This trend would extend into Texas's convict leasing system as sugar and cotton became the leading cash crops for the state—a world that Ledbetter would reveal to his listeners.

Ledbetter's songs become a form of prison praxis that speaks to survival in the midst of constant death. For example, Texas instituted the death penalty in 1923 in large part as a response to lynching, which the governor condemned. Most African American and Hispanic men, particularly those convicted of murder and rape, died while serving long Texas prison sentences. However, after being recaptured and sent back to serve the remainder of his thirty-five-year sentence, Ledbetter eventually found favor with Texas governor Pat Morris Neff. This is a credit to Ledbetter, because, as Perkinson points out, "despite the costs to taxpayers, almost a thousand more convicts entered Texas prisons than were allowed to leave during Neff's four-year reign."[10]

Ledbetter's life revealed the subversive work of black male felons to garner moments of liberty and freedom and to avoid the lynching tree and the electric chair. However, that freedom was not permanent nor was it without conditions, which is in part why his freedom was not long-lasting. Five years after being pardoned by the Texas governor, Ledbetter relocated to Louisiana where he was convicted and sentenced to the Angola Prison Farm on charges of attempted homicide for stabbing a white man in a fight. Music once again proved valuable for Ledbetter during his third adult conviction.

Like in Texas, Ledbetter was able to resist being erased by the prison system by manipulating the structure of incarceration for his benefit. He used music to transform the tactics of incarceration. He also subverted the ideas that typically presented black felons as lacking merit or usefulness. Through his musical partnership with John Lomax, Ledbetter constructed actual concrete moments of Beloved Community

These moments of Beloved Community allowed Ledbetter to overcome the structural erasure that usually occurs when one's identity is repositioned into the category of black male felon. With the assistance of the Lomax's, Ledbetter's musical offering helped to form of creative exchange that surpassed his individual benefit. It also didn't hurt that Ledbetter had a great dose of confidence, charm, and musical talent. Governor Neff and the Lomax family provided him with opportunities that would enable him to detail his life experiences.

TEXAS: A CASE STUDY IN THE REINVENTION OF SLAVERY

After visiting Angola Prison Farm, John and Alan Lomax discovered Ledbetter. They became enthralled by his tenor voice and lyrical expression. They decided to record Ledbetter's music and interview him for the Library of Congress. According to Perkinson, the Lomaxes transcribed his remarks so as to maintain Ledbetter's colorful dialect. In a BBC Four documentary entitled *The Story of American Folk Music*, historian MaryBeth Hamilton contends that John Lomax believed that "when you put black people in isolation, they will revert back to the music that they've grown up with . . . the songs of their childhood . . . the real black music."[11] Eventually, in 1936, the Lomaxes published a collection of songs and interviews with the blues legend in a book entitled *Negro Folk Songs as Sung by Lead Belly*.

The book became a testament to the creative exchange between Lomax and Ledbetter. It also revealed the realities of Ledbetter's world as a black male felon. For instance, within the book, Ledbetter is quoted as saying that "now I been to Lou's'ana, an' Arkansas, Georgia, and Alabama, an' all dem odder states . . . but in Texas got 'em beat for workin'."[12] According to Ledbetter prison work labor was the hardest in Texas. Texas prisons and prison farms were replete with gang labor in the fields, routine brutality, and minimal comfort. Perkinson contends that so entrenched was the institutional culture of masters and minions, even against women inmates, that Texas routinely was criticized by prison investigators for their harsh treatment of prison inmates.

As previously stated, for a black man such as Ledbetter to avoid being lynched or killed in prison speaks to his wit and cunning more so than his brute strength and rugged exterior. It is virtually undeniable that Ledbetter embodied the full stereotype of patriarchal masculinity. He was big and strong and he often got into physical altercation with people that crossed his path. However, Perkinson argues that "not only did [Ledbetter] have a boundless capacity for work and a seemingly inexhaustible supply of confidence and charm, but he was blessed with exceptional musical talent."[13] He used this exceptional musical talent subversively to manipulate power relations.

The ability to manipulate the power dynamic between felon and non-felon gave Ledbetter some personal benefit within white institutional arrangements that others did not receive. For example, although it is uncomfortable and striking for some that Ledbetter's prison pardon comes in part from a black prison praxis that embodied minstrelsy it is undeniable that it came with some benefit. Perkinson points out that "with his boot tapping and strings blazing, the musician hit all the conventional clemency notes."[14] Once again,

Governor Neff was so taken by Ledbetter that he pardoned his total sentence after serving seven years in prison.

Ledbetter found favor with Neff, who also was the ninth president of Baylor University and a deeply religious man, by writing a song for the then governor of the Lone Star State. Perkinson states that "when [Ledbetter] heard that Governor Neff was planning a personal inspection, he composed a special song."[15] Music and songs had two functions. It served as a type of prison intellectual production, and it created spaces for psychological, personal, and spiritual freedom.

In Ledbetter's case, his music and eventual pardon speaks to the way prisoners, particularly black male prisoners, are forced to adopt a certain type of behavior and utilize alternative methods of persuasion to gain agency and voice. After singing the song that he wrote specifically for the governor, Ledbetter states that the governor was "a big, fin-lookin' man," who "sho was crazy about my singin' an' dancin'. Ev'y time I'd sing a new song or cut a few steps he'd roll me a bran-new silver dollar 'cross the flo.'"[16] The ability to sway the governor was not only a remarkable task because he had vowed to not pardon any convicts, but also because Texas did not have a parole system in place at the time.

As it happens, Texas slave plantations are just as valuable in tracing the lineage of American prisons as Pennsylvania penitentiaries are in the North. Similar to Texas slave plantations, Perkinson argues that the Texas prison regime "shows how a uniquely calloused, racialized, and profit-driven style of punishment that developed on slavery's frontier became a model for the nation in the post-civil rights era."[17] Ledbetter's folk song *Midnight Special* actually speaks to this racialized profit driven institution. In *Midnight Special* he says "if you ever go to Houston/boy you better walk right/And you better not squabble/ and you better not fight/ Benson Crocker will arrest you/Jimmy Boone will take you down/ You can bet your bottom dollar, that you are Sugar Land bound."[18] Sugar Land, Texas, a suburb of Houston, is where inmates such as Ledbetter were sentenced to work the Imperial Sugar Factory Farms.

Within the song, Ledbetter shines a light on Texas prison as a profiteering mechanism. Indeed, it is rarely discussed how the prison system in Texas became a vital resource for the State. This profiteering industry dates back to the nineteenth century. Indeed, Texas's desire to take advantage of the resource of free labor that Texas prisons provided largely resulted in the reconstitution of forced labor on the backs of former slaves, particularly black men. This forced labor was dependent on a "democracy" in Texas that was fully grounded in racial subjugation, corporal punishment, and unpaid field labor.

Archival documents from the Freedmen's Bureau records the ways black people were re-enslaved under this new form of bondage. For instance, the

United States Bureau of Refugees, commonly referred to as the Freedmen's Bureau, was established in 1865 by the US Congress to help track and assists free slaves in the South during reconstruction, particularly after the Civil War. However, they found that the Texas prison system had effectively captured enslaved and free blacks, particularly men, back into a system of forced labor and bondage long before the Civil War.

Archival evidence of the different ways black men and women were incarcerated in the state of Texas is included in Texas prison archives. In a document entitled "Freedmen's Bureau Report of an Inspection of Texas State Penitentiary at Huntsville, Walker County", Lieutenant J. F. Kirkman records his inspection of the Texas State Penitentiary in Huntsville. According to Kirkman, of the 411 total men and women confined in the prison 225 of them were "freed people." That is roughly 55 percent of the prison population. Fourteen of the prisoners were black women and 211 of them were black men. That means that roughly 51 percent of Texas prisoners during the time of Freedmen's report were black men. Kirkman writes that "there are no white female convicts (so considered) in the prison though two of the females that are classed as freed people are almost as white as any caucasian."[19]

Kirkman's report shows that freed black men outnumbered every other group of incarcerated bodies in Texas prisons shortly after the Civil War. It also highlights the trivial reasons and long length of sentences that they had to endure. Both accounts become evidence of Texas's racists and corrupt criminal justice system. According to Kirkman, several of his interactions with the prisoners convinced him to do a complete interview with all of the inmates in the prison. He writes that "the majority of them are I am fully convinced and any person listening to simple frank statements and looking into the black honest faces could not believe otherwise."[20]

Although Kirkman did not believe the innocence of all the statements rendered, he did believe most had been unjustly incarcerated. He writes that "in many cases as you will observe the whole cause of the prosecution has for its foundation malice, and is followed up in a spirit of revenge by men embittered disappointment and foiled by the failure of their schemes."[21] In Kirkman's report entitled "Freedmen's Bureau Report of an Inspection of the Texas State Penitentiary at Huntsville, Walker County" he outlines some of the reasons the black prisoners in Huntsville were incarcerated. For example, the report shows that Isaac Lloyd and Richard Childs received the same two-year prison sentence, even though Lloyd is accused of stealing two pigs while Childs is accused of stealing just one.[22]

The Freedmen Bureau Reports illustrates how incarceration began to shape black men, in particular, in the white racist imagination as thieves and criminals. This systemic process of branding black men as criminal helped to justify placing the label of felon on to black male bodies. Like with Nat

Turner, this label became a sign that the state was again protecting its citizens. Yet as the document shows, several of the black men were convicted on very suspicious charges. For instance, in the Freedmen's Bureau Report Henry Richardson of Bastrop was given seven years for "attempted rape." However, according to the document, Richardson was prosecuted by his former slave master.

Stories like Richardson are replete throughout the document. Another example is of Jackson Jones of Fannin, Texas, who is listed in the report. According to the report, Jackson was given a two-year prison sentence for "stealing plow and some corn." Yet Jones, according to the documents, claims that he "was the overseer for his old master who prosecuted him because he would not contract and remain with [him] after being set free." Most of the charges and sentences are random with no reason for the length of the sentence—one could serve the same amount of time for stealing one dollar and stealing ten dollars, ranging from stealing wheat and horses to stabbing and raping. Ultimately for Kirkman, the "trivial" nature of the crimes and the severity of the prison sentences warranted federal government assistance—an assistance that never was fully activated.

In spite of the fact that Texas has one of the largest prison regimes in the United States, its role in expanding and fortifying carceral punishment across the South has remained largely in the margins of penology. This happens in large part because the cultural artifacts that speak to Texas prison regime has largely excluded its most represented group. However, Ledbetter speaks candidly in his song about the relatively quick and easy way police and judges in Houston entrapped black men into penal captivity. In fact, in some live versions of the song *Midnight Special*, Ledbetter actually changes the last verse to say that "the Judge will sentence you/penitentiary bound."[23] In this version of the song, Ledbetter makes a direct accusation to the criminal justice system in Texas.[24]

Furthermore, the song shows the improvisation and creativity of folk music. Regardless of metaphor, both versions of the song highlight the ever-present threat of incarceration for black men in the late nineteenth and early twentieth century. Ledbetter points out that the life course of the black male felon in Texas was often bound to Sugar Land Imperial Sugar Corporation. Even more revealing is that, while some of the land has been sold around the Imperial Sugar Factory, the prison units including the Jester and Carol Vance Units as well as the Imperial Sugar Mill still exists and operate today—making Imperial Sugar one of the leading sugar manufacturing corporations in the country.[25]

The ongoing racialized and profit-driven treatment of incarcerated bodies explains why Perkinson redirects focus from northern penitentiaries, the birthplace of rehabilitative penology, to the South, the progenitors of subjugation and dehumanizing forms of discipline. In *Midnight Special*, Ledbetter speaks to the calloused treatment of inmates by prison officials in the Imperial Sugar Land Convict Factory and Farm. He states that "when you get up in the morning/when the big bell ring/ you go marching to the table/you get the same damn thing/Knife and fork are on the table/ain't nothing in my pan/ And if you say a thing about it/you having trouble with the man."[26] He not only highlights the grueling days of labor without food that imprisoned men endured, he also shines a light on the ways those bodies were intimidated into silence by prison officials.

Furthermore, the close relationship between Texas politicians and former Texas slave holders made it possible for Texas's convict leasing system to emerge in the midst of a country that was fighting to keep its slaves. Like slavery, the state found that the prison industrial complex, particularly during the Civil War, was an almost indispensable financial resource to the state budget. For instance, the prison industrial complex helped solidify a new economy in cotton production after the Union army blockaded the ability of southern ports to transport their abundance of cotton to southern facilities.

Since this impeded most southern states's ability to weave together the necessary tents, supply bags, and uniforms to carry out their war efforts, this apparent barrier to the North proved beneficial for Texas. As a result, Huntsville, Texas, became the number-one textile supplier in the trans-Mississippi West. Perkinson states that "between 1861 and 1863, the prison mill churned out more than two million yards of cotton and woolen fabrics, much of it confederate gray."[27] This, in turn, made Texas the major supplier of goods for the confederate south.

Eventually, this growing convict textile production resulted in a booming commerce for the state that was so lucrative that the Walls Unit, in Huntsville, became Texas's leading source of revenue. Said more succinctly, the prison became Texas's leading commercial industry. Perkinson contends that, "we can never fully understand America's most recent experiment in restricted liberty, mass incarceration, without tracing the story back to the first—slavery."[28] It is out of this context that we come to understand why the historical corrections records in Texas and eventually throughout the South largely consisted of black men that were convicted and confined to prisons and jails for menial and oftentimes unproven criminal charges.

Moreover, the convergence of these political, economic, and social structures that constituted much of the Texas Prison regime makes Huddie Ledbetter's ingenuity and prison praxis an even more valuable resource because it emerges as a type of resistance to the collaborative efforts to erase black male felons all together. Consequently, Ledbetter's value is not only highlighted in his ability to overcome the physical restraints of Texas penal system, but it also illustrates the creative ways he as a black male felon is able to intervene into the politics of the criminal justice system. This primary intervention is illustrated in his ability to negotiate his freedom. He scrupulously subverts widely-held notions of black incarcerated bodies as sentient beings in the white racist imagination to the degree that Governor Neff was inspired to set him free.

Yet overall, profit-driven Texas prisons began to move more black men into another form of legal bondage. In spite of the fact that white lawbreakers were rampant across the state, it was former slaves who flooded the penitentiaries. In fact, "between 1890 and 1904, Texas white imprisonment rate fell by half, but it climbed by twenty-seven percent for black men."[29] This does not suggest that all whites were free from the trappings of incarceration. To the contrary, by 1863 white men convicted of criminal offenses were laboring in prison factories and fields alongside actual slaves. Perkinson points out that "the prison in Huntsville thus became the state's first racially integrated public institution, not by bestowing rights on bondmen but by stripping them from citizens."[30]

Although quite unintentional, the Texas penal system created the very structure that allowed for the creative exchange that we witness with Ledbetter. The integration of black incarcerated men with white felons and white criminal justice and elected officials made possible a form of exchange that other communities across the United States did not necessarily have. Admittedly, most of those creative moments were rare and limiting. However, as Ledbetter shows there are moments of intervention. These rare moments should incite us to seek out and examine more closely carceral spaces.

State officials soon recognized that the integration of white and black felons posed an imminent danger to the prison regime. As a result, elected officials constructed political barriers to fracture any real alignment between the two groups, such as criminal policies that were defined along racial lines. Prison officials created social divisions within the prison to deter any cross-racial alliances and to stifle any possibility of creative exchange between inmates. For instance, the treatment and work details for white convicts was less grueling and white convicts received office and indoor jobs, while black felons continually worked the fields.

Furthermore, white prison convicts received skilled indoor labor jobs that provided them with post incarceration skills while mostly all black convicts worked the fields and rugged terrain of Texas, denying them any real chance for social advancement post incarceration. As was hoped for, the limited opportunities for creative exchange between white and black felons served to advance the structural mission of prison officials and convict leasees. This inevitably created a social hierarchy in the prison that was clearly divided along racial lines.

Yet, Ledbetter was able to expose the social and economic structure of the Texas prison regime through his music, while mitigating for his personal benefit the entrenched racial and economic animus widely held by state officials. He was able to shine a light on the concrete structures and systems that hindered individuals, communities, and groups in Texas from constructing Beloved Community through songs such as *Midnight Special* and others, and at the same time reconfiguring the mode of interaction and exchange between black felons and white political and criminal justice officials for his own freedom.

This was indeed impressive in light of the drastic shift in the political dynamics in Texas. Most certainly, this dramatic shift was due in large part to slave-holding politicians close relationships with convict lease owners. Because of his songs and performance, Ledbetter was able to show how that shift moved Texas from being simply a society with slaves before 1865 to a slave society post-Civil War.

Ledbetter's intersection of music and politics in a creative exchange cleverly inserted black incarcerated bodies into national public and cultural sphere. This intervention ultimately highlights concrete moments of Beloved Community. Although these concrete moments did little to impact criminal justice policy in Texas for all people, it did expose the humanity of black felons to non-felons and impacted the way criminal justice policy was applied to Ledbetter as an individual.

But it is society's continual failure to examine the value that black felons such as Ledbetter offers to Beloved Community that makes the work of justice incomplete. Even as an intellectual exercise it impedes many black radical scholars from linking Texas prison history to the broader discourse on punishment and contemporary prison practices, particularly the privatization of prisons. In addition, it has enabled this callous prison regime to resist many contemporary reform efforts. For example, Texas politicians and prison managers have frequently cut prison reform budgets.[31]

Also, the prison and criminal justice system has been allowed to fortify penal captivity by instituting certain social hierarchies that can be seen in voting rights laws, housing policies, and job discrimination practices. This in many ways enables the prison structure to reify social and political attitudes about incarcerated men and women. Texas prisons have been able to resist reform efforts because the institution gives the false impression that it is the source for enacting public vengeance on behalf of victims of crimes and thus stands as a symbol of our government's commitment to deter criminal behavior.

It even shields corruption within prison walls. It is often overlooked how the growing narrative of prison corruption by prison staff lends to the problem of prison reform. Ironically, these highly publicized incidents have extended penitential disciplines. The actions by elected officers, prison officials, law enforcement representatives, and even felons themselves have inadvertently hindered efforts at reform and reconciliation. For example, the high recidivism rate of felons ultimately validates the idea that their convictions are just and deserved.

Admittedly, it is hard to deny that Ledbetter lends to this argument. He personifies the historically high recidivism rate of black male felons. However, his success as a musical artists with John Lomax, a white musicologist and folklorist who discovered Ledbetter while serving his third adult sentence in Lousiana, also signals to the causes of high levels of recidivism for black men. In other words, a deep investigation of Ledbetter shows that the high recidivism rate of black male felons is not a moral issue as much as it is a structural issue. It occurs because of the lack of opportunity for black men—a structural issue that Lomax helped Ledbetter overcome.

"TELL 'EM I WAS CRYING": LEDBETTER, LOMAX, AND MASCULINITY

Lomax helped construct opportunities for Ledbetter to utilize music for social advancement and economic security. Although the brief eight-month partnership didn't alter Ledbetter's moral attributes, it did keep him from going permanently back into the prison system.[32] Yet again, music became the mode for creative exchange between Ledbetter and Lomax. Moreover, it supports the statistical evidence that putative measures are rarely successful in fighting recidivism. However, these opportunities for creative exchange have been virtually ignored while punitive measures of discipline have been able to go forth practically unchallenged. The notion of prison as punishment has been offered to the public with little public scrutiny, causing black male felons to be more entrenched within carceral spaces.

In spite of his social condition, Ledbetter was able to utilize this restrictive space to garner a type of relative freedom and personal success. However, that success often came at a cost to his personal dignity and humanity. Certainly, it is necessary to point out the social cost because it shows that the expansion of Beloved Community is not without conflict and material sacrifices.

Huddie, like Nat Turner, reveals how black incarcerated men were forced to make choices within a limited space. Some of those choices were good, some were bad, and some were seriously questionable. The truth is that the entrenchment of men and women within carceral spaces do not allow for us to neatly resolve issues of regulative moral behaviors. Rather, they force society to deal with the complexity of human social systems even within Beloved Community.

Even if Ledbetter's black prison praxis was not a way to redeem his personal character, it was a means of subverting the criminal justice system. He demonstrates how this form of prison praxis, particularly his singing and performance, deterred certain harsh punishments and grueling long-term prison sentences. In addition, Ledbetter was able to utilize this form of prison praxis to garner certain entitlements such as the rationing of food or the ability to communicate with family. In other words, he demonstrates concrete moments in time where Beloved Community is actualized through creative exchange.

This creative exchange was not strictly personal. It also signaled the need for society to continue to address the contradictions in human interactions and social systems. For instance, the treatment of prisoners in Texas constituted much of Ledbetter's soulful blues expression. In his song entitled "Take this Hammer" Ledbetter narrates his frustration with working on the prison chain gang. After each verse, listeners can her Ledbetter say "Wow." The quick breath and sharp tone in Ledbetter's phrasing sounds like the whip of the lash. In one chorus Ledbetter says "Take this hammer and carry it to the captain (3x)/ Tell 'em I'm gone/Tell 'em I'm gone." He expresses the tension between his discontent with his forced labor and with his desire to still be free. He goes on to sing about the elusiveness of freedom and the burden of forced servitude in the song when he sings about cornbread and molasses. Cornbread and molasses was not only the meal for inmates, but Ledbetter informs the listener that laughing and happiness was prohibited for inmates. This is why in the song, Ledbetter tells his listener if the captain asks if he was laughing "tell 'em I was crying." This suggests that even the act of misery is the preferred mode of the prisoner's expression.

The problem with this misery, as Ledbetter demonstrates, is that eventually it is no longer an act. Soon, misery becomes the comfortable state of existence for black felons, especially when the hope of any real freedom dims. It is in this way that the true structure of the prison atmosphere is revealed. Prison officials become representations of the atmosphere and culture of prison life. It is within these types of prison songs by nineteenth- and early twentieth-century black male felons that much of the labor and culture of prison confinement might be revealed.

As I said, this is not to say that Ledbetter is not a troublesome figure. He is very troublesome. It is difficult to ignore Ledbetter's criminal history and violent personality. It is also hard to overlook the contention that arises when examining his form of prison praxis. Often, Ledbetter's form of black prison praxis gets labeled as "cooning" or "pandering" by black intellectuals. This critique is often intensified when compared to certain black radicals' praxis by Frederick Douglass and W. E. B. Du Bois. Admittedly, these men resisted common stereotypes held in the white racist imagination.

For some, Ledbetter's praxis is often deemed as not just antithetical to black heroic praxis, but dangerous to black life as a whole. However, historian Marybeth Hamilton points out that the folk music sung by Ledbetter was often considered to be the outsider's music because it was sung by negro prisoners in chain gangs or poor white peasant farmers in the rural South. She states that "that was the world that Ledbelly's songs conjured up. It was just one step away from saying folk music was actually about protesting the way things were."[33]

As a black male felon, Ledbetter illustrates the abstruse nature of black masculinity, even though he is a physically powerful man with a long history of violence. He highlights the ambiguity of black masculinity within carceral spaces. Said another way, Ledbetter demonstrates how, within the confines of white patriarchy and structural racism, black masculinity is open to more than one interpretation.

Moreover, while there is deep religious meaning in the ambiguous experiences of black masculinity, Ledbetter lets us see the very real political and social experiences of black male felons and the various ways they must negotiate black masculinity in the world. For instance, in a documentary film that Ledbetter does with Lomax, we see how his language and performance of black masculinity becomes ambiguous. Although Ledbetter is stout and big, he appears whimsical and subservient to Lomax.

This ambiguity of black masculinity happens because either few viable alternative political choices of black masculine representation have not been created for the black male felon or because they have not been made assessable. In either case, Ledbetter compels black radical scholars to wrestle with the identity of the black male felon within black radical traditions. Moreover, it necessitates that African American religious thought engage in a creative exchange that takes up the ambiguities of black masculinity in order to create a constructive place for it in African American political, religious, and social experience.

Particularly in African American religion, the ambiguity of black masculinity has traditionally been replaced with strong black heroic narratives of black men. Often, this heroic figure is endowed with a Christocentric layer of being that subordinate to the political experiences to the religious. For instance, in African American religious thought, the political engagement by black males has been largely filled with black heroic figures such as Martin Luther King Jr., Ralph Abernathy, Jesse Jackson, and other black male preachers. If we apply these figures to Ledbetter, we begin to see the problem.

Even within the broader black intellectual tradition the political experience of black men has been filled with figures such as Frederick Douglass and W. E. B. Du Bois. These alternative methods of black masculinity are often critiqued for not having the same level of intellectual sophistication as black heroic figures such as Douglass or Du Bois. For instance, Ledbetter willingly and cleverly called himself Neff's "servant" in order to gain favor. We can be certain that Du Bois and Douglass would have shunned such identification. In fact, Du Bois critiqued this type of identification in his writing on black double consciousness.

However, in Ledbetter we also witness a type of vulnerability and humility. For instance, Ledbetter pleaded on behalf of his then girlfriend, even lying to the governor that she was his wife. Unlike the narrative of Douglass who physically fought his captor, Lebetter begged the governor to have "mercy" on him and his thirty-year sentence. This form of pandering does not often align with the hyper masculine images that we ascribe to black masculinity and black heroic figures such as Delaney, Douglass, Du Bois, and others.

For Ledbetter, black masculine representation was not a symbol for black apologetics. It was not meant to "prove" something to white people. Rather, it was a tool to engage in a type of creative exchange. Ledbetter uses black masculinity to symbolically participate with other "deep symbols" in the black world experience. In doing this, he constructs a relational, pragmatic philosophy of African American experience.

Therefore, while Ledbetter's music and black masculine performance brings critique, it also forces us to deal with the reality and life conditions of his world. Ledbetter reveals the relativity and grotesquery of African American experiences as a type of pragmatic philosophy. He integrates felons into a larger unity of life within the creative exchange. His music orchestrates a creative exchange not only between black felon identity and American political ideality and reality but also a creative exchange between the black heroic figures and black male felons.

He also places American notions of justice and democracy in conflict with the social reality of incarcerated men and women. Unlike more popularized black male figures, Ledbetter forces black elites to deal with the hidden realities of black non-elites. This conflict offers space to reimagine both the ideas of incarceration as a form of punishment in American society, as well as the role that late nineteenth- and early twentieth-century black male felons provide to the black radical tradition.

NOTES

1. Scholars such as Daphne Brooks, Patricia Schroeder, and others point out certain black minstrel performances show how the black subject plays into white expectations but subverts them in a coded message to the black audience. Karen Sotiropoulos, Louis Chude-Sokei, and others have pointed out in regard to minstrel performance and coon songs that African Americans often engaged in these cultural

forms as one of the only available outlets for someone who wanted to work in theater or music. Doing so, black performers often engaged in, negotiated, and subverted what Stuart Hall identifies as the cultural signs of a dominant ideology by performing coon songs. Evidence about the concepts of the signifying monkey or blues ideology (classic African American studies ideas from Henry Louis Gates or Houston Baker) also apply to the argument that blacks used minstrelsy to subvert white racism.

2. I expand on Rodriquez's idea of radical prison praxis to speak to also the way music for black felons exposes the penal institutions. For Rodriquez, the radical praxis by these intellectuals destabilizes three foundational American entitlements to include: 1) formal protection under the tenets prescribed as constitutional and civil rights; 2) the intervening work of state juridical, policing, and (para)military structures to protect citizens under the rule and dominion of egalitarian policies and procedures; and 3) the generalized assumption in the United States that individual and collective contain a type of bodily integrity that is free from anticipated or imminent physical suffering, violation, and erasure.

However, in trying to fit the mold of prison praxis into the category of intellectual, Rodriguez limits the scope and work of the imprisoned intellectual to a particular body of imprisoned men and women. For example, Rodriguez takes the political praxis of men and women in the Black Liberation Army (BLA) as the basis of his exploration for radical imprisoned intellectuals. For while Rodriguez argues that "the history and legacies of the BLA reveal precisely how the prison, as a discursive terrain and geographic-institutional production, is at once the emblem of an abstracted and rigorously mystified policing-juridical telos (arrest-prosecution—conviction—incarceration), an approved zone of high-intensity combat (as a place of legitimated capture, interrogation, punishment, torture), and a site of experimentation for new domestic and globalized war-waging techniques" he fails to show how that terrain and interrogation is placed within a context that has a longer standing history of erasing the landscape of radical voices (50). As a result, he narrows the conditions for radical political imprisoned praxis. In doing this, he overlooks earlier instances of creative exchange, and concrete moments wherein Beloved Community is manifested. Indeed, by starting with the BLA he constructs a trajectory for the development and prototype of the contemporary US prison regime that excludes a history of black prison radicals. This history predates the BLA or formal black radical civil and human rights movements.

3. Rodriguez only foregrounds important historical and political conditions of the post-1970s US prison industrial complex. He contends that 1970s radical prison praxis critique: 1) explains how we regard the context, possibilities and historicity of political subjectivity specific to the formation of the prison as a regime of power; 2) forms an idea of praxis by the use of terms that are linked historically to a lineage of imprisoned radical intellectuals; and 3) examines the formation of praxis at the site of imprisonment in order to shift the presumptive political geography of praxis from the juridical and cultural domains of civil society. By moving further back in black incarceration I am showing through the work of Ledbetter that earlier radical prison praxis was taking place that was overlooked. Thus exposing how radical scholars incorrectly narrowed prison praxis to Black Liberation efforts in the 1970s.

4. James Perkinson, *Texas Tough: The Rise of America's Prison Empire* (New York: Picador, 2010), 122.
5. James Perkinson, *Texas Tough*, 121.
6. James Perkinson, *Texas Tough*, 178.
7. James Perkinson, *Texas Tough,* 122.
8. James Perkinson, *Texas Tough*, 3.
9. James Perkinson, *Texas Tough*, 178.
10. James Perkinson, *Texas Tough*, 185.
11. YouTube, "The Story of American Folk Music 1," https://www.youtube.com/watch?v=F9ZNgpb_NkM. Published May 1, 2013. Web (1:37–1:47).
12. James Perkinson, *Texas Tough*, 179
13. James Perkinson, *Texas Tough*, 178.
14. James Perkinson, *Texas Tough*, 184.
15. James Perkinson, *Texas Tough*, 184.
16. James Perkinson, *Texas Tough*, 184.
17. James Perkinson, *Texas Tough*, 7.
18. Lyricsmode, Ledbelly—Midnight Special Lyrics, https://www.lyricsmode.com/lyrics/l/leadbelly/midnight_special.html.
19. The Freedmen's Bureau Online, "Freedmen's Bureau Report of an Inspection of Texas State Penitentiary at Huntsville, Walker County," http://www.freedmensbureau.com/texas/texasstateprison.htm.
20. The Freedmen's Bureau Online, "Freedmen's Bureau Report of an Inspection of Texas State Penitentiary at Huntsville, Walker County," http://www.freedmensbureau.com/texas/texasstateprison.htm.
21. The Freedmen's Bureau Online, "Freedmen's Bureau Report of an Inspection of Texas State Penitentiary at Huntsville, Walker County," http://www.freedmensbureau.com/texas/texasstateprison.htm.
22. A full review of the Freedmen's Report detailing the reasons behind convictions of these black men and the number of years they were sentenced to prison can be found at http://www.freedmensbureau.com/texas/texasstateprison2.htm.
23. An alternate live recording of Huddie Ledbetter singing Midnight Special with different lyrics can be heard on https://www.youtube.com/watch?v=VATKBZrZ4Fc.
24. YouTube, "Lead Belly—Midnight Special Lyrics," https://www.youtube.com/watch?v=VATKBZrZ4Fc. Published September 15, 2013, Web, (1:54–1:58).
25. In a July Houston's CBS news affiliate, KHOU, reported that a recent unmarked mass grave site with over 100 bodies was found during a construction of a new school building near the Imperial Sugar Land Factory in Fort Bend County. The remains are of black men that were in the convict leasing system. A clip of the report can be seen at https://www.facebook.com/CBSNews/videos/10155966636225950/.
26. WEBSITE (lyricsmode.com).
27. James Perkinson, *Texas Tough*, 80.
28. James Perkinson, *Texas Tough*, 46.
29. James Perkinson, *Texas Tough*, 143.
30. James Perkinson, *Texas Tough*, 81.

31. The Institute for Urban Policy Research and Analysis at the University of Texas at Austin published an article in 2015 entitled *Examining the Texas Prison Reform Model: How Texas is Maintaining Racial Disparity and Mass Incarceration* wherein they showed major shortcoming in the states reform efforts despite 2009 claims by the Texas Legislature that incarceration had slowed and that the "state had averted major prison construction." In particular, the study cites for examples of failure 1. "Since the establishment of the Texas prison reform model, the State has failed to reduce the number of individuals it incarcerates or significantly decrease racial disproportionality." 2. "Texas continues to imprison more people than any other state, driving the nation's incarceration rate. While Texas's rate of incarceration has dropped during the last seven years, it still ranks fifth highest in the nation, and first among the most populous states." 3 "In 2013, Texas increased the number of people it incarcerates, despite national trends that indicated decreased incarceration in several of the most populous states." 4. "Texas continues to disproportionately incarcerate African Americans, and 5. "The Texas Model was developed to save taxpayer dollars. While cost savings is a compelling component of prison reform, fiscal austerity reform designs fail to address the underlying drivers of mass incarceration." (http://www.utexas.edu/cola/iupra/_files/Criminal%20Justice%20Brief%20Final%20final.pdf).

32. Ledbetter was arrested in 1940 in Manhattan for stabbing a man however, John Lomax's son helped cover his legal expenses which ultimately resulted in Ledbetter's release.

33. YouTube, "The Story of American Folk Music," 7:20–7:41.

Chapter 4

Twentieth-Century Black Radical Prison Intellectuals

Malcolm X, George Jackson, and the Expansion of Nineteenth-Century Black Prison Praxis

Chapters 2 and 3 highlight the emergence of nineteenth-century prison praxis and its impact on black radical projects by shining a light on black imprisoned radicals Nat Turner and Huddie Ledbetter. Among many things, this investigation reveals how black prison praxis in the nineteenth and early twentieth century was often mediated through white people and white controlled spaces. This mediation impacted the integrity and content of some of the work produced by black imprisoned radicals. In spite of this impact, it is clear that it is impossible to ignore that what comes forth from the black male felon is valuable to our understanding of US politics, culture, and social justice practices.

However, the need to liberate black imprisoned praxis from white institutional control is crucial if society is ever going to work toward Beloved Community. The recognition of this need is why certain black imprisoned men and women began to construct alternate discursive spaces. An excavation of these alternative spaces is necessary in order to gain a better understanding of black male felons' imprisoned praxis.

Therefore, I explore black male felons Malcolm X and George Jackson so that we can move prison praxis beyond the control of white institutional arrangements. Both of these men utilized a form of creative exchange that influenced the language and presentation of black leadership for twentieth-century black liberation movements. This progressive movement shows the subversive role for certain black prison praxis in the twentieth century. Consequently, the construction of these alternative spaces also reveals the subversive nature of the felon to disrupt white institutional arrangements and work toward black freedom and independence.

Malcolm and Jackson constructed a creative exchange that was free from white racist institutions. In other words, while both men appropriated language that emerges from their experience of incarceration to speak about black freedom and resistance, they do so outside of white racist logic. They develop a form of praxis that places blackness as the central experience in their liberation projects. By centralizing blackness as the central experience of their liberation projects, they are able to create a new set of images, metaphors, symbols, and praxis to address black suffering in the United States. Their ideas challenge the popular notion of nonviolence and rethink the idea of pacifism as synonymous with morality. Both of these radical intellectuals believed that nonviolence should be the way people existed in Beloved Community, not necessarily the way we achieved Beloved Community.

Malcolm and Jackson as black radicals argued that freedom from white racism and patriarchy and the establishment of a peaceful Beloved Community would always be met with violence. Like Nat Turner, these men understood that the institution of slavery and segregation necessitated resistance to violent attack. For them, the responsibility for passive resistance to violent assault was not a requisite of Beloved Community. In this light, Malcolm and Jackson shed light again on the importance of the grotesque in creative exchange.

Therefore, in this chapter I place the work of Malcolm and Jackson in a creative exchange in order to show how they help manifest the idea of Beloved Community. Indeed, their work as black male felons helps to expand the way radical scholars can talk about Beloved Community. Their work also moves conversations about black male felons into the discourse on Beloved Community. Thus, centralizing these black male felons reshapes Beloved Community because it requires a social construction of human interaction that does not use white racism as its model. These men, similar to Turner and Ledbetter, help to make Beloved Community active and engaged, as opposed to merely a theoretical utopian idea that marginalizes certain forms of black resistance and protest.

MALCOLM X: THE INFLUENCE OF A BLACK MALE FELON ON BLACK RADICAL PRAXIS

Unlike earlier imprisoned radicals, Malcolm X's radical theory and praxis is well documented. His autobiography and letters, the numerous collections of audio and video taped speeches, and the collection of writing by other scholars concerning his work makes clear that after Malcolm was sentenced in 1946 to the Charleston State Prison that his growing political curiosity flourished. Prison provided space for Malcolm to hone his study of Christian religion and the teachings of Elijah Muhammad and the Nation of Islam

(NOI). He also sharpened his oratory skills and began to develop his political ideology and praxis.

Eventually, Malcolm's move toward the Nation of Islam became a witness to his emerging religious and political ideas. These ideas were intensified by his confinement to prison. This is not to say that prison was beneficial to Malcolm. Rather, it is to suggest that his lived experience within carceral space so magnified his understanding of black experience in the United States that he gained insight that eluded him all the while he remained free from prison.

It is in prison that Malcolm develops a theory about black independent institutional building. It is also in prison that Malcolm develops his critique of black Christianity and the black church. For Malcolm, the black church's dependence on white institutional arrangements made it ill-equipped to effectively address black struggles. In his speech "God's Angry Men" Malcolm writes "Christianity is the white man's religion. The Holy Bible is in the white man's hands and his interpretations of it have been the greatest single ideological weapon for enslaving millions of non-white human beings."[1]

Malcolm wasn't so much against Christianity as much as he was against white Christianity. In *Martin & Malcolm & America: A Dream or a Nightmare*, James Cone points out that Malcolm was not opposed to the creeds, doctrines, and scholarly writings of black or white theologians, but rather to the practices by those who called themselves Christians. The form of Christianity that Malcolm witnessed inside and outside of prison helped to reify the work of the prison regime and helped codify certain black bodies as disposable through the label felon. Therefore, placing Malcolm's writings in creative exchange with white institutions not only reshapes Beloved Community by including the thoughts and experiences of black male felons, but it also highlights how white Western European racist ideas and practices pervade black radical products.

There is a tendency among some scholars to credit other institutions over the prison as the radicalizing location for black radical intellectuals. For example, James Cone writes that "the Nation of Islam was the most important influence on the life and thought of Malcolm X."[2] For Cone, the Nation of Islam was most impactful on Malcolm's worldview and political engagement in much the same way as the black church was to Martin Luther King, Jr. While it is true that Elijah Muhammad and the Nation of Islam played a great part in Malcolm's radical thinking, I contend that Malcolm's confinement in prison served as the lens through which he interpreted and evaluated the message of Muhammad, the work of Garvey, and his critique of Martin Luther King, Jr.

Malcolm also states in the *Autobiography* that access to books and a library in prison changed his life. Thus, to undervalue the prison as a radicalizing location is to both dislocate Malcolm from the lineage of black imprisoned intellectuals and to ignore the ideas that emerge from that space. It is Malcolm's prison experiences that inform his belief that people need both radicalizing spaces and a medium that affirms and mobilizes the radical praxis that emerges from those locations. Without the prison as a radicalizing space for black incarcerated men and women, and without the Nation of Islam to provide a pathway to mobilize imprisoned political praxis, it is hard to imagine that Malcolm Little would have ever become Malcolm X.

The Nation of Islam offered a platform to present ideas that Malcolm had generated in prison. Being a member of the NOI helped to legitimate Malcolm's prison political praxis and his rejection of white essentialism. The Nation of Islam also offered a critique of white institutional structures and nullified the stigma of felon on black bodies. The truest value of the NOI on Malcolm X was the NOI's willingness to mobilize black prison praxis in ways that had been unavailable for previously incarcerated men and women.

So it is certainly true, as Cone states, that the Nation of Islam had a powerful impact on Malcolm. Part of that can be seen in Malcolm's challenge for black religion to construct pragmatic intellectual endeavors. For Malcolm, these radical endeavors better clarify both the practice and interpretations of black churches as radicalizing spaces for black liberation. Ultimately by doing this, Malcolm delegitimizes certain black intellectual discursive practices, particularly those that affirm white racialized ideas.

Malcolm's political praxis highlights the influence of prison as a radicalizing space, and his language informs the nature and foundation from which his praxis derives. Part of that which we get from Malcolm's prison praxis is a pragmatic endeavor that challenges both white and black liberalism. For instance, his perspective and his notion of liberation "by any means necessary" threaten the security of both black and white liberal agendas. This threat is most pronounced on black and white liberal agendas that tend to construct binary options of freedom when speaking about social justice and civic engagement.

Much of Malcolm's imagery, iterations, and terminology derive from this carceral space. He activates a political language that deconstructs the apologetic use of black heroic images as the representational norms for black civic and political engagement. The language he develops re-imagines black value in the body of black thugs, gangsters, and felons.

Furthermore, Malcolm's creative exchange both clarifies and distinguishes black radical imprisoned intellectuals and black prison political praxis from other black intellectuals and their intellectual production. As a black prison intellectual, Malcolm presents a type of tradition that is not often discussed in black intellectual life. His speech entitled "The Ballot or the Bullet" shows the influence prison had on his political praxis, and his defiance to white hegemonic structures. It also speaks to his contempt for black bourgeoisie discursive patterns and their political engagement. Indeed, "Ballot or the Bullet" illustrates both Malcolm's critique of US democracy, and challenges Martin Luther King Jr.'s ideas on nonviolent activism. In particular, he rejects King's traditional nonviolent civil justice practices, and constructs a form of creative exchange that more aligns with other black imprisoned radicals such as Nat Turner and Huddie Ledbetter.

It is not just that Malcolm critiques US hierarchy. Various black radicals have done that. It is not even that his challenge to King's notion of non-violence is so radical. What is more radical is that Malcolm's writings, speeches and civic and political engagement exposes how the technology of the prison allows a type of false contrast between felons and non-felons. It is this falsity of freedom among various groups that is revolutionary—and the prison is the basis of his argument.

In a speech that he offered on November 10, 1963, entitled "Message to the Grassroots" Malcolm contends that the prison became a type of learning chamber for his radical work and ideas. He reconfigured that space to include more than just those physically incarcerated. He states "don't be shocked when I say that I was in prison. You're still in prison. That's what America means: prison."[3] This gave Malcolm a language that talked about freedom and bondage in a more nuanced way.

The prison even introduced Malcolm to ideas by other radicals and revolutionaries which he employed in his work post release. He often cites certain revolutionary movements and activities that influenced his thinking. For example, the activities in the Chinese revolution against the British informed his thinking on the black response to US military aggression against black bodies. It becomes apparent from Malcolm's writings that immobilization is a condition that is not only materialized in the prison industrial complex, but also its effects are felt by other oppressed groups regardless of felon status. For Malcolm these revolutionary movements and activities illustrate the contradiction of US and Western European discourse on violence and colonialism.

Carceral imagery also recurs in Malcolm's rhetoric. These images depict the limited space wherein Malcolm and others are positioned in society. His language continually stressed common struggle over individual differences, but in cramped quarters. He contends that "if we have differences, let us differ in the closet; when we come out in the front, let us not have anything to argue about until we get finished with arguing with the man."[4] In doing this, Malcolm constructs a broad theory of oppression that brings race, poverty, and gender under the umbrella of oppression in the same way that the prison unites all oppression into the same constricted space. By bridging race, gender, and class under the domain of prison oppression, Malcolm unifies structures of oppression to a common cause and goal.

Indeed, the idea that a particular identity can encompass all identities for black liberation such as female, gay, and transgender is problematic. However, for Malcolm, white supremacy traps all of those identities under the structure of the prison regime. So what he in essence shows is that oppressed groups are afforded limited discursive spaces to address their issues and grievances.

This commonality of oppression for Malcolm is crucial for oppressed people in general, and black people in particular. It is vital not only because it illustrates how the prison is indiscriminate in its practice against marginalized and socially oppressed groups, but also because it equips communities of color and oppressed groups to tackle the sophistication of white institutional racism. Malcolm articulates how white oppressive leadership will form alliances over and against their differences to maintain these structures of oppression.

The ability for white oppressive leaders to form alliances in spite of many of their social, economic, and cultural differences affirms the idea of white racial privilege. An example of this can be seen in the interaction between John F. Kennedy and Nikita Khrushchev. According to Malcolm "if the late President Kennedy could get together with Khrushchev and exchange some wheat, we certainly have more in common with each other than Kennedy and Khrushchev had with each other."[5] For Malcolm, as long as whiteness is universalized then oppressed groups, particularly black people, have to unite around a universalizing agenda.

Malcolm's desire to create a symbiosis between differing forms of oppressed groups was not new, but rarely at the time did we see the type of public advocacy that Malcolm presents. The ability to work past differences and form alliances under a common banner of oppression ultimately sets the context for the choice between the ballot and the bullet. Thus for Malcolm, if people of color refuse to unite under a common banner of oppression then they will continue to be oppressed by the unification of white racist agendas and held captive within the restrictive space of white supremacy.

Yet again, the language that Malcolm utilizes to unite all oppression does away with the need for black heroic narratives as a type of social apologetic. Instead, he embraces the felon identity as a subversive to both American politics and black heroic narrative identity construction. For instance, in the "Ballot and the Bullet" he tells his audience that he is not a scholar. Rather, he states that "I'm not standing here speaking to you as an American, or a patriot, or a flag-saluter, or a flag-waver—no, not I. I'm speaking as a victim of this American system."[6] He rejects the European model of scholarship and leadership, and takes on a radical prison praxis as his mode of leadership.

Indeed, Malcolm's experience as both black and felon provides him with a deeper insight into the US democratic psyche. He argues that "I see America through the eyes of the victim. I don't see any American dream; I see an American nightmare."[7] The need to construct constitutional amendments, engage in congressional civil rights legislative filibustering, and conduct radical grassroots social justice campaigns are indicators to the un-Americanness of black people in the United States. In this way, Malcolm ascribes new ways of seeing and critiquing the American political system that derives from the construction of a new discursive space that is less mediated by white institutional arrangements.

Malcolm's ability to create these new discursive spaces not only inspired and influenced later radical political intellectuals such as Dr. Huey P. Newton and Geronimo ji Jaga Pratt, but also influenced less known felons such as Shaka Sankofa, a Texas death row inmate who was executed in December 2001. Sankofa was sentenced to death at the age of eighteen for the murder of fifty-three-year-old Bobby Gant Lambert in Houston, Texas. In a 1996 interview with Gary Graham concerning the movement to free him from death row, Sankofa says "in the spirit of Malcolm, some things you have to take a stand on."[8] For Sankofa and others, Malcolm illuminates how the felon reveals a site for a new type of engagement with the political forces that mobilize US democracy. And like Sankofa, his death also shows how the body of the black male felon is still not fully free from these arrangements.

The very system that mobilizes the prison regime ultimately captures and conditions the bodies inside as political agents and actors that are never fully liberated from the trap of the state. Malcolm X, as a political agent and as an imprisoned radical intellectual, reveals that the construction of his political identity is discursively determined. Moreover, through his prison praxis he contextualizes incarceration as an ongoing system of repression. As Dylan Rodriguez contends regarding political prisoners, this systematized repression "forces [Malcolm X] to map out new 'cognitive territories' within which ways of knowing, feeling, and living the experience unmediated state violence create new spaces and political trajectories of dissent, radicalism, and antisystemic possibility."[9] In other words, the felon is forced to create new ways of existing because of the unnatural crises that the prison and the label "felon" impose.

This unnatural crisis exists for felons both inside and outside of prison units. According to James, the "constant police and FBI surveillance after [Malcolm] served his prison sentence likely increased his radical political and moral presence and inspired activists who would eventually become incarcerated, and in reflecting on his life, spirit, and death struggle to 'reinvent' themselves as political agents, formulating a liberation praxis 'by any means necessary.'"[10] This suggests that the political praxis of felons can be both activated and witnessed both inside and outside of prison.

In spite of the reasons for his incarceration, Malcolm's political activity broadens Rodriguez and James's definition of political prisoners. His impact on political projects in the United States, particularly toward the end of the 1960s and into the 1970s, has influenced radical political production in the sciences, art, and music. For instance, Malcolm's prison praxis greatly influenced the political activity of the Black Liberation Army. Rodriguez reminds us that the BLA "profoundly demystifies and renarrates the formation of the US prison regime as a crisis of the unnatural."[11] Malcolm's political praxis helped shape the identity of the BLA as a black insurgent group and informed much of their rhetoric for resistance.

Malcolm's influence on the BLA is most profoundly evidenced in the language many of their leaders used to address police violence against black bodies. BLA leaders such as Assata Shakur and Geronimo Pratt routinely utilized Malcolm's imagery to talk about white police, systemic racism and black intra-class struggles. For instance, in an interview with Heike Kleffner, Pratt appropriates Malcolm's analogy of the house and field negro to address the class struggle within black liberation movements. In *The New Abolitionists: (Neo) Slave Narratives and Contemporary Prison Writings*, James records Pratt telling Kleffner as it relates to black radical political activity that "[black elected officials] like to individualize prisoners, because, by and large, they buy into the system's propaganda that there are no political prisoners."[12]

While the actions that led to Malcolm's arrest were not political in nature per se, his eventual incarceration is an act of political activity. In other words, the nature of prison and the impact incarceration has on black bodies highlight the political significance of black prison praxis and the construction of the felon as a political agent. Although in *Imprisoned Intellectuals: America's Political Prisoners Write on Life, Liberation, and Rebellion*, James admits that "Malcolm X was not a "political prisoner" in the restrictive sense in which [she and Rodriguez] use the term . . . he transformed or 'reinvented' himself as a political agent while imprisoned."[13] Through Malcolm we see how and why the felon, as a captive agent of the state, becomes a site for black radical intellectual traditions. The politicizing impact prisons have on imprisoned bodies ascribes to felons a type of political agency. Thus, the activity that leads to incarceration is not the activity that defines political prisoners, but rather it is the interconnecting work of a criminalizing system to constructs the prisoner in the first place that makes the prisoner a political agent.

Malcolm also demonstrates the trans-Atlantic influence that US black radical imprisoned intellectuals have on the link between knowledge production and activism. His prison praxis expands the reach and scope of black imprisoned intellectuals past the shores of the United States. He was not only able to capture the attention of an international audience, but also invited them into the language and experience of a black world that had not been fully revealed outside of US black inner cities. For this reason, much of his political influence can be seen in both the Civil Rights Movement in the United States and in the Free South Africa Movement in the 1980s. This is important because it illustrates how Malcolm X, as a black male felon, moves black prison praxis, particularly the impact of incarceration on black bodies, into a trans-Atlantic discourse. His work shows how the use of the prison regime is used as a tool for global terror against certain communities.

In this light, it is clear that Malcolm's political ideas and activity closely align with the ideas and activity of early imprisoned political praxis that is seen in the work of Nat Turner and Huddie Ledbetter. His direct confrontation with white supremacy, his threat of violence as a response to white aggression, and his ability to fully understand the role and significance of imprisoned radical intellectuals as a subversive to US political structures resonates with many nineteenth- and early twentieth-century black radical imprisoned intellectuals.

However, wherein Ledbetter, for instance, utilized music as a form of black prison praxis and publicly strayed away from overt political engagement, Malcolm X constructed a form of black prison political praxis that directly took on political and social theory. This is an important distinction because it indicates that imprisoned political praxis is both complex and dynamic. No one person can adequately serve as the standard bearer for all radical imprisoned intellectuals.

For Malcolm, the immobilization experienced by black people is materialized in the construction of prison buildings. In other words, prison symbolizes black people's inability to live their everyday lives as constitutive moral agents. Therefore, the structure and confinement experienced in the prison industrial complex frames Malcolm's thinking and his political praxis as it relates to the whole of black life in the 1960s.

Furthermore, we can see through the life and work of Malcolm how confinement in this space ascribes onto the black body a type of experiential knowledge. He illustrates how black people are continually being radicalized through oppressive structures in complex and diverse ways. Without question, the prison is the material evidence for one of those radicalizing spaces.

Thus, it is vital to investigate the role the prison has played as a radical political transformative space for other imprisoned men and women. The impact that the prison has on black bodies makes it important for scholars in black radical intellectual traditions to avoid suggesting that Malcolm is an anomaly of imprisoned men and women. It is more likely that Malcolm is indicative of other imprisoned men and women who are trapped in these carceral spaces.

It is probably more accurate to suggest that he helps to frame the conditions of oppressed people in various spaces.

Indeed, Malcolm's political praxis solicits a deeper investigation of this space in order to reveal new transformative spaces that might be valuable for other social identity groups. In this light, Malcolm X becomes a more expansive representation of black imprisoned men and women. This representation causes us to think more about other oppressed identity categories.

Lastly, he shows how the prison, and by extension the felon, becomes a hermeneutical lens through which society can examine and interpret black life in the United States. Malcolm and other felons become the embodiment of a new hermeneutical approach. This new approach reshapes our concepts of Beloved Community.

GEORGE JACKSON AND THE RECONSTRUCTION OF CARCERAL SPACES FOR BLACK RADICAL PRODUCTION

George Jackson was born in Chicago on September 23, 1941. From his earliest adolescent years to his young adult life Jackson had various encounters with state confinement. Indeed, his personal narrative is replete with instances of aggression, violence, and crime. He makes no attempt to shy away from or diminish the unsettling aspects of his young felonious lifestyle.

Admittedly, when one first reads Jackson's work it is very jarring—almost as jarring as depictions of Nat Turner killing children during his rebellion. His language about his parents, women, black institutions, even the early civil rights movement is disturbing at the very least. However, if one studies Jackson and his work as representation of the grotesque, then he forces one to really look deeply into the United States and black and white culture and institutions that emerge from this society. In particular, he forces one to examine how gender, class, and racial ideology are all conditioned to exist and operate in a particular space. For Jackson, this space dictates how we see the world, and how we engage it.

Ultimately, Jackson's body of work as a representation of the grotesque—and by this I mean the set of principles that underline Jackson's action, ideas, and practices in response to certain injustices and oppression—engages black people to see how we advance an agenda within a system that is structurally designed to limit and suppress black agency. This also requires, then, that black radicals wrestle with all his imperfections and contradictions. He compels those who read his work to address the deepest areas of human hurt and fears. This requires readers to examine how the history of oppression in the United States shapes our perspective of the world, both the black world and the white one. In this way, Jackson engages in a creative exchange of the grotesque within black life to expose the deep wounds that keep black people from being fully committed to their liberation.

Consequently, Jackson's creative exchange constructs concrete moments where we see Beloved Community as fully engaged with the grotesque. For example, in those concrete moments readers see Jackson apologize to Angela Davis for his language and statements about women. This also occurs in letters wherein he apologizes to his mother. Indeed, by exploring Jackson we see a man grow and expand in his thoughts and feelings as he seeks a Beloved Community that is shaped by the realities of prison life. In this way, George Jackson illustrates a type of creative exchange that allows Beloved Community to remain open to contestation, doubt, and opposition. This type of creative exchange affords opportunity for others to exist and grow in their own time and through their unique experiences of the world.

Throughout his personal memoir, *Soledad Brother: The Prison Letters of George Jackson*, Jackson gives an unapologetic account of his violent and criminal past. He writes "I could play the criminal aspects of my life down some but then it wouldn't be me. That was the pertinent part, the thing at school and home I was constantly rejecting in process."[14] Jackson embraces his criminal past in part because he wants to reshape the black heroic apologetic narrative tradition. He is fully aware that this rejection of the black heroic apologetic narratives makes it easy for some to marginalize his form of black representation and to reject the usefulness of his intellectual offerings to black radical political intellectual traditions. Nevertheless, Jackson's political theory and praxis provides access to explore the construction of new discursive terrains for black radical production.

Jackson's insightful critique of the carceral state and the construction of black boys as felons illustrates why it is a mistake to overlook or dismiss him from black radical intellectual traditions. For instance, he admits that prison was a type of rite-of-passage for him and many other black and brown boys growing up in his neighborhood. According to Jackson, the allure of prison permanently entrapped many young black male bodies into structures of penal captivity. Consequently, it is not very surprising that Jackson would fall victim to this allure. However, the impact prison would have on him and to the construction of his radical political praxis was surprising.

Indeed, it was not until Jackson was sentenced to prison that he discovered that the allure of prison was a systemic condition within black communities. While in prison he came to realize this his behavior as a youth was a response to the structural and systemic ways incarceration captivated the black youth imagination. Jackson recognized the sophisticated ways that structural racism imprisoned black boys' thoughts about life chances and social opportunities. This thinking not only grasped hold of many black and brown boys' imagination of life, but served as the pathway to a life of penal incarceration. Lastly, it was during his incarceration that Jackson discovered how ill prepared he was growing up to resist the allure of prison.

So as not to give the idea that I am justifying bad or criminal behavior, let me be clear on a few things. One, saying that Jackson's behavior was a response to structural racism and the systemic allure of prison is not to suggest that Jackson is making excuses for his behavior. It is important to point out that Jackson is not excusing or diminishing his behavior prior to incarceration, but rather he is placing his behavior within a frame and context in order to better understand the conditions that influenced it. Prison offered Jackson a language to articulate the context of his behavior and it provided resources to help him address the complex structures of black male incarceration.

Furthermore, the ability to understand the conditions that influenced Jackson's behavior brings forth a new language and a new set of tools to address the enticement of penal captivity. In this way, Jackson helps us to understand the dynamics of the prison because it informed his thinking about himself and the community from which he came. The prison also became the site that helped Jackson identify and address structural and systemic racism.

Jackson links his status in prison to the overall status of African Americans who are forced to live in a white supremacist world. This, at times, left African Americans vulnerable to epistemic violence and family disintegration. Jackson speaks to some of his own vulnerabilities and the lasting effects. For instance, he was not educated or motivated by his parents toward political or civic engagement. In several of his letters, he criticizes his parents for capitulating to white racism and the impact that capitulation had on him and his siblings. In a letter he wrote to his father in July 1965, Jackson contends that "the same forces that have made your life miserable, the same forces that have made your life senseless and unrewarding, threaten me and all our posterity. I know the way out. If you cannot help, sit back and listen, and watch."[15]

Prior to prison, there is little in Jackson's childhood to suggest that he would one day become a political revolutionary. Indeed, with his multiple youthful encounters with the police, there was more to suggest he would have been killed as a youth. However, by 1971, Jackson was fully invested in tearing down the walls of social indoctrination. While in prison he became deeply entrenched in a political movement that sought to challenge structural racism. These activities are the direct result of being situated in an alternative space that provided him access to new ways of thinking about the world.

Jackson's creative exchange places black imprisoned men and women at the center of their liberation. Moreover, as opposed to the black church, Jackson uses the prison as the context for thinking about the principles of Beloved Community. For instance, in a letter that Jackson wrote to his father on July 13, 1967, he states "in the passing of these last couple of years, I have completely retrained myself and my thinking to the point now that I think and dream of one thing only, 24 hours of each day."[16] This is significant to the idea of Beloved Community because it ensures that representation continually comes from the margins of society.

Jackson also refigures both the images that we use to think about community and the resources we access to talk about justice and liberation. Later in that same letter Jackson writes "there can be no ties of blood or kinship strong enough to move me from my course. I'll never, never trade my self-determination for a car, cheap mass-produced clothes, clapboard house, or a couple of nights a week at the go-go."[17] In this light, the idea of the Beloved Community as a black intellectual product can be seen as a more radical intellectual endeavor.

In addition, Jackson was able to meet other revolutionary thinkers while in prison. For example, he met W. L. Nolan, a major figure in the Black Panther Liberation Movement. Nolan introduced Jackson to the writing of other black imprisoned intellectuals such as Black Panther leader Eldridge Cleaver. In solitary confinement, Jackson began to read the work of Karl Marx, Friedrick Engels, and Mao Tse-tung, and other political theorists.

The isolation of the prison provided opportunity for Jackson to connect with earlier radical thinkers. In one of his letters to Greg, the editor of his autobiography, Jackson states that "I met Marx, Lenin, Trotsky, Engels, and Mao when I entered prison and they redeemed me."[18] He quickly began to believe that liberation for black people in the United States required a type of sacrifice that persons who are not fully conscious of their captivity are unable and unwilling to give.

Furthermore, while in prison these theorists motivated Jackson to form the Black Guerilla Family with other inmates. He believed that knowledge was the liberating factor for black people both inside and outside of prison. For Jackson, knowledge revealed the structural ways black people are confined to carceral spaces. This belief was grounded in the notion that prison was merely one physical location of the carceral state and that the only true form of freedom was resistance. Consequently, Jackson's ability to draw a mass appeal and his desire to respond to the prison regime incited Jackson, Fleeta Drumgoole, and John Clutchett, commonly referred to as the Soledad Brothers, to organize a guerrilla warfare strategy in prison as a mode of resistance.

Inspired by Marxism, the Black Guerilla Family began to advance the idea of black prisoners' rights to self-defense and prison abolition. Indeed, within the confines of the prison, these inmates along with other followers of Jackson became radicalized in their political and social ideas. Rodriguez contends that "this epistemology of resistance and insurgency structured Jackson's political praxis, and his refusal to indulge banal discourse of idealized, hopeful, and (racially) reconciliatory civic 'peace' or 'coexistence' was amplified by his pedagogical commitment to stating the grounds of that principled refusal."[19] This resistance required a new type of thinking at the intersection of black captivity and liberation.

Fortuitously, Jackson emerges at a time when the prison movement was gaining traction within the black liberation movement of the 1970s. Much of this emergence happens around the expansion of the Black Panther Party Movement. As the movement grew, the spirit of the movement became more revolutionary in its beliefs about the means of addressing structural racism and inequality. More radical figures such as Malcolm X, Marcus Garvey, and black separatists of the nineteenth and early twentieth century had sway on the thinking of the leaders of the black liberation movement. As Cone states, "during the period of the 'nadir' and the 'long dark night' of black people's struggle for justice in America, Henry McNeal Turner, a bishop of the AME Church, and Marcus Garvey of the Universal Negro Improvement Association (UNIA) articulated nationalist perspectives that were more directly linked with the subsequent philosophy of Malcolm X."[20] These two occurrences and the form of resistance that it promoted had profound impact on Jackson's thoughts and actions. Therefore, it is not surprising that Jackson's political praxis was more informed by the ideas of militarism and resistance. These forms pushed up against those more pronounced ideas espoused by earlier civil rights figures and organizations during the 1950s and 1960s.

However, Jackson's thinking did not just contest the way early black radicals and civil rights groups thought about liberty and justice. He also thought about how European migrants engaged in their campaigns for freedom. In a letter that he wrote to his father on May 28, 1967, he reminded his father that "in the 1770s the Europeans over here wanted to pull away from the Europeans of England. They called it a freedom fight. Now we men of color here in the U.S. want to pull away from these Europeans and they call it subversion, irresponsibility, etc."[21] For Jackson, the idea of freedom and liberty is intrinsically a human condition that black people are being asked to deny. So he pushes against these forces and their attempt to deny him the full benefit of humanity.

Like other contemporary imprisoned intellectuals of his time, Jackson embodied Nat Turner's spirit of rebellion against state-sponsored violence onto black bodies. He appropriated Huddie Ledbetter's talent to attract white liberal supporters, and advanced Malcolm's critical offerings on political theory for liberation. Also like Malcolm, Jackson's theory of resistance and prison praxis included seeking national media attention. The national media attention helped to connect his work to a broader audience.

His radical theory challenged reformist traditions that often used the language of black survival as opposed to black martyrdom to speak about black social justice and human rights projects. For Jackson, any black liberation movement that did not take into account the history of white supremacy to kill the leaders within black liberation movements denies the very structure that maintains white supremacy. Yet, what is most impactful about Jackson's use of the national media was his desire to change the prison from a place of isolation to a space for black imprisoned praxis. In particular, Jackson changed the prison into a public spectacle for punishment as opposed to a private administrative site for punishment. This form of prison praxis would later influence other prison revolutionary leaders such as Monster Kody, Assata Shakur, and Mumia Abu-Jamaal.

Jackson also knew the power of the national media to build movements. He consistently spoke to and highlighted attempts to physically and materially erase the prison liberation movement. In *Soledad Brothers* he contends that the prison liberation movement "is structured in such a way as to allow us to exist and continue to resist despite the losses we absorb."[22] Furthermore, Jackson understood that organizing the movement in this way would necessitate that revolutionaries would continually seek to build collaborations with other oppressed groups. This radical theory differed in its language and presentation from the civil rights movement of the 1960s wherein much of the movement was built largely on the backs of select black leaders to represent the movement.

Indeed, Jackson's representation of black imprisoned intellectuals not only challenged traditional black civil rights models, it also challenged popular depictions of imprisoned people as uncivilized and unlearned. For example, in an interview that he gave with a reporter for KRON News, Jackson articulated a theory of revolution that is grounded in international freedom movements. He contended that "the principle point behind the prison movement is to prove to the establishment that the concentration camp technique, the reversion to the second dimension of Fascism, the terrorist face. We got to prove that the terror won't work on us. It won't stop our movement . . . not actually short of death."[23] Jackson constructed a form of representation that could resonate with other marginal communities both inside and outside of the United States. In doing this, he united black radical engagement with international forms of resistance, thereby confronting the idea that the only way to advance black liberation projects was through the promotion of black respectability politics.

It is not simply that Jackson created new ways of thinking about the representation within radical social movements. His radical prison praxis became the means of achieving black racial freedom. Rodriguez contends that "for Jackson, radical freedom was beyond the realm of possibility in a social formation that defined and reproduced the 'free world' of civil society against the violent unfreedom that was at once the bane of his existence and the core of his political intellectual identity."[24] Indeed, he defied the entirety of black bourgeoisie representation as the primary mode through which black radicals might create space for black liberation.

Jackson also challenged the idea that educational pedigree and intellectual rigor are synonymous. This became another way to defy appropriating black bourgeoisie imaging. For Jackson, such imaging capitulated to a white patriarchal system that required a docile form of black male representation.

By reconfiguring the image of imprisoned men and women, he not only challenged the docile and conformist representational model that was often utilized throughout the 1960s for the more popular civil rights movements, but he also repositioned black imprisoned bodies into black life and culture. This was important for Jackson, because it highlighted the continual need to broaden black representation and the spaces wherein that representation is located. In other words, Jackson shows that the way we think about black representation is a direct reflection of the way we think about who has been involved in black radical projects.

Ultimately, the composition of black radical projects directs the types of black political activities that society will bring to the public's attention. According to Jackson, there must be a representation within black radical projects that directs attention to everyday poor and marginal people in the world. He contends that "the nature of the function of the prison within the [prison state] police state has to be continuously explained, elucidated to the people on the street because we can't fight alone in here."[25] For Jackson, presenting black imprisoned intellectuals removed a type of isolation that is imposed on imprisoned bodies by the prison state. Jackson's work offers a theory of black political representation that invites a larger group of marginalized and oppressed people to participate in black radical projects.

In his attempt to rethink radical social movements, Jackson continued to push against more normative ideas and perspectives that mobilized some of the earlier black social justice and human rights projects. For instance, in addition to challenging black bourgeoisie imaging, Jackson rejected the way black religion was used within black human rights projects. He argued that the religious underpinning of earlier black reformist movement largely served to advance the work of white supremacy. Much of his critique was based on the idea that those movements traditionally relied on black churches and black pastors to lead the cause for justice. For Jackson, not only is black religion illogical to black liberation movements, but it also seeks to promote a movement to constrain black men to a particular social position.

Ultimately, Jackson constructed a theory largely of black liberation that critiqued black churches, black religion, as well as black feminism. He suggested that the work of black religion and black motherhood within black liberation projects ignored the broad spectrum of experiences of black males. In Jackson's estimation, black religion and black feminism lacked a theory of black genocide, particularly as it relates to black men. He contended that this form of genocide not only erases black male bodies, it also limits the range of black male representation. In Jackson's opinion, the erasure of more diverse images of black male representation allowed for the emergence and acceptance of the black masculine that was more susceptible to institutional assault.

These institutional assaults of black male representation advanced these apologetic ideas that the surrendering of black men's full constitutive moral agency to white patriarchal hegemonic social orders was noble. Moreover, it was necessary for survival. According to Jackson, these ideas were largely advanced by black religion. Resistant to this idea of black surrender, Jackson calls those of us interested in black liberation into a creative exchange that invites a broader range of black males into the conversation. This invitation to other black male representation allows more black men to define themselves based on their own experiences without the need or want to re-present themselves in the likeness of some European imagination of black men.

Jackson's more controversial ideas came from his assertion that the emasculating work of the black church was largely advanced by black women. This process of emasculating black men and the social condition of the black community led Jackson to challenge the theory of black church as a liberative idea. Moreover, in Jackson's mind, the idea of God within the black community authorized black suffering and allowed that suffering to go forth as a type of virtue. However, for Jackson, that type of virtue was only meant to relegate black men to a permanent subservient role within a white patriarchal structure. In a letter to his mother on July 28, 1967, Jackson spoke about the impact the black church has on black male identity construction. He claimed that "the theory of an existing and benevolent god simply doesn't make sense to anyone who is rational. A benevolent and omnipotent god would never allow such imbalances as I see to exist for one second."[26]

Jackson's critique of the black church is in its inability to centralize the notion of theodicy at the core of black religion. In other words, Jackson contended the vindication of divine goodness and providence as represented in the black church had been passive in view of the existence of evil as witnessed in white supremacy. Jackson set black incarceration and the suffering of black imprisoned men and women at the center of black religious ideas and practices to illustrate the black churches social impotence. This also highlights the absence of black prison suffering and mass incarceration within black liberation theologies and black religious studies. In the end, it placed that discourse on the black church and black liberation theologies in contradiction with their ideas about God, freedom, and justice.

Indeed, for Jackson, the only justifiable way to maintain the idea of an omnipotent and benevolent god to uphold a theology that affirms the notion that blackness is, by nature, corrupt. He stated that "if by chance I am wrong, however, I must then assume that being born black called for some automatic punishment for sins I know nothing about, and being innocent it behooves me to defy god."[27] Ultimately, this calls black liberation theologians and black religious scholars to more pragmatic and liberatory ways of thinking about God, particularly as it relates to the social position of black male felons. The very idea of Beloved Community as an exercise of "creative exchange" is impossible if the social position of black male felons are absent from black religious and black liberation theological discourse.

Jackson's analysis of black religion also led him to a critique of black motherhood. It was largely based on his belief that black religion is advanced primarily by black women and that the natural tendency of men to reject servitude is hindered by the social conditioning of black boys by their mothers. This critique is also largely absent from earlier investigation of black civil rights movements. In his letter to his mother, he wrote, "as a woman I can understand your being naturally disposed to servitude. I can understand your feelings but what I can't understand is why you would have me feel the same, considering that I am a man."[28] He contended that black women must have an affinity to servitude and that the use of religion becomes a tool to also place black men in the position of servant as well.

Throughout his earliest arguments, Jackson contended that black women's "natural" disposition is the result of their capitulation to white supremacy for black survival. They have become products of their environments and have succumbed to circumstantial and situational pressures. However, Angela Davis would eventually challenge him on his position of black women, causing him to later apologize for some of his criticism of black women and their "natural" disposition to servitude.

Notwithstanding his apology and capitulation to Davis, Jackson held to the idea that white racism transmutes the natural tendency of black women and men for freedom. He argued that the natural tendency by some black women, particularly black mothers, to be subservient is a result of their submission to being "reduced to nothing" by a "foolish man grown heady with power and made drunk, dizzy drunk from the hot air that inflates his ego."[29] In other words, for Jackson, black men as well as black women are victims of their own submission to white racism.

Jackson's openness to creative exchange, however, led him to shift his assessment of the grotesque from something he blamed black women for to something he looked to black women to help solve. Certainly the work of Angela Davis and other black radical women became a type of feminist intervention that he believed is necessary for the liberation. For example, in a letter to Davis he said:

> In our last communication I made a statement about women, and their part in revolutionary culture (people's war). It wasn't a clear statement. I meant to return to it but was diverted. I understand exactly what the woman's role should be. The very same as the man's. Intellectually, there is very little difference between male and female. The differences we see in bourgeois society are all conditioned and artificial.[30]

In these words, we see that Jackson does not have an issue with women, but rather he is frustrated with white patriarchal structure that subjects men and women to subservient roles of being.

The more radical feminist theory by Jackson can be seen in both his writings to Angela Davis as well as in the readings within Black Panther publications. For example, in *Good Mothers with Guns: Framing Black Womanhood in the Black Panther, 1968–1980*, Linda Lumsden contends that the Black Panther's publications continually evolved the framing of black womanhood from a restrictive essentialist stereotypes that was promoted largely in black churches to empowering portrayals of female resistance. Lumsden contends that "the newspaper's evolving frame of black women makes it an important artifact of the culture of resistance regarded as the foundation of black feminist thought."[31] For Lumsden, the Black Panther Party's newspaper served as a counter-hegemonic artifact for depicting alternative frames on women's issues such as women in prison. Jackson greatly believed that Angela Davis embodied that form of radical black feminism.

The BPP newspaper places in context Jackson's letter to his mother and his framing of black womanhood. It sheds light on Jackson's belief that the "silent" and "reformist" approach does not work for black men and is detrimental to the black liberation movement. In other words, Jackson's "hypermasculinity" is a response to what he initially felt was an assault by black mothers to diminish black men's response to white patriarchy. For example, in another letter that he wrote to his mother on March 27, 1967, he apologized for being harsh. In the letter, he attempted to explain the foundation of his and her misery. He contended that, "I believe sincerely that you will be a very unhappy and perplexed woman for as long as you try to pretend that you have anything in common with this culture, or better, that this culture has anything in common with you."[32]

Jackson offers a complex way of thinking about mothering, particularly the notion of love and obedience, as tools used to keep black sons safe from violence and death. Yet, this depiction of Jackson is not to suggest that certain practices and beliefs that he puts forth should be submitted without critique. Nor is it meant to try to present Jackson as perfect. There are moments that his theory denies black women full participation in the black liberation movement within the Black Panther Party. As Lumsden points out, "the Panther's public rhetoric about women . . . obscures private intraparty gender battles, a common tension in social movements."[33]

However, it does show where and how black male felons such as Jackson enter, into the discourse on black feminism and helps map the discursive practices within black liberation movements. For instance, female Panthers routinely challenged sexist practices and stereotypes and, by 1969, the BPP's newspaper framed black men and women as equals. According to Lumsden, the portrayal of black women as equal to black men in BPP's verbal and visual rhetoric offers traditional and radical frames of womanhood. This also suggests that the involvement of black male felons reveals a way of not only thinking about black feminists discourse, but offers new spaces wherein verbal and visual rhetoric of black women might be discovered and investigated.

In spite of Jackson's feminist controversy, he was unyielding in his religious stance. He stood steadfast on his position of the black church and its role in limiting black liberation efforts. For Jackson, the black church is the institutional embodiment of the victimhood and submissiveness that he initially held of the shoulders of surrendered black men and black women. For Jackson, this capitulation of the black church was self-evident.

Yet overall, we see through Jackson's prison praxis how the prison regime operates as a technological tool of immobilization. Moreover, his work signals the various ways the state authorized contemporary forms of forced labor and servitude. For example, in his letters and interviews Jackson often equated the prison regime to military concentration camps. In an interview he gave to Karen Wald in 1971, he said "we're all familiar with the function of the prison as an institution serving the needs of the totalitarian state. We've got to destroy that function; the function has to be no longer viable, in the end. It's one of the strongest institutions supporting the totalitarian state. We have to destroy its effectiveness, and that's what the prison movement is all about."[34] For Jackson, any black liberation movement is co-dependent on the success of the prison liberation movement—a liberation effort that was largely composed of black men and women.

This codependency between black liberation and prison liberation explains why Jackson wanted to make clear that any discourse around black radical politics must not only include work on prison abolition, but must also effectively engage black prison praxis. According to Rodriguez, Jackson [and Angela Davis] "offers a useful mode of entry into the body of praxis generated by captive political workers who have since sustained and strengthened the political intellectual insurgency embodied by Jackson and Davis."[35] In other words, imprisoned men and women offer an embodied philosophical perspective that allows for greater insight about the tools white supremacy utilizes to keep certain person from full participation in the US democratic project.

As mentioned earlier in the chapter, Jackson's appeal drew a wide and diverse audience. His book sparked a national dialogue around law enforcement and the criminal justice system. From inmates in California and New York to celebrity spokespersons such as Jane Fonda, Jackson built a community of resistance, which strangely began to draw prisoners from other racial backgrounds. Moreover, his advocacy for a type of prison guerrilla warfare would spark a type of revolutionary strategy for other imprisoned men and women across the country. To the discontent of governors and prison officials, Jackson provided a voice for people that are often marginalized in society.

Thus, Jackson illustrates how black imprisoned men and women expand the people involved in social and political movements. Ultimately, this expansion brings forth new ways of thinking about institutional assault on black bodies. Indeed, his ability to give a voice to a silent and oppressed group lent to a groundswell of grassroots activists. These activists gathered around issues from police brutality to corruption in the criminal justice system. Much of the grassroots activity helped to also expand the idea of unifying common oppression among diverse groups.

But we also can't deny that Jackson's imprisoned praxis came at a great cost. It not only cost Jackson his life, it also cost the state financially. Both of these things served to limit what we know of Jackson and his movement. For instance, the Black Guerrilla Family's intellectual and political praxis goes largely unnoticed. This happens not solely because of their radical philosophy, but because of the political structure that holds their bodies and their political praxis captive to a particular location. If we are not more engaged within black intellectual discourse to investigate these locations, then this silence will continue to exist.

Even where there is inquiry into carceral spaces, the details are superficial at best. Unfortunately, much of the work around the black guerrilla family and other black imprisoned bodies gets caught in a discourse on spectacles of violence, the impact of criminality on communities, and the link between prisons and other social inequities. While those things are important, too often the current discourse within black radical intellectual traditions allows a type of reduction and simplicity to both the work and being of those bodies that have been labeled felon. As a result, the discursive tendency around black felons presents these figures as merely products of the prison regime and not as moral agents that stand in opposition to a larger carceral regime.

Even in light of mass incarceration, the ongoing killing of unarmed black people, and Jackson's own prison praxis, the discursive tendency with black radical traditions allows for the prison to go unnoticed as a production site for oppressed groups. The tendency to allow the prison to go unnoticed has several implications. First, the reduction of the prison diminishes the spaces available wherein black males are engaged in the discourse as equal agents for liberation and change.

Second, when the prison is diminished as a space of interrogation for black radical production, the erasure of black incarcerated bodies is referenced merely as the by-product of men and women who are victims of their own negligible choices. In other words, for many people the capture of black bodies within the prison regime is the result of a set of choices that could have been avoided as opposed to a structural and systemic technique for black immobilization. Yet, Rodriguez reminds us that "the context of Jackson's assassination . . . compels an extended theoretical engagement with genocide as the logical, dynamic, and constantly reproduced condition of racism and white supremacy."[36] Therefore, the death of black felons becomes another technique for disposing of black bodies in the United States and masking the spaces that inform black intellectual production.

Yet, this didn't stop Jackson from influencing those held within prisons and jails. His call for prison abolition and radical freedom attracted inmates from various racial groups. The appeal to a broad group of prisoners allowed his ideas to spread rapidly throughout the prisons in California. Furthermore, his effectiveness as an organizer and educator to other prisoners was also felt across the country. For instance, shortly after he was killed at San Quentin Prison, inmates in the Attica State Prison in New York organized a prison uprising with many of the same demands and critiques that Jackson put forth in his writings and interviews. For this reason, Rodriguez contends that "as Jackson's political stature and reputation grew among imprisoned people within and beyond California, in part through the celebrated publication of *Soledad Brother: The Prison Letters of George Jackson* (1970), he became a liability to state authorities because of his effectiveness as an organizer and educator to fellow prisoners."[37]

Similar to *Soledad Brother*, Attica's written Prison Manifesto not only detailed the injustices in the New York prison regime, but also gave evidence to the organizational and creative work of imprisoned men. The prison praxis by Attica inmates would eventually lead to structural prison reform in New York. Jackson's nephew, Jonathan Jackson, Jr., contends that the mainstay of George's brilliance was his ability to make his personal experience come across as universal. In the foreword of *Soledad Brother*, Jackson states that, "when [George's] collection of letters was first released in 1969, it brought a young revolutionary to the forefront of a tempest, a tempest characterized by the Black Power, free speech, and antiwar movements, accompanied by a dissatisfaction with the status quo throughout the United States."[38] Ultimately, the Soledad Brothers, which consisted of Jackson, John Clutchette, and Fleeta Drumgo, helped to propel a prison movement that brought the criminal justice system and the treatment of imprisoned men and women under national public scrutiny.

NOTES

1. Malcolm X, "God's Angry Men," in *Malcolm X Speaks: Selected Speeches and Statements*, ed. George Breitman Merit (Publishers: New York, 1965), 166.
2. James Cone, *Martin & Malcolm & America: A Dream or a Nightmare* (Ossining, NY: Orbis Books, 2012), 14.
3. Malcolm X, "Message to the Grass Roots," in *Martin & Malcolm & America: A Dream or a Nightmare*, ed. James Cone (Ossining, NY: Orbis Books, 2012), 8.
4. Malcolm X, "The Ballot or the Bullet," in *Imprisoned Intellectuals: America's Political Prisoners Write on Life, Liberation, and Rebellion*, ed. Joy James (Lanham, MD: Rowman & Littlefield Publishers, 2003), 51.
5. Malcolm X, "The Ballot or the Bullet," 51.
6. Malcolm X, "The Ballot or the Bullet," 52.
7. Malcolm X, "The Ballot or the Bullet," 52.
8. Joy James, *The New Abolitionist*, 281.
9. Dylan Rodriquez, *Forced Passages: Imprisoned Radical Intellectuals and the U.S. Prison Regime* (Minneapolis: University of Minneapolis Press, 2006), 105.
10. Joy James, *Imprisoned Intellectuals: America's Political Prisoners Write on Life, Liberation, and Rebellion* (Lanham, MD: Rowman & Littlefield Publishers, 2003), 15.
11. Dylan Rodriguez, *Forced Passages*, 55.
12. Geronimo ji Jaga, "The Black Panthers: An Interview with Geronimo ji Jaga Pratt," in *The New Abolitionists: (Neo) Slave Narratives and Contemporary Prison Writings*, ed. Joy James (Albany: State University of New York Press, 2005), 243.
13. Joy James, *Imprisoned Intellectuals*, 15.
14. George Jackson, *Soledad Brother: The Prison Letters of George Jackson* (Chicago: Lawrence Hill Books, 1994), 3.
15. George Jackson, *Soledad Brother*, 69–70.
16. George Jackson, *Soledad Brother*, 122.
17. George Jackson, *Soledad Brother*, 122.
18. George Jackson, *Soledad Brother*, 16.
19. Dylan Rodriguez, *Forced Passages*, 120.
20. James Cone, *Malcolm and Martin*, 11.
21. George Jackson, *Soledad Brothers*, 118.
22. George Jackson, *Soledad Brothers*, 231.

23. YouTube, "George Jackson Speaks! 1971 Interview," https://www.youtube.com/watch?v=P8Va-wxoJYQ. Published May 22, 2015, Web video (0.00–0:35).

24. Dylan Rodriguez, *Forced Passages*, 116

25. George Jackson, *Soledad Brothers*, 230

26. George Jackson, *Soledad Brothers*, 126.

27. George Jackson, *Soledad Brothers*, 126.

28. George Jackson, *Soledad Brothers*, 126.

29. George Jackson, *Soledad Brothers*, 127.

30. George Jackson, *Soledad Brothers*, 298.

31. Linda Lumsden, "Good Mothers with Guns: Framing Black Womanhood in the Black Panther, 1968–1980," in *Journalism and Mass Communication Quarterly* (Thousand Oaks, CA: Sage Publications, 2009), 900.

32. George Jackson, *Soledad Brothers*, 111.

33. Linda Lumsden, "Good Mothers with Gun," 901.

34. George Jackson, *Soledad Brothers*, 230.

35. Dylan Rodriguez, *Forced Passages*, 117.

36. Dylan Rodriguez, *Forced Passages*, 122.

37. Dylan Rodriguez, *Forced Passages*, 119.

38. George Jackson, *Soledad Brothers*, xiv.

Chapter 5

Prison Prophets

Twenty-First Century Black Male Felons on Race, Religion, and Mass Incarceration

On Thursday August 16, 2015, Grammy, Golden Globe, and Academy award-winning singer-songwriter John Legend spoke with a body of Texas State Legislatures as part of his multiyear campaign initiative, Free America. Legend launched the Free America campaign to bring awareness to the issue of mass incarceration in the United States, and to construct legislative reform policies to address the hyper-incarceration rate, particularly of nonviolent drug offenders. In an interview with the *Texas Tribune* he stated that he launched Free America because he believes that mass incarceration is a serious problem in America.

Legend talked about the high numbers of people living behind bars. He told the *Tribune* that "every day 7 million people are under correctional control, which means being in prison or jail or on probation or parole." According to Legend, many of these prison sentences are the result of policies enacted over the last forty years. These policies impact sentencing for various acts, including nonviolent crimes. He explained to the Tribune that he started this new initiative because he believed it was time to reverse the trend of incarceration, particularly the impact is has on communities of color.

Legend realized that his notoriety as an artist gave him a platform to make change in criminal justice policies. He concluded the interview by saying that:

> we want to help create awareness for the efforts that are already ongoing, help amplify them and support them and really get America to pay attention to this issue, because a lot of times people that are incarcerated are forgotten about. We kind of put them in prison and forget about them and forget about the fact that they are people with families, with histories, with stories, stories that are meaningful and we can all learn from. We need to pay attention to them again and try to end this system that has really destroyed so many lives and so many communities.[1]

The introduction of John Legend into the public discourse on mass incarceration and felons begs the question to both the future role of the artist as social justice and political agent as well as the future role of the artist as prison intellectual. John Legend encourages us to think critically about other source materials that scholars might interrogate as it relates to the imprisoned intellectual in the twenty-first century. Although Legend has never been incarcerated or convicted of a felony charge, there are several twenty-first century urban musicians and hip hop artists whose lives exist at the intersection of artist and felon. Thus, it seems only appropriate to explore what cultural production twenty-first century black felons as artists offer to black radical traditions.

The unique insight of oppressed groups to perceive new ways of understanding the human experience has been widely discussed in black radical traditions. For instance, scholars from W. E. B. Du Bois to Angela Davis to Anthony Bogues to Joy James have critically examined how certain identity categories lend to black history and culture. In addition, many of these scholars have explored the roles that black radicals as pastors, prophets, gospel singers, Rastafarian musicians, and educators have played in order to counter hegemonic ideologies and practices.

One of those practices within black radical traditions is the use of music and art to express ideas about identity, justice, and life meanings. For example, Anthony Bogues re-situates radical Jamaican Rastafarian musician Bob Marley within the prophetic black radical intellectual tradition in order to show how certain radical ideas are reshaped, particularly within black culture, through a process of cultural commodification. In re-situating Marley, Bogues contends that the process of commodification captured "the light skinned Jamaican Rastafarian who in transcending racial boundaries and countries also moves beyond race, and therefore belongs no longer to the black radical tradition out of which he sprang."[2] Thus, without intervention, both Marley's music and identity are expunged and his legacy within the black radical traditions is erased.

In much the same way, hip hop and urban artists are often deleted from the terrain of black radical cultural production and their artistic expressions are overlooked for their offerings. Like the case of Marley, the radical body of knowledge that it produces becomes lost in the milieu of pop culture. These artists within hip hop culture not only get lost because of the commodification of hip hop by mainstream capital industries, but also because of the misogyny and violent imagery within hip hop's lyrical content.

Furthermore, there is a pervasive belief among some that hip hop culture's artistic expression has little value as source material for academic inquiry. This is often due to the narrow constraints, definitions and considerations that regulate what some call scholarship. Lastly, this belief regarding the cultural value of hip hop happens because certain bodies are just simply discounted or overlooked as sites for intellectual life. Dylan Rodriquez makes the observation in *Forced Passages: Imprisoned Radical Intellectuals and the U.S. Prison* that "imprisoned people have no 'right' to exist as political beings or social subjects."[3] Yet, if we move past these narrow ideas, we can see through a close examination of felons within hip hop culture and urban music how these artists raise questions and present theories that are important to black political and cultural life.

OVERCOMING DUALISM: THE CHALLENGE FOR BLACK CULTURAL PRODUCTS WITHIN THE AMERICAN IMAGINATION

Both W. E. B. Du Bois and Alain Locke understood the value that black cultural production and black aesthetics played in bringing about political, religious, and cultural change. While neither Du Bois nor Locke examined the experience and cultural production of the felon explicitly, their work on black art and folk music is nonetheless impactful to how black radicals would come to validate black experience and the cultural materials that they produced. Moreover, while it is unfair and slightly inaccurate to suggest that W. E. B. Du Bois and other black radicals of the twentieth century made it impossible for certain black artists and their work to find a place within black intellectual life, it is not too far reaching to suggest that they created a standard and atmosphere within black intellectual life that narrowed the body of work studied among black cultural products. This narrowing of black art made it difficult for modern forms of black cultural expressions such as hip hop to forge a path as a true artistic expression and potential site for black radical intellectual traditions.

African American music and cultural expressions that arose out of cotton fields and urban ghettos faced many difficult challenges, particularly their ability to garner popular acceptance from mass audiences. This difficulty was due in large part to racist and classist notions that contended that certain black people were not worthy to be seen as cultural producers. We saw this in the Harlem Renaissance among the selection of blues and jazz artists and later in the music of the 1960s with Motown, whose desire was to distinguish black pop music from black soul music as a means of garnering a large white consumer base.

To their credit, much of Du Bois's and Locke's work in the early twentieth century was invested in the belief that black cultural production such as music, art, and literature could validate black people's humanity. They used the songs, writings, and artistic expression of black artists to demonstrate the value and worth of black lives. However, from their work there still lingers a complex and troubling idea about black people and their cultural products. For instance, even though hip hop is one of the most popular musical expressions in the world today it is still often marginalized for its political and religious offerings. The men and women who produce this genre of artistic expression are seldom seen as political or social justice agents.

The marginalization of hip hop and its value as both political and religious artistic expression happens for many of the same reasons that black blues and jazz artists of the early twentieth century died with little to no recognition. Similar to the belief regarding Bessie Smith and Huddie Ledbetter, hip hop artists get largely critiqued based on the preconceptions that society holds about these artists as thugs, gangsters, felons, and the like. Few extol their value as social and political agents.

As a consequence of this, hip hop is viewed largely through the lens of urban folk art. It is interpreted largely as the experience of poor black urban city youths. This narrow perception of hip hop reveals urban experience largely through the context of poverty and race and in our society who wants to listen to poor black youth. While the focus of hip hop may center on poverty and race, the interpretations of these experiences are shallow at best.

Also, the relegation of hip hop's cultural aesthetic as a type of folk or street art and the preconceived notions of the artists that produce the music has hindered a more full assessment of the knowledge production that Du Bois and Locke make concerning the value of black cultural production. Again, this marginalization occurs in large part because of the way Du Bois and Locke situate the discourse on black culture and artistic expressions in the early twentieth century.

Du Bois and Locke helped frame how scholars would come to analyze and interpret black artists and the cultural products they produced. This type of framing as a consequence gives little consideration to the role hip hop plays in the development of political, religious, and cultural theory. Some again might think that it is far-reaching to argue that Du Bois's and Locke's early approach to black expression is in part why hip hop is not widely recognized for its artistic and cultural value. However, our total focus cannot be on Du Bois and Locke as black cultural critics per se; rather, we should give some attention to the process and intention behind their exhibition and critique of black cultural products.

If we stop for a moment to investigate the intentions and motivations behind Du Bois's and Locke's work, we can see how much of their work was meant to make a statement about black life and culture over and against white supremacy and racism. That type of examination reveals their work served as an apologetic function. This is not a totally bad function for black cultural studies. However, when black cultural studies operates mostly as an apologetic function to white supremacy, it does not allow black cultural products to speak fully on its own terms and in its own language. Instead, it is constantly being made to appropriate the language of its oppressor in order to find meaning and value.

That being said, it is also clear that Du Bois and Locke understood that black cultural production offers more than just cultural apologetics. For instance, in *The Souls of Black Folk*, Du Bois expresses both the importance and impact that certain forms of black cultural expression, namely blues and gospel, had on articulating the black experience in America. He admits that these earlier forms of black cultural production were "neglected, it has been, and is, half despised, and above all it has been persistently mistaken and misunderstood."[4] He knew that this cultural expression revealed the hiddenness of black experience.

Hip hop and contemporary urban music provide many of the same offerings that Du Bois's makes regarding blues and Negro folk songs. Similar to those black cultural expressions, hip hop and contemporary urban music, reveal the hidden world of African Americans. We see this most vividly when we examine the prison industrial complex through hip hop and urban music. In addition, these genres, like their predecessors, give voice to many African American artists that felt marginalized in the world. According to Du Bois, "the Negro folk-song—the rhythmic cry of the slave—stands to-day not simply as the sole American music, but as the most beautiful expression of human experience born this side of the seas."[5] Nothing less can be said of hip hop and the soulful sounds of black urban musicians.

However, the misunderstandings regarding this art form derive largely from the preconceived notions that the larger society has about the people who created the art. Thus, Du Bois's work is significant because it calls for a deeper engagement and examination of the cultural production of marginalized and oppressed groups. This deeper engagement requires black cultural critics and scholars to refocus our attention to: 1) the human experience of the artists as forms of knowledge production; 2) to the social structures and systems within society that mitigates how the work of the artists is framed; and 3) how the artists is positioned in community and how that community operates within a larger social structure.

Engaging black cultural production through this type of method is useful for a few distinct reasons. First, the experiences of these artists will help to spotlight any contradictions between social ideology and government practices. Spotlighting these contradictions creates moments of creative exchange that otherwise might not be available. Second, focusing on structures within a society help define who within the community is given constitutive moral agency. Constitutive moral agency ultimately reveals who within a society is considered human and, thus, valuable. Third, focusing on how the artist is positioned in community and how that community exists in relation to the broader community reveals aspects and features of social and systemic situations and problems. The revelation of these situations and problems shines a light on certain dimensions of the human experience, which ultimately can be understood as part of the knowledge collective about issues on justice, politics, and race.

Du Bois goes into great detail to talk about how African American's experiences must be understood through at least two dimensions to include a knowledge of self within the larger society and knowledge of self within its particular community. He contends that "the history of the American Negro is the history of this strife—this longing to attain self-conscious manhood, to merge his double self into a better and truer self."[6] For Du Bois, this concern is most prominently articulated in his theory on African American's double consciousness.

Ultimately, by exploring this hidden space we are able to locate the essence of this music's origin. Indeed it is the hidden aspect of black life that lends to the creativity and the uniqueness in this cultural expression. For Du Bois, the study of black life and culture is pivotally significant because it reveals his idea that these cultural products arose from the "twin souls" of black folks in America. This twin soul—Du Bois's notion of double-consciousness, spoke to the hidden portions of black identity from the masses in America. As a result of Du Bois's work on black people's cultural production, scholars are able to better understand the value these cultural products have on both cultural and political discourse.

In much the same way as blues and gospel music, hip hop also reveals similar political, religious, and social value. Yet hip hop music also reveals the hidden experiences of certain black people in America that wrestle with more than a mere "double consciousness." In other words, hip hop reveals a people struggling with not only being black in the United States, but also being black and a felon in the United States. Thus, hip hop music reveals a multifold oppression to include what it means to be black and a felon in America, which adds another layer to the black experience in America.

Like Du Bois, Alain Locke believed that black cultural production aided in the recognition and acceptance of African Americans to the broader society. The desire to provide cultural resources that witness to African American value is in part why Locke became one of the original innovators of the Harlem Renaissance. Indeed, the Harlem Renaissance garnered its greatest appeal largely because of the New Negro Movement in the early and mid-1900s. According to Locke, these new artists within the Harlem Renaissance, particularly the writers, had the ability to best express the quality and value of black people.

As a result, Locke helped redefine what it meant to be black in America by uplifting particular types of black artist and their work as evidence of black humanity. In an article entitled *Alain Locke and the New Negro Movement*, Eugene C. Holmes claims that Locke ascribed to these new set of artists a type of "spiritual wealth."[7] This wealth came not only from their writings and artistic expression but also from the experiences that informed those expressions. Furthermore, as Holmes points out, Locke believed this new wealth would usher forth a "new judgment and re-appraisal of the race."[8] Holmes contends that, the "New Negro Movement coincided with an ever increasing interest in Negro life and character in the twenties."[9]

Locke's desire to position black experience within mainstream American culture meant that much of the art championed by Locke served a dual purpose. However, Locke did not ascribe the same value as Du Bois did to black folk art and folk music. For Locke, the Harlem Renaissance was ideally a vehicle to shine a light on black creativity and ingenuity as well as a way to impact society's perception that blackness was void of cultural value. As a result, Locke in many ways capitulated to Western aesthetic values.

Often, these two desires work in opposition with each other. Thus, Locke not only highlights the two divergent missions of black artist and black radicals but also, inevitably, he calls attention to the duality of black radical projects. In *Alain Locke and American Art Criticism*, Mary Ann Calo contends that "as an art critic, Locke sought to historicize, analyze, and classify African American art and to position it in relation to both black experience and mainstream American culture."[10] Consequently, advocates of hip hop culture are challenged with reconciling the dual nature within black radical political projects if they are going to show how hip hop is a viable resource for black intellectual life.

Much of the value of hip hop is obscured, particularly for the felon, because it lacks a fuller investigation of hip hop's third mission, which is to expose the trappings of the criminal justice system in America. According to Calo, Locked advocated for a form of black cultural production with "authentic national populist expression [while] rooted simultaneously in personal and communal experience."[11] However, this personal and communal experience did not always authenticate national populist expressions in the same way as Western European American art. For example, Calo contends that Locke "was simultaneously a classic American critic of his generation and a unique voice; that is to say, he had much in common with other American critics of the interwar decades, but he had a different job."[12] The problem didn't rest so much in Locke's job. The problem rested in what he thought of as black art.

Locke was very clear about how and what he considered black artful expression. The most evident considerations can be seen in the selection and analysis of the black cultural products that he gave his greatest attention. His cultural definition on black art and creativity not only hindered black rural and urban artistic expression but it ultimately helped to solidify European aesthetic values normally expressed in Romantic and neo-romantic literature and writing.

As a result, this narrow lens influenced the way the larger society came to accept black artistic expressions, as well as the method through which black cultural critics did their work. Holmes contends that Locke, along with other black intellectuals of the twentieth century "helped in hastening the demise of Negro dialect poetry" which they "believed was only a continuation of the stock stereotypes about gentility, humility and buffoonery, and an evasion of all of the realities of Negro life."[13] Indeed, the intrinsic dual work of black cultural production, as witnessed through Locke's New Negro Movement, had negative implications and collateral consequences.

In addition, the dual nature within black cultural production highlights the tension between Locke's radical work with black artists and his theoretical notions about black art. This conflict is actually very promising for the inclusion of hip hop. Calo contends that "scarcely anyone who has taken a serious look at Locke's critical priorities fails to recognize the conflict in his thinking between competing notions of the specific and the general."[14] For instance, in *Values and Imperatives*, Locke argues that, "the blind practicality of the common man and the disinterested impracticality of the philosopher yield similar results and rationalizations."[15] This means that, wherein Locke indeed might advocate for a particular type of artistic expression, his pragmatic philosophical approach as expressed through his value relativist theory allows for the potential advocacy for and inclusion of the type of folk art that makes way for hip hop as a radical pragmatic intellectual endeavor.

Although Locke held to a strict artistic prototype to represent black cultural value, his relativist theory concerning value makes it hard to think of his beliefs of black art as an ontological ideality. Locke's New Negro Movement was largely based on his belief that both the philosopher and the "common man" are not in any position to hold a value standard that can and should last throughout time for every generation. For Locke, these "transvaluations of value" supports a more relativistic approach to values and norms. In other words, scholars overlook how Locke's relativistic approach is open to a creative exchange that gives access to new forms of black cultural expression. Therefore, customs, beliefs, values, and traditions must always be examined and reexamined by successive generations. Moreover, Locke's divergent notions between thinking and doing create a space for a reexamination of black aesthetics and cultural production.

Certainly Locke and Du Bois both were concerned with the social structures that define who is considered human within in a democratic society and how the expression of that humanness is transmitted and validated. Thus, this reexamination calls for an evaluation of the methods that have been used to critique and analyze black cultural products. This is most helpful for those black cultural products that have traditionally been thought to lack political and religious value for black radical traditions such as certain forms of hip hop.

Ultimately, both Du Bois and Locke illustrate how knowledge is rejected in society when certain marginalized groups are not given full constitutive moral agency. Lock sought to address this issue. He reminds us that "we are warrantably alarmed to see these vigorous, new secular absolutisms added to the older, waning metaphysical and doctrinal ones to which we had become somewhat inured and from which, through science and the scientific spirit, we acquired some degree of immunity."[16] One most notable consequence of this marginalization is that any cultural work produced by and from these groups is thought to have no value.

Thus, a reflexive examination of black cultural products allows scholars who study black radical history to situate the felon as artist into the broader discourse on black cultural productions. Despite their internal conflicts, both Locke and Du Bois understood the correlation between what experiences society deemed as valuable resources for knowledge production and the need to secure some type of social and political well-being for African Americans. Therefore, a more thorough reflexive examination of these men is vital for the sake of black radical traditions.

In addition, a reflexive examination on black cultural production makes clear how the felon as artist is restricted. It shows the various ways in which his/her choices become limited by structured discursive practices. These structures inevitably limit the space available for black felons to do their work. Furthermore, the space wherein these artists do their work limits the set of choices available to them. In other words, the felon as artist is situated within a set of creative choices that are framed within a larger systemic structure—one that both condemns, isolates, and conceals the identity of felon from the broader society.

Consequently, hip hop reveals both the constrictive structures wherein felons are assigned, and also the ways contemporary urban music articulates cultural remembrance. In other words, felons as artists utilize hip hop to reveal the complex ways black bodies have historically been isolated through penal captivity. It is for this reason that Anthony Bogues contends that, if we are going to fully appreciate the complexity of black popular music, we must dispense with the "high" and "low" distinctions within black cultural production. According to Bogues, "as an art form, black popular music in the New World functions [as] cultural memory."[17, 18] Therefore, to fully appreciate the felon as artist, scholars within black radical traditions must engage in a creative exchange with their cultural production in order to displace the distinctions that separate and isolate the felon and his/her cultural production.

A NEW BORDERLAND: THE BLACK MALE FELON AS CULTURAL CRITIC AND PRAGMATIC PHILOSOPHER

The discourse on urban music in general and hip hop music in particular is grounded in a set of intellectual debates. Many of those debates range from hip hop commercialization and its relationship to large capitalist industries to its intellectual value and scholarly contributions. Notwithstanding these significant debates, it is hard to deny that hip hop's artistic work has played a significant role in giving voice to the experiences of persons and communities impacted by mass incarceration in ways other artful expressions have yet to capture. For instance, in the 1990s, groups such as Public Enemy and NWA continuously spoke about police brutality and racism within the criminal justice system in graphic language and imagery.

In this role, hip hop has also been able to depict how the democratic ideal of America and the democratic mechanism by which it operates stand in continual opposition to each other. This democratic tension between the ideal of democracy and the practice and administration of democratic ideology has been the critique of black radicals, cultural critics, and pragmatic philosophers such as Frederick Douglass, Martin Luther King Jr., John Dewey, and others. For instance in *The Search for the Great Community*, Dewey highlights this tension by contrasting his great community with Western democracy. He details the foundation and significance of a great society and how that society differs from the system of government in the United States. According to Dewey, even though the two are connected, there is a "distinction between democracy as a social idea and political democracy as a system of government."[19]

Similar to Dewey's work in *The Search for the Great Community*, numerous hip hop artists have addressed radical distinctions between social and political ideology with social and political practices. Indeed, the experiences of felons within hip hop lyrics highlights Dewey's general thesis regarding the notion of democracy as a social ideal and democracy as a political exercise.

The subject of felon within hip hop lyrical content reveals how systems of government operate contrary to the social idea of democracy as a liberative political construct. In this light, hip hop emerges as a pragmatic philosophical body of knowledge within the larger discourse on democracy and justice. By presenting itself as a pragmatic philosophy, hip hop exposes a type of knowledge, reality and existence of being in the world. This revelation is most evident in the role hip hop plays in articulating the lived experiences of felons.

Furthermore, as a pragmatic philosophy hip hop frames the content for investigating the fundamental nature, causes, and principal realities that inform society about the world out of which many persons who are labeled felon exists, particularly black male felons. It articulates in pragmatic ways how democratic practices form discursive spaces wherein and through which persons labeled felon come to make meaning out of life. Furthermore, as a pragmatic philosophy, hip hop becomes a form of cultural criticism in the tradition of Locke, DuBois, West, Bogues, and others within black radical traditions.

Indeed, the understanding of hip hop as a pragmatic philosophy is in keeping with what early twentieth-century pragmatic philosopher John Dewey believes is necessary for the survival of philosophy. In particular, hip hop spotlights an experiential knowledge that translates to the mass of society. Dewey argues that not only is experiential pragmatic philosophy vital for the resurgence of the usefulness of philosophy but he claims that "any account of experience must now fit into the consideration that experiencing means living; and living goes on in and because of an environing medium."[20]

It is precisely because hip hop can translate the experience of living between and among communities that it lends itself to creative exchange. For example, hip hop articulates the crises of felon disenfranchisement in ways that other philosophies do not. According to Dewey, a true "pragmatic philosophy means that philosophy shall develop ideas relevant to the actual crises of life."[21] In other words, for any type of philosophy to really be useful it must consist of ideas that can significantly address crises within communities and can be verifiable in their relevance to those communities.

There are few crises in contemporary American culture that rise to the levels of mass incarceration in United States, particularly for African American communities. So pervasive is incarceration in the African American community, that its impact hits nearly 1 in 10 families in black communities. Mass incarceration embodies and intersects with almost every social dilemma that plagues communities in the US social and political life. Hip hop expresses the crises of mass incarceration and depicts how education, poverty, race, gender, and class all lend to the issues.

Ultimately, hip hop's relationship to incarcerated black men and women uniquely situates the art form in a creative exchange that allows for the actualization of Beloved Community. In other words, hip hop reveals both the ethical principles of Beloved Community as advanced in black religion, as well as those brief but concrete moments of freedom and communal relations that speak to the political and economic dimensions of Beloved Community. Through this actualization of Beloved Community, we can see how to apply Beloved Community more thoroughly.

Indeed, hip hop's ability to translate the experiences of black felons to a mass audience is why Richard Shusterman argues for the use of hip hop as a tool for pragmatism. In *Art in Action, Art Infraction: Goodman, Rap, Pragmatism*, Shusterman contends that "rap philosophers continue the pragmatist tradition not merely in their metaphysics of material, historical flux, but in their noncompartmentalized aesthetics that highlight cognitive function and embodied process in the pursuit of productive practical reform."[22] The experiences of black males in the criminal justice system highlights the most cognitive function and embodied process than any other experience in the hip hop lexicon.

Hip hop not only constructs narratives to address issues of identity and being within a changing world, it also embodies a type of protest against social and political structures in material ways. This protest becomes the representation of the grotesque that makes hip hop useful in creative exchange and for the manifestation of Beloved Community. Certainly, Shusterman is making a similar claim for hip hop that Alain Locke and Du Bois made for black cultural music during the Harlem Renaissance. As Eugene C. Holmes claims in *Alain Locke and the New Negro Movement* regarding Harlem Renaissance artists, hip hop's rap philosophers substantively transform black bodies "as subject and as artist from the old stereotype into the New Negro, militant, no longer obsequious, more of a paragon because he had shown that he was nearly on equal terms with his white counterpart."[23] At that moment of equality, Beloved Community becomes manifest.

In addition, hip hop challenges the class distinctions within intellectual life. It confronts the false notion that certain modes of experience provide a greater landscape for the construction of knowledge. According to Shusterman, "rap's positive infractions have been so obscured by its media-hyped image of monstrous gangsterism that we must recall its history, aesthetic, and progressive purpose in order to regrasp its rich socio-cultural potential and its import for the notion of philosophical life."[24] Even John Dewey recognized that classical philosophy must turn from a system of divided schools of thought to a pragmatic body of lived experiences. Dewey states that "to learn to be human is to develop through the give-and-take of communication."[25, 26] Therefore, if artists have always been the real purveyors of news as Dewey claims, then hip hop artists, particular the artist as felon, must be counted as a conduit for knowledge and experience.

Ultimately, Dewey's experiential philosophy provides a way to look at agency for all persons. This notion extends an invitation to scholar-activists to explore hip hop as pragmatism within their respective disciplines, particularly in the field of sociology, cultural studies, and black radical traditions. This is essential in order to develop a great community that bridges aspiring democratic ideals and rarely experienced democratic practices.

In this light, hip hop helps us to understand the vast wealth of human experiences within society. Its ability to articulate the moral agency of marginal and oppressed groups also highlights the structures wherein these lived experiences take place. Moreover, hip hop helps us define what it means to be human within these structures. Understanding these structures and the lived experiences of those that dwell within them is crucial to the radical and pragmatic work that Du Bois and Locke hoped to shine a light on.

Certainly, Dewey never actualizes how Du Bois's double consciousness impacts his pragmatic philosophy and his notion of the great community. Therefore, in light of both Dewey and Du Bois's work, I appropriate various human dimensions of experience within black radical intellectual tradition to produce a less-talked-about body of knowledge. This rare knowledge production reveals how society comes to thinks about and understand black male felons. For instance, it is apparent that within Dewey's great community he privileges a certain transmittance of experience. This experience is grounded primarily in his experience of whiteness.

Furthermore, the experiential knowledge that Dewey transmits doesn't just affirm who is considered human in that community, it also translates that experience into knowledge that is useful for the broader community. Yet, Dewey finds little need to challenge his own social position. He avoids interrogating his position in society. The inability or unwillingness to do both of these informs his notion of experience and knowledge.

I briefly make note of this here to highlight three particular issues regarding Dewey's conception of the Great Community and why we must take seriously Du Bois's theory of double consciousness. First, Dewey's conception of the great community is articulated and generally perceived through a position of privilege and power. Therefore, a certain type of knowledge through experience is ignored or misinterpreted in Dewey's theory if left unchallenged.

Indeed, Dewey does not fully address in his description of the great community how the social position of certain people within a society influence the way we transmit, develop, and sanction lived experiences as knowledge production. However, hip hop pulls us into a creative exchange with those that tend to ignore their privileged positions in society. This creative exchange highlights conflicts and social inequalities in ways that Dewey's great community does not. Moreover, the experiences of those persons labeled felon in the United States as articulated through the lyrics of hip hop music challenge contemporary scholars in similar ways.

Thus, I find it vital to engage felons in a creative exchange that would allow scholars to see the various ways power and privilege manifest itself both inside and outside of black spaces. Second, the tools that Dewey articulates as vital for transmission are not accessible to all groups. Therefore,

I attempt to illustrate through hip hop music how certain identity groups lack certain resources to transmit its experiences as it relates to other groups.

The use of hip hop as a type of subaltern experience and catalyst for knowledge production help to resolve aspects of Dewey's work. Both Locke and Du Bois recognized that it is impossible to build the type of great community that Dewey desires to advance when certain practices construct ontological notions of a person or group. These ontological categories cause society to reject certain experiences without conscious awareness.

Admittedly, it would be unfair and inaccurate to suggest that Dewey is wholly complicit in the construction of these ontological notions. In fact, he notes that "whatever obstructs and restricts publicity, limits and distorts public opinion and checks and distorts thinking on social affairs hinders the great community."[27] Dewey recognizes that the inability or unwillingness to view certain types of experiences impedes the public's ability to receive new knowledge. However, what Dewey doesn't fully recognize is what Du Bois points out concerning the way hierarchies and systems of oppression impact how experience and knowledge are translated by all persons within a given society.

Du Bois understood more fully how systems of oppression and hierarchy impact the way marginalized and oppressed groups transfer knowledge. Moreover he understood how that knowledge is often received by the larger community. For this reason, Du Bois is not just concerned with the way groups of privilege understand themselves, but also the way marginalized and oppressed groups construct their identity independent of the larger group.

Independent black identity construction is not only hidden but is often inaccurately understood by the larger society. As such, Du Bois concentrates much of his thinking on how African Americans as a marginalized group understand their identity in relation to the larger group, as well as the means whereby they might translate that experience within the structure of society as a whole. The introduction of felons and their use of hip hop helps do the work that Du Bois suggests and fills the gap as it relates to Dewey's theory of the great community.

If hip hop is going to fill this gap, two things will be necessary to move through this notion of Great Society, or what I call Beloved Community. First, it is necessary to look at black male felons as constitutive moral agents. This means understanding the role that black male felons play as subjects, persons, and citizens in society. Second, it is necessary to understand that felons are not monolithic. Thus, it is vital that we examine the diversity and complexity of all felon identity categories, including women, gays, and other ethnic and class groups within the classification of felon.

Hip hop allows us to expand Dewey's notion of the great community, while at the same time challenging the US philosophical model of democracy, particularly its assertions on liberty, justice, and the pursuit of happiness. It also confronts contemporary forms of knowledge that focus the discourse on these issues. As a correlation, the black male felon challenges knowledge held by those within the larger community in general and within black communities in particular.

We also can't deny that the preconceived social image of felons distorts the transmission and interpretation of the felon's experience and ultimately its usefulness as knowledge production. Furthermore, certain experiences through race, gender, and class as a consequence of felon biases dismiss the uniqueness of the felon experience. Therefore, the use of black felons' cultural productions is vital in order to show how even within communities differentiation takes place. This is useful because it challenges certain assumptions that individuals within society hold about certain groups when race, gender, and class may not be the distinguishing dimensions of existence in the world. As Dewey contends, "we must . . . renew our protest against the assumption that the idea [of political democracy] has itself produced the governmental practices which obtain in democratic states: General suffrage, elected representatives, majority rule, and so on."[28] Ultimately, the use of hip hop to articulate the experiences of the felons offer a unique experiential lens—a lens that is often excluded from the discourse on social justice within black radical intellectual traditions.

BRIDGING THE MULTIPLE DIVIDES: RACE, RELIGION, AND HIP HOP

Scholars, hip hop activists, and community leaders, such as Imani Perry, Patricia Hill Collins, Emmett G. Price III, Michael Eric Dyson, Tricia Rose, and others have argued both the value and the problems of hip hop culture and music in revealing the conditions within communities of color.[29] For instance, in *Holler If You Hear Me: Searching for Tupac Shakur*, Michael Eric Dyson depicts how hip hop articulates the crisis of race, poverty, class, and even gender in American democracy. Dyson utilizes the creative work of hip hop artist Tupac Shakur to shine a light on the hidden world of not only African American communities, but the impact poverty, disenfranchisement, and violence within many African American communities has on the way certain groups come to understand themselves and the world around them. Through his relationship with convicted men and women, Shakur prognosticates the systematic exclusion of felons in the African American community.

Through his lyrical content, Tupac expresses how felons lose their ability to exist as full citizens in the United States. Indeed, Shakur outlines the various methods that hide the experience of felons in society. For example, in his song "Keep Ya Head Up," Shakur states that "I'm tryna make a dollar out of fifteen cents/It's hard to be legit and still pay the rent/And in the end its seems I'm headed for the pin/I try to find my friends but they are blowin' in the wind."[30] According to Shakur, the hiddenness of the felon is deeply rooted in the US principal realities of governmental practices. He goes on in "Keep Ya Head Up" to say that "you know it's funny/when it rains it pours/They got money for wars/but can't feed the poor."[31]

The web of incarceration diminishes the experiences of the felon from the larger society in general and the black community in particular. According to Shakur, "We ain't meant to survive, because it a set up." However, Shakur doesn't move to a philosophy of fatalism, but rather engages in a type of pragmatism that sees hope and reality as vital tools for Beloved Community. For this reason he tells those that are trapped within this structure of oppression that "even though you are fed up/you gotta keep your head up."

Ultimately, Shakur's work is not pragmatic merely because it embodies the world of many urban city black youth, but because it desires to understand why such a world exists in the first place. Through Shakur's lyrics we hear an embodied philosophy by men and women in a world that is hidden in plain sight. Tupac's lyrics become an example of pragmatism because, as Locke states, "it rejects equally trying to reduce value distinctions to the flat continuum of a pleasure-pain economy or to a pragmatic instrumentalism of ends-means relations."[32] For instance, in one verse of "Keep Ya Head Up" listeners hear Tupac praise his mother, claiming that "she nearly gave her life/to raise [him] right," and in another verse hear him say that he "blames [his] mother for turning [his] brother into a crack baby." Yet again, Tupac illustrates how the grotesque in creative exchange is not without conflict. Rather, it highlights conflict in order to address actual structures that impede Beloved Community.

Furthermore, Shakur's song "Life Goes On" speaks to the web of mass incarceration that Alexander speaks about in her book *The New Jim Crow*. In "Life Goes On" he recalls the life of a friend who has been killed. In the commemorative rap narrative, Shakur ask the question "how many brothers fell victim to the streets." For Shakur, life in many poor black neighborhoods is a trap that not only seeks to incarcerate African American men in particular, but ultimately kills both them and the spirit of their communities. He raps about the impact incarceration has on the spirit of the community in the chorus of "Life Goes On," when he states that it would "be a lie, if I told ya that I never thought of death." He invites the listener to reimagine issues of violence against black male bodies and to contemplate the psychological impact it has on them.

Tupac also highlights structures in society that delegitimize the experiences of black bodies in life and death. As Shusterman argues, rap, more than any other genre, "forcefully demonstrates art's important political dimensions, socio-ethical states, and practical consequences."[33] Tupac shows how rap engages in a form of creative exchange that makes Beloved Community possible even while highlighting the real despair and structural racism within carceral spaces.

Many other hip hop artists such as Lyfe Jennings adopt the social underpinnings of Tupac's narrative rap style. However, unlike many other hip hop artists, Lyfe Jennings's music is less harsh in sound and tone. Thus, it represents a segment of the hip hop community that is often ignored because of the expanded marketing of neo-soul, a contemporary pop genre that blends elements of hip hop, jazz, urban rhythmic patterns, and R&B.

Jennings's work is strongly influenced by hip hop music and culture. Throughout his entire musical repertoire, Jennings encompasses the style, lyrical expression, and musical improvisation of hip hop artists such as Force MDs, Whodini, and Tupac Shakur. In fact, Jennings appropriates the musical composition of Shakur's rap single "Can You Get Away" for his single "Must Be Nice." Even on his sophomore album, Jennings gives tribute to the legacy of Shakur. On the CD entitled *The Phoenix*, Jennings sings Shakur's rap song "Lift Ya Head Up." Similar to Shakur, Jennings utilizes hip hop to offer a depiction of life for many inner city youths. More specifically, Jennings thoughtfully narrates a set of events and activities that produce the felon as a new category in black urban life. Lastly, similar to Shakur, Jennings extends an existential hope for those currently trapped in penal captivity.

In addition to revealing the hidden experience of the felon, hip hop artist such as Shakur and Jennings explore the tension between democracy as a philosophical ideal and democracy as a pragmatic exercise. Indeed, through much of their lyrical content, these artists illustrate how the fundamental nature of American society is at best a social and political contradiction. *In The Hip Hop Wars: What We Talk About When We Talk About Hip Hop—And Why It Matters*, Tricia Rose contends that "debates about hip hop have become a means for defining poor, young black people and thus for interpreting the context and reason for their clearly disadvantaged lives."[34] In other words, social and political preconceptions about certain bodies structure the debate around hip hop in ways that diminish the desire to meaningfully explore the various identities that constitute black urban experience as seen in the complex representations of Shakur and Jennings. Ultimately, these preexisting ideas about the communities wherein these bodies exist become the basis for much of the analysis about the people and their conditions. As a result, the complex meanings within hip hop are overwhelmingly interpreted through the narrow construction of race, gender, and poverty and ignores how hip hop signals to the systemic arrangements that lend to the construction of new identity categories within those communities.

Moreover, the narrow conceptions regarding the complex meanings embedded within hip hop can be linked to its relationship with large, mainstream corporations. Indeed, the interconnection of hip hop with corporate entities has caused much of hip hop to transform from a cultural expression that narrates black life and experiences into a cultural product that is marketed to largely white teenage consumers. This change lends to some of the problems and critiques levied against the art form, particularly the production and marketing of hip hop. In this way, black experience in general and black felon experience in particular become again trapped within mediated spaces. Even in the twentieth-first century, hip hop is cast into carceral spaces, which make it easy to overlook its full political value.

Indeed, since the 1980s the mass distribution of hip hop has been controlled by Wall Street corporations. In addition, global corporations such as Disney and McDonald's have appropriated hip hop to market and sell everything from clothes to fast food to movies. Many of these corporations have sought to capitalize on black cultural products. In their attempt to gain advantage in the marketplace, numerous corporations have helped to advance fetishized ideas about black urban life for largely white, suburban, teenage hip hop consumers. In *Prophets of the Hood: Politics and Poetics in Hip Hop*, Imani Perry states that "the commodification and commercialization of hip hop has forever altered the art form, at times challenging its integrity."[35]

It also can't be overlooked how the global commodification of hip hop and its natural hybridity creates a debate around ownership and originality. This is not unique to black cultural production. Many black artists such as B. B. King, Muddy Waters, and others have been victims of creative plundering by white artists and racist music executives. Even the experience of "ghetto" life has been popularized and sanitized for a broader consumer group. In spite of this, many scholars have failed to sufficiently mine how the category of felon influences hip hop as a black cultural and intellectual product. Indeed amid the debates, hip hop culture and urban music has arguably been the chief form and method that black felons have used to translate both experience and theory.

Moreover, scholars within black radical intellectual traditions have failed to interrogate how the felon as an identity category expresses ideas, beliefs, political, social, and religious meanings and values through hip hop. This is because the transmission of political, social, religious, and cultural theory within hip hop music and culture as presented through the lens of black felons has not been deemed valuable. According to Rose, "the hyperbolic and polarized public conversation about hip hop that has emerged over the past decade discourages progressive and nuanced consumption, participation, and critique, thereby contributing to the very crisis that is facing hip hop."[36] As a consequence of this, many scholars within black radical intellectual traditions also fail to articulate the roles that felons play as fathers, mothers, prophets, preachers, and educators.

The failure to articulate the full range of felons' humanity is most evident in the hyperbolic analysis of hip hop. Often, the analysis on hip hop not only limits the space wherein felons as artists are allowed to occupy, but it also limits the social, political, and religious conversations that the music articulates. This polarization within the public conversation allows black radical scholars to overlook multiple identities of the felon and the ways the black felon, in particular, utilizes hip hop to advance social, political, and religious meanings.

In addition, the erasure of black felons through hip hop's commodification has enhanced the tenuous relationship between hip hop culture and urban music to black religion. In other words, the commodification of hip hop music and culture lends to the divide between black religious life and the complete work within black radical intellectual traditions. The absence of the black felon has shielded many scholars that study black religion from examining the theological and religious significance that black felons offer to black intellectual religious life, particularly through the medium of hip hop.

This current marketing and promotion of hip hop only exacerbates the divide between the sacred and the secular. This isn't to say that hip hop created the divide. In truth, the divide between the sacred and the secular is a long-standing debate. According to Perry, "the division between the sacred and the secular transitioned into one between that presented as the face of respectability, often marketed to the mainstream, and that which was music for dark, smoky nightclubs."[37] However, hip hop culture and urban music provide witness to black experience in many of the same ways as Negro spirituals and thus requires equal examination by black religious scholars. Black Christian rapper Lecrae is a great example.

Furthermore, ignoring these dimensions within hip hop culture has implications on the whole of black intellectual life. For instance, in *The Black Church and Hip Hop Culture: Toward Bridging the Generational Divide*, Emmett G. Price III contends that "no previous generational divide has been as extreme, volatile, and destructive as the present divide between the Civil Rights Generation and the Hip Hop Generation."[38] For Price, the Civil Rights Generation, unlike the Hip Hop Generation, has largely constructed its cultural ethic through black religious ideology and meanings. According to Perry, "this division in part served as a civil rights strategy; it was necessary to have a clearly demarcated space of respectability that could provide an unmarred example of the denial perfect citizens experienced in a racist society."[39]

However, the overlooking of felons as a strategy to uphold black respectability politics has real consequences that can be felt across the whole of black life. Specifically, when black felons are overlooked in hip hop it mutes any expression or articulation of their subjectivity, personhood, and citizenship within society. As Howard Thurman argues concerning Negro spirituals, hip hop culture and urban music is also a "source of rich testimony concerning life and death, because they are the voice, sometimes strident, sometimes muted and weary, of a people for whom the cup of suffering overflowed in haunting overtones of majesty, beauty and power."[40]

This also reveals why voices in hip hop music have been critical and suspicious of black intellectual religious products, particularly the black church, and vice versa. However, this suspicion and critique doesn't mean that we should do away with black religion and black religious cultural products. Indeed tenets within Black liberation theology and black religious discourse are commonly expressed in hip hop culture. Ideas about liberation from oppression, the call for unity within black communities, the affirmation of blackness over and against white patriarchy, and the articulation of a god of the oppressed are concepts that are widely shared and can be found at the intersections of hip hop, black religion, and black liberation theology.

Instead, what hip hop calls to attention is the growing de-radicalization of black liberation theology and black religious discourse. This gap between the black sacred and secular spaces is only widened with hip hop's increasing commodification. Also, the constriction of hip hop culture and urban music only widened the divide between these black intellectual and black cultural products. Therefore, Shakur and twice-convicted felon and hip hop and R&B artist Lyfe Jennings and their music not only bridges the conversation between black religion and black theology to hip hop music and culture, but their music also illustrates how the black male felon emerges as a hermeneutical lens within black radical intellectual traditions.

Certainly, one of the themes that is consistent throughout Jennings's music is the role and significance of black religion in shaping the life experience of black felons. Yet for Jennings, black religion aids in the marginalizing effects of black felons through oppressive religious language, imagery, and ideology. In highlighting this, Jennings's music challenges the intellectual and pragmatic discourse of black religion as a liberating notion. In several of his songs, Jennings takes issue with the status of black religion as an authentic and requisite mode of human experience and expression for all black people within the black community. He disavows the notion that black religion in its current state stands fully on the side of all those oppressed. In doing this, Jennings constructs an alternative mode for thinking about the role of black religion as a liberative ideology. Thus, as a hermeneutical lens, Lyfe Jennings signals to another stream of black radical intellectual production that expands Bogues's discourse regarding the prophet and the heretic, namely the felon.

NOTES

1. The news article with the *Texas Tribune* can be found at http://www.texastribune.org/2015/04/15/john-legend-tt-interview/.

2. Anthony Bogues, *Black Heretics Black Prophets: Radical Political Intellectuals*, (New York: Routledge, 2003), 188.

3. Dylan Rodriquez, *Forced Passages: Imprisoned Radical Intellectuals and the U.S. Prison Regime* (Minneapolis: University of Minneapolis Press, 2006), 36.

4. W. E. B. Du Bois, *The Souls of Black Folk* (New York: Barnes and Noble Classics, 2003), 178.

5. W. E. B. Du Bois, *The Souls of Black Folk*, 178.

6. W. E. B. Du Bois, *The Souls of Black Folk*, 9.

7. Eugene C. Holmes, "Alain Locke and the New Negro Movement," in *Negro American Literature Forum* 2, no. 3 (Autumn 1968): 60.

8. Eugene C. Holmes, "Alain Locke and the New Negro Movement," 60.

9. Eugene C. Holmes, "Alain Locke and the New Negro Movement," 60.

10. Mary Ann Calo, "Alain Locke and American Art Criticism," in *American Art* 18, no. 1 (Spring 2004): 91.

11. Mary Ann Calo, "Alain Locke and American Art Criticism," 90.

12. Mary Ann Calo, "Alain Locke and American Art Criticism," 90.

13. Eugene C. Holmes, "Alain Locke and the New Negro Movement," 60.

14. Mary Ann Calo, "Alain Locke and American Art Criticism," 93–94.

15. Alain Locke, "Value and Imperatives," in *The Philosophy of Alain Locke: Harlem Renaissance and Beyond*, ed. Leonard Harris (Philadelphia: Temple University Press, 1991), 35.

16. Alain Locke, "Value and Imperatives," 53.

17. Anthony Bogues, *Black Heretics Black Prophets*, 193.

18. Samuel A. Floyd, Jr., *The Power of Black Music* (Oxford: Oxford University Press, 1995), 8.

19. John Dewey, "The Search for the Great Community," in *The Later Works, 1925–1953*, vol. 2 (1984), 325.

20. John Dewey, "Historical Roots and Reflections," in *The Philosophy of John Dewey*, (Chicago: The University of Chicago Press, 1973), 61.

21. John Dewey, *The Middle Works of John Dewey, 1899–1924 Volume 10: 1917–1917: Journal Articles, Essays, and Miscellany Published in the 1916–1917 Period*, ed. Jo Ann Boydston (Cabondale: Southern Illinois University Press, 1980), 43.

22. Richard Shusterman, "Art in Action, Art Infraction: Goodman, Rap, Pragmatism," in *Practicing Philosophy: Pragmatism and the Philosophical Life* (New York: Routledge, 1997), 145.

23. Eugene C. Holmes, "Alain Locke and the New Negro Movement," 66.

24. Richard Shusterman, "Art in Action, Art Infraction: Goodman, Rap, Pragmatism," 136.

25. John Dewey, "The Search for the Great Community," 332.

26. Although I agree with Dewey that human experience brings with it a vast wealth of knowledge, I contend that Dewey does not take into account the social

construction of what it means to be human within a society. He does not explore in great depth how certain experiences are disregarded. Thus, his argument that experiences may be "socially transmitted, developed and sanctioned" runs the risk of being narrowly conceived (Dewey, 334).

27. John Dewey, "The Search for the Great Community," 339.

28. John Dewey, "The Search for the Great Community," 326.

29. For additional information regarding the debates on hip hop music and culture, read Imani Perry, *Prophets of the Hood: Politics and Poetics in Hip Hop* (Durham, NC: Duke University Press, 2004); *The Black Church and Hip Hop Culture: Toward Bridging the Generational Divide*, ed. Emmett G. Price III (Lanham, MD: Scarecrow Press, 2012); Patricia Hill Collins, *Black Sexual Politics: African Americans, Gender, and the New Racism* (New York: Routledge, 2005); Michael Eric Dyson, *Holler If You Hear Me: Searching for Tupac Shakur* (New York: Basic Civitas Books, 2001).

30. Tupac Shakur, *Keep Your Head Up*, SONG LYRICS (lines 43–46)

31. Tupac Shakur, *Keep Your Head Up*, SONG LYRICS (lines 51–52).

32. Alain Locke, "Values and Imperatives," 47.

33. Richard Shusterman, "Art in Action, Art Infraction: Goodman, Rap, Pragmatism," 142.

34. Tricia Rose, *In The Hip Hop Wars: What We Talk About When We Talk About Hip Hop—And Why It Matters* (New York: Basic Books, 2008), 5.

35. Imani Perry, *Prophets of the Hood: Politics and Poetics in Hip Hop* (Durham, NC: Duke University Press, 2004), 3.

36. Tricia Rose, *The Hip Hop Wars*, 5.

37. Imani Perry, *Prophets of the Hood*, 5.

38. Emmett G. Price III (ed.), *The Black Church and Hip Hop Culture: Toward Bridging the Generational Divide* (Lanham, MD: The Scarecrow Press, 2012), xiv.

39. Imani Perry, *Prophets of the Hood: Politics and Poetics in Hip Hop*, 5.

40. Howard Thurman, *A Strange Fruit: The Best of Howard Thurman on Religious Experience and Public Life*, ed. Walter Earl Fluker and Catherine Tumber (Boston: Beacon Press, 1998), 56.

Chapter 6

Expanding Beloved Community

Black Churches, Black Felons, and Mass Incarceration

In *26 Years 17 Days, Stick Up Kid, and Made Up Mind*, Lyfe Jennings highlights how the intersectionality of black churches, the criminal justice system, and the prison industrial complex limits the lived experiences of black male felons by confining them to narrow social spaces. In particular, he finds that the intersection of these institutions situates black males within a space that limits their access to black communal life. Ultimately, these narrow spaces can be located through the identity categories that Jennings assigns to black male figures in his music.

Throughout the CD, he accentuates only three black male identity categories: the thug, the felon, and the preacher. All three of these identity categories impose limitations on black male agency. For example, in highlighting the black preacher, Jennings shows how the representation of black males as moral agents in his symbolic world order is trapped to the imaginary space of black religious consciousness. In other words, the perception of black males as moral beings in Jennings's social world is framed largely through Christian language and imagery. In this light, Jennings shows how, often, the religious consciousness and social sensibilities within black communities mythologizes black male preachers to the extent that black masculinity becomes constrained to narrow black religious heroic stereotypes.

Indeed, the narrow religious image of the black male preacher in Jennings's world has far-reaching implications on the notion of Beloved Community. First, as it relates to Beloved Community, it implies that black communities are conditioned to perceive the moral representation for black masculinity as largely the domain of black religion. In doing this, the idea of Beloved Community is restricted to a set of moral and ethical ideas that is advanced through patriarchal religious iconography. For this reason, men such as Howard Thurman, Martin Luther King Jr., Jesse Jackson, TD Jakes, and other black male preachers arise in prominence because of the ways black religion lays claim to black cultural imagination. Even figures such as Elijah Muhammad, Malcolm X, and Louis Farrakhan function under the banner of black male religious iconography.

Consequently, representations of black masculinity that do not conform to the black preacher image are recognized as a subaltern part of black community life. Therefore, black male felons such as Huey P. Newton, Mumia Abu Jamal, and Monster Kody are situated to the margins of black communal life because they do not speak under the covering of black religion. The narrow perception of black male religious figures over black political imprisoned radicals explains in large part why Beloved Community lacks a structural and systemic form of economic and political engagement that benefits black male felons.

In addition, the moral personification of black masculinity embodied in black male preachers is significant because it suggests that the other identity categories available to black males in Jennings's world, namely the thug and the felon, lack significant moral agency. As a result, enmity develops between black male preachers and black male thugs and felons. This enmity can be heard in Jennings's song *Stick Up Kid*, wherein he states:

> See lately I've been thinking bout saving my soul/And do prayers make it to Heaven from the ghetto/I asked all my friends but they all say they don't know/ It's all bad ya'll/And the preacher talking bout some stuff he don't know/When church done became a fuckin' fashion show/And they won't let a nigga in with these timbos/It's all bad ya'll.[1]

In the verse, listeners can hear the distinct ways that Jennings expresses his entrapment. First, his lyrics highlight the distinct ways that poor black people are marginalized through a type of cultural and religious hegemonic structure. As a result, Jennings and his friends are left without answers to their social condition. For Jennings, the church as an institution does not allow certain people full access and membership. This is also clear in his statement about not being allowed in because of his "timbos," referencing the shoes stereotypically ascribed to thugs and felons.

Second, he suggests that the black male preacher advances a particular language within the church that reifies isolationist tendencies. In this way, the language of the church not only contradicts the historical mission of the black church, but also misdirects the church's strategic work by casting blacks into class categories. For Jennings, the language constructed by black preachers entraps poor black felons to an additional carceral space inside the ghetto. Therefore, he offers a critique of the black church, particularly as it relates to poor black males.

In offering a critique of the black church, Jennings lifts poor black people from carceral spaces and re-situates them in the center of black religious discourse. This transitioning of poor black people highlights the inconsistencies between the language of black church and the language of Beloved Community. Furthermore, by lifting poor black people out this carceral space and re-situating them into Beloved Community, Jennings also reveals how the black political and social class structure within black churches has appropriated certain larger social stereotypes and social barriers.

Jennings argues that black male preachers and black churches impede the personal and social progression of black male felons by casting felons as irredeemable social agents with little to no moral core. For Jennings, much of that impediment occurs because the church allows black heroic religious iconography to go forward without challenge. Therefore, he deconstructs the fantasy images of black male preacher within black religious consciousness in order to show the value of black male felons within black sacred spaces. Indeed, Jennings's resistance forces his listeners to reengage how they think about black male identity in this social world order and to reassess the black church's practice of Beloved Community.

The reassessment of black churches and black male identity is the central focus of Jennings's creative exchange. This exchange is evidenced in both *26 Years and 17 Days* and *Made Up Mind*. Within the songs, Jennings shows how the division between the black thug and felon subvert the use of black heroic imagery as the basis of black religious consciousness.

Lastly, Jennings's animosity toward black male preachers not only causes distance and conflict to arise between Jennings and the black church, but also it dislocates Jennings from the God of that community. This dislocation is heightened within this social world because the black male preacher is perceived as the embodied representation of God. In this sense, Jennings's dislocation from community, church, and God illustrates a tripartite excommunication.

The beginning of this excommunication is first heard clearly in his song *26 Years 17 Days*. Jennings states "I was looking for God at my grandmother's house/underneath the cushions on the couch/I looked all around side to side up and down/that man was nowhere to be found."[2] At the very beginning of the song, listeners can hear how Jennings's inability to connect with God causes him personal turmoil.

THE DISLOCATED FELON

Indeed, Jennings's tone of voice and his lyrics reveal his desperation and urgency to find meaning in his life in a world with no meaning. This trauma may come from a feeling of loss with community, family, and self-identity. Furthermore, it is worth noting that Jennings searches for a God that is not only patriarchal and anthropomorphic in its operation and its representation, but also absent and distant from the black male felon. For this reason, it should not be overlooked that the absence of this patriarchal father God mirrors the dislocation of an earthly father in Jennings's social world.

The dislocation of the black male felon within the black church is significant because it calls into question the work of the black church in addressing structural and systemic barriers. For instance, Jennings illustrates how the dislocation of black male felons from the communal life of black people functions in similar ways to the prison industrial complex. In *26 Years 17 Days*, he continuously repeats that "It's done been 26 years 17 days/been to five different prisons got two babies on the way/and they say it'll be a waste of time to pray/seeing that I'm going to hell anyway."[3] In the refrain, Jennings suggests that the black church, similar to the prison, imposes restrictive social barriers on black male felons. Ultimately, he links the carceral effect of incarceration to black religious institutions.

Furthermore, the idea that Jennings has been to five different prisons highlights the ways incarcerated bodies move through the prison industrial complex with little notice or outcry. This movement of incarcerated bodies not only dislocates incarcerated people from families and communities, but also places undue financial burdens on poor people. Therefore, by speaking to the five different prisons he has been assigned and his children that are on the way, Jennings signals to how the dislocation of black male felons from the black church speaks to the political and social ineffectiveness of black religious institutions to address the social position of black male felons in society.

Additionally, Jennings makes the subtle claim that black religious institutions have appropriated certain political ideologies and maintained certain religious practices within black sacred spaces that work to oppress black male felons. He highlights the various ways these two institutions operate in synergy with each other. In addition, by linking prison and black churches in this way Jennings points to the intersectionality of black religious and juridical discursive practices.

Through Jennings's work, we can see how both of these institutions develop language that helps to marginalize black male felons. For example, in the song, Jennings illustrates how the theological notion of sin correlates to the juridical notions of guilt. This correlation impacts black male felons' lived experiences in very acute ways. In other words, the theological notion of sin and the juridical notion of guilt become interlocking terms that work to exclude black male felons in sacred and secular spaces. Therefore, by highlighting the intersectionality of religious and juridical language, Jennings is able to point to unique ways carceral spaces exclude black male felons from both religious and political life in ways different from other black people.

Moreover, it is apparent from Jennings's lyrical conversation with his grandmother that he desires to have an encounter with God. It is important to note that Jennings knows about the God of his grandmother. However, through his lyrics he reveals how that form of knowing separates the black felon in the community. For instance, when Jennings is unable to find God he says:

> So I called my grandmamma on the phone/said old lady you best get home/ cause God ain't where you said he would be/and there's something that I really need to speak to him about immediately."[4] [5]

Indeed, the lyrics show the extent Jennings goes to find meaning in his life. The metaphorical use of his grandmother's house represents both the black church, and the community in which he grew up as a child. However, he finds as a black male felon that neither of these spaces as they exist now offers him any access to God.

In addition, Jennings's conversation with his grandmother highlights a generational divide in the black community. When Jennings highlights this divide he draws a dichotomy between his grandmother's generation and the younger generation. Indeed, for Jennings to repeatedly express his age in the song "26 Years 17 Days" along with the number of times he has been to prison speaks to this younger generation's experience with God, church and incarceration. Consequently, the conversation with his grandmother invokes a set of ideas that indirectly indicts the church. For example, the belief that the black church has a set of practices that speaks to older black people, but does not translate to this generation of black youth.

This generational divide shows how the influence of the church in the lives of black people has changed. For Jennings, this divide shows a schism in the black community. It also indicts the black church for not having a concerted effort or strategic plan to address the issues faced by the black male felon. Therefore, when Jennings says to his grandmother that "God isn't where you said he would be" he highlights the role of the church in the life of young black people—in particular, black men. Jennings brings to the fore the need for a generational dialogue—a creative exchange that expands the role and importance of the black church in the twenty-first century.

Ultimately, Jennings illustrates how the isolation of black male felons within black churches and black communities restricts our understanding and practice of Beloved Community. Indeed, these structures and regulative tendencies bind creative exchange to a limited black population. Moreover, he highlights how a fuller notion of Beloved Community is stifled when the black male preacher is authorized to stand as the gatekeeper for both black sacred and secular spaces. This authoritarian role denies the democratic notions of Beloved Community.

Furthermore, this social and religious practice leaves black male felons vulnerable to racist attacks by institutions such as police departments and criminal courts. Consequently, this violence happens in large part because the black church has failed to shield black male felons from the ongoing assault of white racism and patriarchy in the same way that it has for other categories of blackness. However, it should be noted that it is not just that the black church leaves black male felons susceptible to violent assault outside of black sacred spaces, but also the ways the black church as an institution does violence to black male felons within black sacred spaces. For example, since black male felons are perceived as not worthy of communion with God, then the black male preacher becomes the sole arbiter to black communal life. This suggests that the imagined role of the black male preacher impacts our notion of Beloved Community along categories of both gender and incarceration.

Ultimately, Jennings's conversation with his grandmother, his disdain for black male preachers, and his inability to locate God in his social world order diminishes his faith in the black church as a liberative institution. This intense disregard for the black church leads him to excoriate black religious institutions in the lives of black people in general and black felons in particular. For instance in *26 Years and 17 Days* Jennings states that "I done smoked weed with the best of ya'll/shot at all the rest of ya'll/my heart hurts like an old man with high cholesterol/the preacher said I'm the dirtiest dude he ever saw/shouldn't even be livin/and he a Christian."[6] In particular he condemns the church for situating black felons to a restrictive space that leaves them vulnerable to racial assault.

Jennings's critiques of the black church also shows the various ways the black church erases the vulnerability of black male felons from the experiences of black communal life. This erasure happens because, as Jennings says, "the preacher" has said that he is "the dirtiest dude he ever saw" and that he "shouldn't even be livin'." In this light, Jennings uncovers the way the black church functions as merely another type of institutional overseer for black regulatory behavior. Therefore, he begins the process of deconstructing black heroic religious iconography and black religious practices as a means of re-situating certain young black males within black communal life and struggle.

Jennings's dissatisfaction with the social position of black male felons manifest every time he is faced with having to acknowledge his existence in the world. This social world limits the black male felon's ability to function as a constitutive moral agent. Therefore, part of the way that Jennings re-situates black males, particularly black male felons within black communal life and struggle is by highlighting the intersection between penal institutions and black religious discourse.

Jennings shows how the intersection of penal institutions and black religious discourse posits the black male felon to exist at the margins of black communities. In doing this, he is also able to show how black religious consciousness allows the role of black male preachers to go forth with little reflexive thinking. This practice inevitably creates one space for black male preachers and an alternate space for black thugs and felons.

Furthermore, the interplay between the political and the religious situates black religious institutions in unique ways. For instance, the black church is allowed to determine who can and should publicly represent the black community in both political and religious spaces. This explains why black churches are largely viewed as the epicenter for political candidates and elected officials. It is hard to deny the influence that black churches hold on black people's view of elected officials and the policies that black communities support. For this reason, the black church is able to take black figures, particularly black male preachers, and posit them in positions of power within institutional structure to ensure a black communal form of justice.

However, as Jennings illustrates, that justice actually helps to maintain the same institutional arrangement that caused the hyper incarceration of black bodies in the first place. Indeed, often times these elected officials and public policies helped to do violence to black male felons. Thus, for Jennings, the black church becomes an agent of the criminal justice system that operates to maintain a type of control over black male felons. In this light, the black church helps construct a form of justice that has dehumanizing effects on black male felons.

Moreover, he is able to point out how these restrictive and oppressive spaces condition society's perception of black male felons as subversives of both sacred and secular institutions. Yet, by re-situating black male felons, Jennings is able to show how the subversive actions of many black male felons occurs as a response to racialized social and political attacks on black male bodies by black churches and the US criminal justice system. For example, in *26 Years 17 Days* he states "shoulda been dead like 17 times for 17 crimes I committed/took 'em all to trial and got acquitted/ Left wavin' my middle finger in the air whispered in the prosecutor's ear, yeah I did it."[7] Jennings's lyrics express both the constant threat of death that he faces and his defiance against it. In the end, he shows how his life as a black male felon becomes the opposition to discriminatory institutional practices, particularly as it relates to the US judicial and criminal justice system.

This adversarial relationship reveals something far more profound than just Jennings's deviance. For instance, Jennings recycling in and out of criminal courts shows how the criminal justice system fails to serve as a deterrent to criminal behavior. This means that "get tough on crime" legislation and bills have little impact on crime statistics. Second, it reveals how contention develops between certain communities and law enforcement agencies and the ways that contention mirrors the enmity between black male felons and black churches. His music spotlights the relationship between black religious institutions and political institutions.

Ultimately, Jennings illustrates the need to institute an alternative form of engagement. We see this alternative form of engagement in his song *Made Up Mind*. Jennings decides to take on these issues by confronting the black church and its impact on black male felons. The introduction of the song is in fact a dedication "to all [those] good church going people, talking about folks and don't be livin' right [themselves]."[8] Listeners hear Jennings's frustration with the black church and the ways it marginalizes black felons. In particular, he confronts the acute ways the black church denies black male felons access into black Christian faith communities and its tendency to construct black religious figures that ultimately presents the black male felon as void of moral agency.

It is also interesting to point out that before engaging the church, Jennings enters into a conversation with God. This private conversation comes after his final imprisonment. He talks to God about the exclusionary practices that he has experienced from the black church. In a breathless but raspy tone Jennings says:

> Lord they really think they fooling you by coming to church on Sunday/praying and laying hands on folks stomping and jumping around faking the Holy Ghost/ but it's a thin line between walking it and talking it/living it and giving it or just pretending it's alright.[9]

Using words such as "fake" and "pretending," Jennings challenges the work of the black church. Through his conversation with God, the listener gets a chance to understand Jennings's motivations and concerns as it relates to the black church and black church people.

Jennings continues to detail in the song his reasons for disrupting the current discursive practices in the black church. He says:

> so I've made up my mind I'm a go to church on Sunday/and sing a song that may hurt somebody's feelings so that maybe/thy will, will be done/on earth as it is in heaven/and hopefully they will see/how much they really be discouraging a little old sinner like me.[10]

Jennings's discontent with the black church and black male preachers leads him to disrupt black religious spaces for the sake of repositioning black male felons within black community life. He wants the church to recognize that the communities wherein black male felons are situated is not welcoming or liberating.

Made Up Mind initiates a new conversation into the discourse on black religion. Part of that includes constructing a narrative within black religion that provides a sense of belonging, redemption, and hope for the felon. Jennings continues throughout the song to show how the condition and objectification of the felon is sustained through black religious discursive practices. He illustrates why incarcerated people and those related to incarcerated people feel discouraged and ostracized from the black church. Thus, in creating a new language within black church discourse allows for a reimagining of felons within history, religious traditions, and biblical hermeneutics. This explains why, at the end of the song, Jennings inserts the popular refrain of soul artist Pattie La Belle's rendition of "Someone Loves You Baby."

A CREATIVE EXCHANGE: THEOLOGY AND HIP HOP

Consequently, ignoring the conditions of the felon illustrates the black church's inability to impact real change in the communities where they exist. It is important to point out that Jennings doesn't reject the significance of the church and its role in defining the value of black lives. Rather, he contends that the church's present condition and practices hinders its ability to extend its radical work to the black felon. For instance, in the song, he speaks to God and asks "and did they really think that they could pull the wool over your eyes lord/did they really think that by faking they were saved that they would get this same reward."[11] Although Jennings's question is rhetorical, it does direct the listeners' attention toward the performance of black church and how that performance motivates or detracts any substantial work toward black incarceration. This critique also explains why, in *Made Up Mind*, Jennings repeatedly declares that:

> this be the realest thing I ever wrote for sure/after this a lot of folks won't like me no mo'/but after this I gotta go answer to you Lord/so I've made up my mind I'm a go to church on Sunday/and sing a song that may hurt somebody's feelings so that maybe/thou will, will be done/on earth as it is in heaven/and hopefully they will see/how much they really be discouraging a little old sinner like me."[12]

Through his lyrics, Jennings illustrates how a creative exchange with the grotesque establishes a concrete instance of Beloved Community. Indeed, Jennings's creative exchange places the black male felon directly in confrontation with the injustices in both black secular and sacred spaces.

By challenging the liberative work of black churches, Jennings offers a critique of black religion that is useful for scholars of black religion and black liberation theology. Black liberation theology is charged to not only continue the discourse about white racism on the black experience for the construction of Beloved Community, but Jennings incites it to engage a new discourse about the marginalization of black felons within black communities.

Jennings is not merely wanting to know "what Jesus Christ means when blacks are confronted with the brutality of white racism" as Cones suggest, but he wants to know how to speak of God in light of his experience as a black male felon.[13] In particular, his creative exchange constructs a new type of dialogue concerning the link between black liberation theology and social justice. In this way, Jennings expands the function of black liberation theology to include the black male felon.

For Jennings, the church's religious practices are ineffectual because they are so disconnected from the lived experiences of black male felons. Jennings's CD suggests the need to construct a black theology that "arises not only from the need of blacks to liberate themselves from white oppressors," but also from the need of black felons to liberate themselves from black oppressors. Ultimately, Jennings's creative exchange invites a conversation that expands Cones notion of black theology by illustrating the ways black churches work to maintain traditionally white racist practices.

Jennings's lyrics also challenge James Cone and other black liberation theologians assertions of Black experience as the source in black theology. If "black theology is a theology of liberation because it is a theology which arises from an identification with the oppressed blacks of America," then to exclude black felons from that identified group means that black theology must investigate more fully the experiences of all blacks.[14] This means, for instance, that the meaning of revelation within black theology that Cone presents has to begin to "define revelation in such a manner that the definition will, on the one hand, retain the essence of the biblical emphasis and, on the other, be relevant to the situation of oppressed blacks" and felons.[15]

The unique experiences of black male felons must be seen as a vital source for black liberation theology. Indeed, if Cone is correct that "there can be no black theology which does not take seriously the black experience—a life of humiliation and suffering," then it is vital that the experiences of black male felons must become a part of that source material.[16] Otherwise, the marginalization of the black male felon within black liberation theology and black religion places the domain in contradiction with itself.

Moreover, the displacement of the black male felon's experience from black religion is why Jennings believes that the black church has abandoned its mission. This accusation hits at the core idea of the black church within black liberation theology, particularly that the black church has been a liberating space for all black oppression. Although Jennings is not the first person to allege these types of charges against the black church, he is one of the few black male felons to use hip hop music to do so.

Just as Cone argues that "we cannot lose sight of the contemporary situation and what this situation means to the oppressed in the land" in the 1960s and 1970s, we have to expand that to the black felon in the current age. We have to ensure that we are examining all areas of black oppression, including poor, unwanted, female, and felon. Only in doing this can black liberation theology continue to claim that "revelation is God's self-disclosure to humankind in the context of liberation."[17] We are forced to accept the new reality that the black church is no longer a black liberative space without the black felon. Through Jennings's work we can see how the absence of the black felon within the contemporary black church fails to give a sense of hope to the black male felon in the same way it had traditionally given hope to other identities and earlier generations within blackness. Through hip hop, he entreats the church to initiate a new set of practices. His creative exchanges make Beloved Community open to more categories and experiences of blackness.

Certainly the means and mode through which Jennings makes his claims on the black church is made even more powerful because he speaks as a black male felon. The intersection of blackness, masculinity, and felon provides a new terrain for understanding and articulating the black experience in the United States. This new terrain becomes a source for black liberation theology, particularly in its ability to illustrate the value of black male felons. For without the black male felon, the discourse within black religion only serves to perpetuate negative ideas about black criminality within black communities.

Thus Jennings's challenge to black religious scholars and black liberation theologians to become more critical of black religious experiences for black religion deepens the meaningfulness of the work. This deeper, more rich study emerges largely because Jennings calls for black radical scholars to investigate alternative spaces outside of the black church that might also illustrate others forms of black oppression. His music opens opportunity for black liberation theology and black religious studies to examine the interplay between the US criminal justice system and black religious discourse, thus once again making black religion and black religious study a political exercise.

It is by doing this type of work that black liberation theology is able to develop new notions of identity that address citizenship and personhood. Thus, Jennings's creative exchange with hip hop music and theology shows why it is vital that black theology create an exploration of criminal behavior. This exploration begins to construct a new discourse on redemption and restoration within black sacred cosmos to now include the black felon.

In addition, by focusing attention to the intersectionality of blackness, masculinity, and felon identity, Jennings invokes new ways of imagining religious imagery and the social work of black religious institutions as it relates to black felons. Jennings's lyrics resituate the role of the felon in society in new ways. Part of this process of reimagining black male felons is dependent on an increased sensitivity to the conditions of the felon. The increased sensitivity and compassion for black male felons becomes the construction of Beloved Community.

Furthermore, Jennings allows for the development of a new hermeneutical principle for the Doctrine of God. It is not that Jennings creates a point of departure with black theology's perspective concerning the doctrine of God, but rather, he broadens the notions of who is oppressed. Consequently, in doing this he also calls into question the prophetic role of the black church, and recasts the prophetic function of the black male preacher onto the black male felon. In other words, for Jennings the heroic black male preacher figure is no longer the manifest representation of God. Instead, the black male felon emerges as the new voice. He becomes the representation of a liberating God that sits on the side of the oppressed. As a result, the black male preacher becomes the symbol of white institutional desire to regulate black radical behavior. In this light, Jennings reframes conventional black moral representation within black religious consciousness. Jennings also illustrates the idea of the grotesque in creative exchange by recasting the role of the black preacher and the black male felon. This reimagining of the black male felon again points to concrete moments of Beloved Community because the marginalized oppressed person becomes a central part of the community.

Therefore, as black liberation theology continues to ask "how do we dare speak of God in a suffering world, a world in which blacks are humiliated because they are black" it must expand that question to speak of felons who are humiliated simply because they are felons. The questions become enlarged in this way, and the field becomes challenged to deal with oppression in unique ways that signal to its desire to liberate people from the United States's modern-day form of slave. Indeed, Jennings's creative exchange allows for a reimagining of God, black males as preachers and felons, and the contemporary role of the black church.

Furthermore, as a black male felon and artist, Jennings utilizes his music to reimagine black leadership within black churches. His critique of black churches and black church leaders becomes more prevalent as he continues to narrate his personal quest for agency and self-discovery. He creates a discursive space that allows the voice of the felon to be heard. One of the things that becomes clear in this creative exchange with the black church is Jennings's growing belief that the institution has become a social and cultural contradiction. However, the inclusion of the black male felon resolves many of these contradictions.

In light of Jennings's work, I offer a framework wherein we might not only interpret the work of felons as artists through the lens of a new identity category that has yet to be explored by black religious scholars, but also to motivate an exploration for other cultural products such as quilts, paintings, and literature that signify the felon as a symbol of objectification through both political and religious discourse. Scholars such as Charles Long, Edward Wimberly, Anne Streaty Wimberly, and Anthony Pinn have long contended for other hermeneutical approaches to the study of black religion. These alternative hermeneutical approaches attempt to engage deeper meanings and possibilities for thoughts that are rooted in the religious experience of black traditions for the masses of black people in the diaspora.

Jennings's music helps to address the problematic meaning of religion for people in general and black people in particular. This occurs because his music is situated at the intersection of political and religious discourse. Long, Pinn, Wimberly, and other scholars not only argue for the need to resource more diverse black cultural products and artifacts for the interpretation of their religious significance, they also illustrate the need to situate those creative artifacts within the various intersections of human experience in order to show the complexity of human identity.

In *Significations: Signs, Symbols, and Images in the Interpretation of Religion*, Charles Long offer a collection of essays to detail an interpretative methodology that he calls a hermeneutic of ontological dimensions. His hermeneutic conjoins people's social and religious experiences in order to engage his notion concerning the "sacred." In doing this, he avoids a lot of the pathological language that has traditionally defined black religious experience in the history of the study of religion. For Long, this methodology is rooted in an epistemological theory that entreats scholars of religion to take seriously both the social and religious experience of people.

Both the religious and the social inform how people come to understand themselves in the human world that they encounter. Ultimately, Long attempts to make sense of religious phenomenon and interpret the complicated meanings of the religious experience of African Americans in particular.[18] He argues that "religion thus becomes the locus for a meaning that carried an archaic form; it was a root meaning and could thus become the basis for radical critical thought."[19] For this cause, Long sets in motion a renewed conversation between scholars of religious studies and scholars in the human sciences, particularly black scholars within social and human sciences whose work all too often expresses religious and ethical concerns.

Jennings's lyrics points out this complex relationship between the claim of black religion as a radical theoretical construction and the practice of black religion as he experiences it as a black male felon. Through Jennings's music, I find contradiction and contradistinctions between the theoretical formulations of black religion as a liberative project and black religion as a radical pragmatic exercise. It is because of these types of complex experiences that Long highlights the role and influence signification plays in the total hermeneutical discourse for the forming of theoretical formulations.

In addition, those cultures that have endured through political, religious, and militarized power has lasting effects on the work of religion as both a liberative idea and a pragmatic exercise. As a historian, Long begins his study of the history of religion with the nature of religion in the post Enlightenment world of the West. According to Long "there is a complex relationship between the meaning and nature of religion as a subject of academic study and the reality of the peoples and cultures who were conquered and colonized during this same period."[20] This is important for Long because the idea of religion as an "authentic" mode of the human experience has served as the basis for much of its work.

Ever since black people arrived in the West, black religion has faced the persistent task of responding to political structures that were undergirded by Western religious ideals. This normativity was interpreted first through the structural categories of race and class and later through gender and sexuality. Long's contention regarding this complex relationship between nature of religion as the subject for academic inquiry and the reality of people that exists within the structure of society wherein that religion is practiced helps illustrate how the felon, particularly the felon as artist, gets hidden. For Long, this largely occurs because religion, particularly black religion, had to compete with other realities "for the role of normativity regarding the nature and destiny of the human being."[21]

However, the identity of the black felon as an emerging category within these structures was either unrealized or all together ignored. As a result, the reformist structure of the Enlightenment set in place various intellectual structures concerning racial theories and forms of "color symbolism" that justified both economic and military conquest of various people and cultures which required a type of preoccupation by those groups with more widely used structural categories. Long argues that "in this movement both religious and cultures and people throughout the world were created anew through academic disciplinary orientation—they were signified."[22]

In this sense, signification becomes one way in which names are given to certain social realities and locates people within a set of categories, particularly as it relates to colonial and military conquests of groups. In doing this, signification highlights how the process of objectification of those named within these structural categories and concepts engage in complex power arrangements. For Long, these power arrangements are both manifest and latent. First "it is manifest in the intellectual operations that exhibit the ability of the human mind to come to terms with that which is novel."[23] In other words, the fascination with the discovery of the other conditions the intellectual activity which ultimately objectifies categories of people and cultures through the naming process.

Ultimately, failing to critically explore the structures wherein this objectification take place, religious or otherwise, allows for the continual dismissal of other signified identity groups. This power dynamic inevitably appears as one group stands in the position of disinterested conqueror striving to produce knowledge about the conquered other. The conquered "other" is only known by its signified self—an identity which is largely prescribed through some form of militarization. Second, Long argues that power, "is manifest in the manner of passivity that is expressed in the process wherein the active existential and self-identifying *notae* through which a people know themselves is almost completely bypassed for the sake of the conceptual and categorical forms of classification."[24]

Yet, signification is also obscured and undergirded by pervasive latent power dynamics. Ultimately, this dynamic allows the intellectual desire for knowledge of the other to mask the political, economic, and military arrangement that forms the context of the confrontation between the signifier and the signified. As a result, the authentic state of cultural exposure and interaction is never brought into full view within the context of intellectual formulations. Instead, what is ultimately exposed is the ability of intellectual power to merely clarify and describe commonality and difference between the signified and the signifier. These commonalities and differences are revealed through defined categories and procedures. For Long, these "descriptive and analytical categories and taxonomies form the basis for an accusatory or compensational order of meaning."[25] For example, on a descriptive level as in the case of the black male felon, one cannot deny that there are black people who break laws, and groups and communities that have higher rates of incarceration compared to other groups.

We know that communities with higher crime rates and arrest records often express different meanings regarding their orientation in the world. Yet often, those different meanings are accused of being shaped by bad behaviors and lack of responsibility. These descriptive and analytical categories reveal a way of defining groups and communities as subordinate to the controlling group. Rarely do we shine a light on the phenomenon that forms these differences.

Jennings's music illustrates how the existence of the felon is obscured in discourse and how the nature of those labeled felon and their different world views are explored from the lens of non-felon identity categories. For instance, one does not gain much in-depth knowledge about why higher rates of incarceration happen in one community more often than another. The investigation of felons rarely sparks one to fully engage in understanding the types of laws that are broken relative to communities. Indeed, Jennings suggests that rarely does anyone, particularly within black religious context, attempt to locate the cause and effects of criminality on individuals and communities. According to Long, the differences that bring a culture or a people to the attention of the investigator are "the nuances and latencies of that power which is part of the structure of the cultural contact itself manifesting itself as an intellectual curiosity."[26] In this light, Jennings's lyrics emphasize the manner in which black male felons are created as products through the complex signification that Long presents.

The cultural and political situation of the black felon in the United States is one such heritage that African Americans have longed since been forced to address in personal and communal ways. However, the legacy of racial slavery, Jim and Jane Crow, and the heritage of gendered inequality have prescribed for scholars of religion a specific context that has set in motion a preoccupation in the study of religion. This preoccupation has been centered on a set of theories that limit its exploration concerning other ways that black bodies are signified. Long tells us that we should not simply be concerned with representing in outline form the critical responses to the process and influence of signification of signs and symbols that appear through cultural contact.

The emergence of the black felon reminds us that we should be particularly concerned with how the religion of African Americans as a source for new modes of thought has been narrowly interpreted. This is the significance of Jennings's music. He calls African American religion into a creative exchange that opens Beloved Community up to a new mode of being black in the world. For Long, the religion of African Americans has been so encompassed within the cultural categories of American reality that it has overlooked other sites for African American religion. He contends that "Americans of African descent have been forced to deal with several heritages—those of Africa, those of the New World in the form of the cultural and political situation of the United States, and the heritage of a distinctive culture created in this country from this amalgam."[27] This is most pronounced in Jennings's work wherein he critiques the black church and its perception and treatment of black male felons as outsiders of the black church ethos.

The idea of religion as orientation both expands the use of "extra church orientations" such as folklore, music, and lifestyle to understand African American religion as well as address some of the deeper religious issues regarding the situation of black communities that are not commonly demarcated by church leaders and pastors. This challenge to seek out "extra church orientations" provides a measure of space for the insertion of hip hop music and culture and the felons that produce them. Certainly for Long, the black church is not the only context for the meaning of religion in black communities. As a historian of religion he offers other forms of religion in the history of black communities.

I utilize the work of hip hop artists, such as Jennings, to challenge scholars of religion to seek out and interrogate other sites for the meaning of religion that might not be readily apparent through the normative structures that influence inquiry and interpretation. By highlighting the black male felon, I extend the notion of black religion beyond common regulative definitions and norms. For this reason, I appropriate Long's definition of religion to mean orientation in the ultimate sense of the human condition. In other words, according to Long, religion as orientation denotes "how one comes to terms with the ultimate significance in one's place in the world."[28] In this light, Long expands past Christian language as the only example of language for the meaning of religion. I do this by inserting hip hop as a language of black religion and black religious experience.

I also do this work to show the gaps between black male felons and other groups. These gaps highlight how the social condition of the black felon gets muted in the study of religion and the ways and means by which that religious and political discourse gets disconnected. Long's hermeneutical approach is most useful for this project because it helps address the gaps in contemporary hermeneutical approaches for the study of black religion. As Long points out, the problem with many scholars of religion is the tendency to construct frameworks for the study of religion that put at odds the work of sociologist, ethnologists, and anthropologists with the work of phenomenologists and morphologists.

Moreover, the discussion concerning the life conditions of religious people is often not engaged with the discussions of those same people's religious beliefs and practices. Long contends that contemporary studies of religion force students of religion to choose between either the work of sociologists, ethnologists, and anthropologists that focus on practical existential responses to the economic, social, and political conditions of communities or the work of the phenomenologists and the morphologists that interpret religion through the religious experience of the communities that practice them. The former discussions are often expressed without need of a referent or deity and the latter relies on a mystical discourse that tends to ignore the social context of the people within the religious tradition.

It is through the expression of symbols and myths that humans come to understand the world around them. However, wherein symbols express the imaginative experience "through which a new form of the world is discovered by the human consciousness," myths highlight a rupture in cultural life by expressing the concrete ordering of a world that carries with it the idea of permanence. In order to address these gaps, Long contends that scholars of religion must have a different methodological approach to interpret the more complex reality of human experience. In other words, there needs to be a way to interpret concrete forms of cultural life that more fully reveals the complex longing of humanity's search for a more full life. These concrete forms of cultural life are revealed to the human consciousness through the expression of symbols and myths.

By highlighting the link between black male felons' experiences and concrete forms of cultural life, I locate the locus of the rupture between black felons and the world they experience. According to Long "the recitation of the basis for the human condition through the language of myth is a sign that the first step toward human autonomy has already taken place, not simply because the myth tells the story of a rupture but equally because language itself, even the language of myth, is a premonition of human autonomy."[29] In other words, the ideas and stories that black felons utilize to explain and make sense of their social condition highlights their longing to find self-determination within a predetermined structure. This is the start of radical equality for the construction of Beloved Community.

Moreover, this context of human self-determination within ontological structures is the rupture that myths make known. The ability to locate these ruptures and interpret them needs to be the work of scholars of religion. Locating these ruptures also helps define the complex ways that symbols and myths operate as cultural artifacts in understanding human identity. In other words, when humanity encounters the limits of a concrete ordering and meaning in the world it lends to its dependence to an ontological reality that does not provide the fullness of space to express their full imaginative experience. Long argues it this way when he states that " all aspects of culture, or, rather, the manner in which culture is experienced through the forms of language, social structure, work, dance, and so on, convey a sense of creativity and dependence on an ontological dimension."[30] It is within this context of striving for a sense of creativity or autonomy with a dependence on an ontological dimension that Long suggest scholars of religion must begin to interpret this complexity within human cultural artifacts, particularly if we are to resolve the tension between scholars of religion with scholars within other human sciences.

Indeed, a hermeneutic of ontological dimensions help interpret cultural artifacts by engaging the complex ways black felons experience structures of social reality and probing cultural structures for what they say about their source. In *Terror and Triumph: The Nature of Black Religion*, Anthony Pinn contends that Long's "approach works from the presupposition that the sacred—the referent for religion—is manifest in the context of history and gives depth to all modalities of human consciousness and experience."[31] In other words, Long's comparative sensibilities grounds theological concepts in a historical discourse that seeks to understand those concepts through the material reality that is found in humanity's everyday lives. According to Pinn, this approach helps humanity live fuller lives because it involves a critical engagement with the world by exploring the "roots of human perception."[32]

The examination of these communal realities helps to not only construct a better understanding of one's self-consciousness, but also helps communicate the underlying impulses that motivates humanity to grasp the fundamental bases for human presence. Although Pinn contends that Long's work relies too heavily on the notion of sacred and suggests that there are enough "natural" resources available to humanity wherein we might access these inner impulses without need to refer to a sacred space, he still argues that Long's hermeneutic is an "important methodological development because it explores consciousness and historical action in terms of an underlying genius, the prevalent feeling or impulse as genesis of the black liberation broadly conceived."[33] Long's hermeneutic promotes a clearer vision concerning the questions of meaning and purpose that beset humanity.

Long's approach takes as its locus the actions of oppressed groups to perceive and respond to structures of oppression as full moral agents. The ability to do this makes Beloved Community, in this moment, concrete. In this sense, African American people come to be perceived as subjects of history that are consciously addressing systems of power. Thus, they are viewed as the center of their liberation experience. This centrality constructs the way oppressed people exist in Beloved Community.

Both Long and Pinn highlight a way wherein we might become sensitive to the political, religious, and social genius of individuals that are not dependent on existential and doctrinal ideas alone. I utilize this hermeneutical approach as a guidepost to interpret the ways cultural artifacts express secular and religious ideas and notions about what it means to exist at the intersection of three distinct ontological categories—namely black, male, and felon. Indeed, scholars of religious studies and black liberation theology have virtually ignored examining this third category, thus limiting the radical components of the black religious project. As Pinn suggests, "a hermeneutic of the ontological dimensions helps sensitize us to that which through history we often ignore."[34] This approach ultimately allows scholars to investigate the elemental genius of black religion that Jennings's music attempts to seek out.

In addition, this approach is helpful as I interpret the work of Lyfe Jennings and its impact on black radical intellectual production. A hermeneutic of ontological dimension situates the felon at the center of his/her own religious, social, and political reality. As such, Lyfe Jennings's experience and mode of human consciousness as both black male felon and artist reveals within the context of history what it means to be black and male and felon. In this context, Jennings's work confronts Pinns's question regarding, "what is religious about black religion."[35]

Consequently, I also illustrate the manifest and latent power relationships that exist both inside and outside of black cultural spheres. In other words, Jenning's music and lyrics help clarify the "sacred reality" of black male felons that are bound to historical experiences. These experiences clarify an ordering of social structures and realities that highlight the political and religious context wherein black male felons are situated. In doing this, Jennings makes clear what Pinn means when he argues that there is more to the fundamental essence of black religion than just the understanding of religion as historical liberation.

Jennings's music, particularly his challenge to the black church, represents this yearning for a new and complex interpretation of his subjectivity and personhood as it is shaped and impacted by both political and religious discourse. As such, this involves moving beyond simply exploring the way constructs such as churches, mosques, and synagogue structures life meaning within black intellectual life to investigating less explored spaces and structures such as prison, jails and detention facilities as a location for an emerging stream of black radical intellectual production. This emerging stream of black radical intellectual production provides an additional lens wherein we locate new radical agents who represent black imprisoned intellectuals that are often ignored or viewed primarily through race, gender, and class.

The idea of the black felon as a stream within black radical intellectual production entails the broader array of intellectual and creative work that is produced by persons labeled felon, criminal, convict, or other connotations through juridical discursive practices. This stream of black radical intellectual production not only broadens the representation within black radical intellectual traditions but also clarifies the debate on imprisoned intellectuals by offering a more diverse array of people labeled felon within the United States. It also allows scholars to examine how members within this stream articulate ideas about religious, social, political and economic justice issues through historical modes of disenfranchisement and punishment within the United States.

NOTES

1. Chester "Lyfe" Jennings, "Stick Up Kid," recorded January 2004, Columbia Records, track 10 on *Lyfe 268-192*, compact disc.
2. Chester "Lyfe" Jennings, "26 Years 17 Days," recorded January 2004, Columbia Records, track 12 on *Lyfe 268-192*, compact disc.
3. Lyfe Jennings, "26 Years 17 Days," compact disc, Lines 14–17.

4. Lyfe Jennings, "26 Years 17 Days," compact disc, Lines 5–8.

5. This inability to find God begins to impact Jennings's faith. He tells his grandmother that "God ain't where you said he would be." This threatens Jennings's very reality. Yet, in spite of the elusiveness of the "father" God within black institutions, Jennings never gives up his longing to encounter God. His persistent struggle suggests that any theory of black male suffering has to investigate the various moments and ways black males resist erasure, particularly their need to create liberative spaces for their personal and group satisfactions.

6. Lyfe Jennings, "26 Years 17 Days," compact disc, Lines 18–23.

7. Lyfe Jennings, "26 Years 17 Days," compact disc, Lines 24–26.

8. This is mostly ad lib that is recording for the CD.

9. Lyfe Jennings, "Made Up Mind," recorded January 2004, Columbia Records, track 13 on *Lyfe 268-192*, compact disc.

10. Lyfe Jennings, "Made Up Mind," compact disc, Lines 10–15.

11. Lyfe Jennings, "Made Up Mind," compact disc, Lines 5–6.

12. Lyfe Jennings, "Made Up Mind," compact disc, Lines 7–15.

13. James H. Cone, *A Black Theology of Liberation: 20th Anniversary Edition* (Ossining, NY: Orbis Books, 2005), 23.

14. James Cone, *A Black Theology of Liberation*, 5.

15. James Cone, *A Black Theology of Liberation*, 45.

16. James Cone, *A Black Theology of Liberation*, 23.

17. James Cone, *A Black Theology of Liberation*, 45.

18. Long appropriates much of his understanding on phenomenon from Geradus van der Leeuw definition. To better understand Long's thinking on the influence of experience with phenomenon, read Geradus van der Leeuw, *Religion in Essence and Manifestation*, trans. J. E. Turner (London: George Allen & Unwin, 1938). Also, Charles Sanders Pierce, *Collected Papers of Charles Sanders Pierce*, ed. Charles Hartshorne and Paul Weiss (Cambridge, MA: Harvard University Press, 1931), vol. 1; William James, *Essays in Radical Empiricism and a Pluralistic* Universe (Gloucester, MA: Peter Smith Publishing, Inc., 1967); Richard J. Bernstein, "Action, Conduct, and Self-Control," in *Perspectives on Pierce* (New Haven, CT: Yale University Press, 1965), 66–91.

19. Charles Long, *Significations: Signs, Symbols, and Images in the Interpretation of Religion* (Aurora, CO: The Davies Group Publishers, 1995), 8.

20. Charles Long, *Significations: Signs, Symbols, and Images in the Interpretation of Religion*, 4.

21. Charles Long, *Significations: Signs, Symbols, and Images in the Interpretation of Religion*, 3.

22. Charles Long, *Significations: Signs, Symbols, and Images in the Interpretation of Religion*, 4.

23. Charles Long, *Significations: Signs, Symbols, and Images in the Interpretation of Religion*, 5.

24. Charles Long, *Significations: Signs, Symbols, and Images in the Interpretation of Religion*, 5.

25. Charles Long, *Significations: Signs, Symbols, and Images in the Interpretation of Religion*, 5.

26. Charles Long, *Significations: Signs, Symbols, and Images in the Interpretation of Religion*, 5.

27. Charles Long, *Significations: Signs, Symbols, and Images in the Interpretation of Religion*, 7.

28. Charles Long, *Significations: Signs, Symbols, and Images in the Interpretation of Religion*, 7.

29. Charles Long, *Significations: Signs, Symbols, and Images in the Interpretation of Religion*, 34.

30. Charles Long, *Significations: Signs, Symbols, and Images in the Interpretation of Religion*, 35.

31. Anthony Pinn, *Terror and Triumph: The Nature of Black Religion* (Minneapolis: Fortress Press, 2003), 186.

32. Anthony Pinn, *Terror and Triumph: The Nature of Black Religion*, 187.

33. Anthony Pinn, *Terror and Triumph: The Nature of Black Religion*, 187–188.

34. Anthony Pinn, *Terror and Triumph: The Nature of Black Religion*, 187.

35. Anthony Pinn, *Terror and Triumph: The Nature of Black Religion*, 188.

Conclusion

Where Do We Go From Here?

Felons in Gender, Education, and Sexuality

The black male felon as radical political intellectual is often shrouded in a rather longstanding debate regarding the role and function of black captivity through racial slavery and segregation. This debate overshadows the impact that criminal justice policies and the prison regime have on black males' constitutive moral agency. It is because of this concealment that I used the cultural production of black male felons to construct a creative exchange that places their experiences, ideas, practices, and beliefs at the center of political and religious discourse. Centralizing the cultural production of black male felons reshapes our notions of Beloved Community.

By utilizing black male felons and their cultural work I am also able to resituate the locus for Beloved Community. In doing so, I move Beloved Community beyond the realm of religion and spirituality to develop a theoretical notion of Beloved Community that more completely encompasses the black freedom struggle. By engaging black male felons, I not only open Beloved Community to new ideas, experiences, and spaces, but also I reshape the way Beloved Community is understood as a black radical product.

Certainly, King understood and expressed in his later speeches and writings, such as "Where Do We Go From Here," how the concept of Beloved Community was not merely about religious and spiritual experiences. For instance, King speaks about the triple evils of racism, poverty, and militarism, and how they work to maintain forms of domination and oppression. According to King, "our only hope today lies in our ability to recapture the revolutionary spirit and go out into a sometimes hostile world declaring eternal opposition to poverty, racism, and militarism."[1] King believed that a commitment to these goals would challenge the ills in our society and make way for Beloved Community.

In talking about these threats to Beloved Community I show how black radical scholars have avoided adequately addressing black male felons and the ways in which the black male felon has helped to work toward the goal of Beloved Community. I suggest that the work of black male felons encourages us to think about their intellectual and aesthetic contributions to the black freedom struggle, as well as how that work helped to reimagine particular categories of blackness. Both the contributions of black male felons and the reimagining of their value to society reshapes our ideas and practices of Beloved Community.

Among other things, this creative exchange illustrates how black male felons reveal experiences of black people that are not often addressed. Also, placing their cultural production in creative exchange reveals the complex ways black male bodies are targets for incarceration in the United States. For instance, black male felons' cultural production reveal how criminal justice practices help to construct a language on crime that incriminates black males and frames black male bodies as dangerous. However, creative exchange helps to reframe black males in general and black male felons in particular.

Indeed, placing the cultural work of black male felons in creative exchange highlights moments of resistance from carceral spcaes. These spaces have historically limited black males to restrictive discursive realms. Locating those moments of resistance helps to build the liberative language for black radical intellectual traditions. This liberatory language contributes to concepts of freedom and agency which makes Beloved Community possible. Thus, certain black male felons and their cultural production not only serve to reshape Beloved Community but also illustrate how black felons create these liberative spaces for themselves. In other words, the language that emerges from the creative exchange with black male felons helps to broaden the political, social, and religious conceptions of Beloved Community as a liberative discursive space.

Ultimately, I show that inserting the felon into the black radical traditions allows scholars to rework the theory of intellectualism, particularly the idea of the public intellectual, by adding another category of intellectual. Indeed, the addition of the felon refocuses scholars' attention away from the narrow conception of black heroic images and engages scholars to think more about the broader ideas, belongings, and workings within black history.

Reshaping Beloved Community supports my primary argument that the cultural production of black male felons is source material for black radical traditions. These cultural products differentiates the experiences of black felons from black people without felony convictions, and reveals alternative ways that black male felons throughout early US history have resisted racism and social injustice. For this reason, throughout the chapters I show how, when the social and political theories of black male felons are placed in an exchange with other ideas and institutions, the development of concrete structures are made real in the lives of people. We can see most apparently moments where Beloved Community is concretely manifested as theories of black male felons are deployed in a creative exchange with the grotesque.

Therefore, each chapter highlights how and why a creative exchange with black male felons is important for the manifestation of Beloved Community. Chapter 1, "Slave and Free: The Mapping of Race, Religion, and Punishment in the New World," shows how the Beloved Community became closed to diverse experiences of blackness as the expansion of the prison in the nineteenth century began to structure public conversations on race and impact ideas and practices in Christian religion. I show how the experiences of black males and incarceration statistics combined to construct ways of talking about black men and confines them to various forms of carceral spaces.

In addition, through a reflexive interpretation of Nat Turner's Rebellion I show how the institution of slavery not only obliterates the human being, but also how it uses the prison as a tool to justify that obliteration process. As such, chapter 2, "The Construction of Nineteenth-Century Black Prison Radicals," illustrates how placing Nat Turner's radical work in creative exchange highlights how carceral space limits the set of choices available to certain people. In other words, this reflexive interpretation proves how the prison and the criminal justice system helped to diminish black radical praxis. Ultimately, placing Turner's Rebellion in creative exchange constructs new ways of thinking about racial assault and injustices.

In chapter 3, "A Challenge to Black Heroic Images: Huddie Ledbetter and the Politics of a Black Male Felon," I utilize archival material to show how states like Texas reconstructed another form of slavery through the criminal justice system and the way black male felons such as Huddie Ledbetter developed a type of creative exchange to subvert the mission of the prison to entrap black males. Moreover, I show the value of black music to the work of black radical traditions, particularly as a means of locating the cultural production of black male felons.

In chapter 4, "Twentieth-Century Black Radical Prison Intellectuals: Malcolm X, George Jackson, and the Expansion of Nineteenth-Century Black Prison Praxis," I examine the work of black male felons Malcolm X and George Jackson to show how these black male felons utilized the experience of incarceration to inform their social justice work and the way their work influenced later liberation movements. I continue in chapter 5, "Prison Prophets: Twenty-First Century Black Male Felons on Race, Religion, and Mass Incarceration," to show how black male felons as artists utilize hip hop as a means of articulating new ways of thinking about race, religion, and mass incarceration. In particular, I show how hip hop operates as a type of pragmatic philosophy. Lastly, in chapter 6, "Expanding the Beloved

Community: Black Church, Black Felons, and Mass Incarceration," I explore in depth the music of hip hop artist Lyfe Jennings. In doing this, I show how his work in a creative exchange with the grotesque makes possible new ways of thinking about Beloved Community.

However, the evolution of black radical traditions must continue to find new ways to unite experience with knowledge and knowledge with pragmatic solutions in order to provide a space wherein other oppressed people, particularly black incarcerated bodies, can continue to address socio-cultural and socio-political dehumanizing practices. In particular, black studies must evolve in many of the same ways and guided by many of the same pragmatic and theoretical philosophical notions found within American hip hop, particularly the way hip hop becomes both a form of cultural criticism and an extension of the black prophetic tradition.[2] As James contends, "given its mission and longevity, black intellectualism has become the form of American intellectualism best adept and well versed in truth telling about democracy crippled by racism."[3]

This book endeavors to apply black studies to activists and popular culture more thoroughly and persistently by highlighting black male felons in the person of Nat Turner, Huddie Ledbetter, Malcolm X, George Jackson, Lyfe Jennings, and others. It does this to show how black male felons are a site for black radical traditions. In highlighting these black male felons, I show how black radical traditions can begin to access new ways of thinking about felons and incorporating men labeled as felon through a more constructive lens.

Indeed, over the last thirty years, the increasing rate of incarceration has lent to an ever-growing disparity. This disparity is felt in every aspect of black life across class and gender lines. This has negatively impacted the vitality of some the United States's most vulnerable and marginalized groups. More distressing to the trend of incarceration in the United States is that the Department of Justice Bureau of Justice Statistics concluded that if the incarceration rate does not make a substantial change in direction, then they anticipate approximately 6.6 percent of all persons in the United States born in 2001 will serve time in state or federal prison during their lifetime. According to Arditti and Parkman's study, "lived meanings around dependency on family as a result of incarceration ran counter to young men's self-definitions of adult manhood."[4]

Therefore, scholars of black radical traditions must continue to work in this area in order to bring to light the various ways incarceration impacts American life and culture in general and black people in particular. Certainly, the next step in this investigation of incarceration of black people has to explore other categories of black felons. For this reason, a deeper investigation of black women felons is integral to future inquiry. Indeed, scholars must expand beyond merely black male felons to show the diversity within the category of felons. This is crucial if we are to engage the fullness of this new identity group.

Since the construction of the felon is not limited to black males, and since black women are the fastest growing population of people going into prison, scholars must begin to take seriously the work of black female felons as well. Although the empirical numbers are not equal to black men, the growing trend of black women in prison and jails might offer further insight on black captivity and mobilization.

Most importantly, this book tries to show how removing the cloak of invisibility on black incarceration requires being intentional about listening to the voice of felons both men and women. Breea C. Willingham, in her article *Black Women's Prison Narratives and the Intersection of Race, Gender and Sexuality in US Prisons*, argues that in order to address intervention and policy changes in the criminal justice system, particularly for black female felons, "it becomes especially important to hear their stories to increase our understanding of their prison experience."[5] Indeed, disregarding the particular voice of felons by gender hinders the "unique insight into interlocking patterns of oppression that contributes to their incarceration."[6] This new voice develops a new and creative space to hear felons in their own words and highlights unique discriminatory practice against felons as it relates to race, gender, and sexuality. [7]

Furthermore, both male and female felons complicate binary concepts that are largely upheld within black religion, particularly black liberation and womanist theology. As Willingham contends, "learning about imprisonment from the people experiencing it raises key issues that go beyond an immediate concern with the institution of the prison, as prisoner writing interrogates notions of captivity, racism, classism, and oppression."[8] Black female felons stretch the boundaries beyond the borders of persistent notions as prescribed in ontological blackness.

The advent of the black female felon further liberates blackness from racial and gender oppression. So, while the narrative for the felon in this project began with the history of incarceration itself and its impact on the identity, voice, and personhood of the black male felon, we have to track that history through gender. For instance, "whereas white women prison writers are 'doubly marginal' . . . black women suffer threefold—as a woman, prisoner, and African American."[9] Within this track, we might discover the way gendered felon identities express themselves and move through society in ways that speak to feminist and masculinity discourse.

In the end, I move Beloved Community past regulative religious ideals and language that emerge from a black southern freedom movement that was preoccupied with a set of human conditions in which domination does not exist. Although I show respect for that historical context, I emphasize a set of practical political and economic goals in order to show the ways in which human beings have to continually struggle to construct a more humane world. In this way, Beloved Community takes on a type of pragmatic dimension. In other words, Beloved Community is a place that humans will always have to struggle to find because it is constantly moving. It does not have a fixed goal or normative idea to it, but rather, has a set of practices that people have to engage in order to construct a better place. This pragmatic dimension, particularly in relation to the grotesque, highlights a lineage of Beloved Community that is not often explored.

I show how this notion of Beloved Community emerges most prominently from a radical black agency that is most strongly linked to black religious figures within Prince Hall Masonic Orders. Indeed, linking Beloved Community to these earlier black radicals not only connects Nat Turner, Huddie Ledbetter, Malcolm X, George Jackson, and Lyfe Jennings to Beloved Community, it also reshapes the traditional notions of Beloved Community. In other words, reshaping Beloved Community to a longer intellectual history allows black radical scholars to employ a new language and a different set of metaphors for the construction of Beloved Community.

Thus we must continue to address the social complexity of discrimination and marginalization that arises because of incarceration. It is my hope that this project sparks a new conversation with a broad and diverse audience of scholars, activists, and popular culture in order to address the needs and concerns of felons in the United States. It is my hope that this project helps to make others aware of the need to connect humanitarian work to social science projects, particularly in education, health, and public policy.

The need for this interdisciplinary work is evidenced in the various statistics that expose the harsh reality of people and communities impacted by incarceration. Indeed, in their phenomenological study on young male felons, Arditti and Parkman reveal that "reentry [of felons] was a developmental paradox that embodied contradictions about employment, maturity, and dependence on family."[10] The empirical statistics regarding incarceration in the United States is not only staggering, but the cultural production of black felons reveals the stigma associated with imprisonment. In addition, their cultural production informs the way cities develop communities and support capital industries in particular areas. In other words, their cultural production helps make the Beloved Community concrete.

NOTES

1. Martin Luther King, Jr., "Where Do We Go From Here: Chaos or Community?," in *A Testament of Hope: The Essential Writings and Speeches of Martin Luther King, Jr.*, ed. James M. Washington (New York: HarperCollins, 1991), 632.

2. For more information about the Black Atlantic Traditions correlation to American Pragmatism, refer to Cornel West's *The American Evasion of Pragmatism* and Eddie Glaude's *In a Shade of Blue.*

3. Joy James, *Transcending the Talented Tenth: Black Leaders and American Intellectuals* (New York: Routledge, 1997), 3.

4. Joyce A. Arditti and Tiffaney Parkman, "Young Men's Reentry After Incarceration: A Development Paradox," *Family Relations* 60, no. 2 (April 2011): 205.

5. Breea C. Willingham, "Black Women's Prison Narratives and the Intersection of Race, Gender, and Sexuality in US Prisons," *Critical Survey* 23, no. 3 (2011): 55.

6. Breea C. Willingham, "Black Women's Prison Narratives and the Intersection of Race, Gender, and Sexuality in US Prisons," 56.

7. In addition, this method has roots within the work of black womanist theology which desires to expands black experience past masculine experiences. Similar to what Willingham suggests in liberating black female felons, womanist ethics argues that "the Black woman's literary tradition is the best available literary repository for understanding the ethical values Black women have created and cultivated in their ongoing participation in this society" (Cannon, 7). The unfortunate case, however, is the voices of black female felons is not significant in the lexicon of womanist ethics. Just as womanist theology and ethics "makes regulative a womanist consciousness that includes within itself a privilege of difference" so too does the voice of black female felon help to construct a separate yet vital constitutive category (Anderson, 104).

8. Breea C. Willingham, "Black Women's Prison Narratives and the Intersection of Race, Gender, and Sexuality in US Prisons," 57.

9. Breea C. Willingham, "Black Women's Prison Narratives and the Intersection of Race, Gender, and Sexuality in US Prisons," 57.

10. Joyce A. Arditti and Tiffaney Parkman, "Young Men's Reentry After Incarceration: A Development Paradox," 205.

Bibliography

Alexander, Michelle. *The New Jim Crow: Mass Incarceration in the Age of Colorblindness*. New York: The New Press, 2010.

Anderson, Victor. *Beyond Ontological Blackness: An Essay on African American Religious and Cultural Criticism*. New York: Continuum Publishing Company, 1995. Print.

———. *Creative Exchange: A Constructive Theology of African American Religious Experience*. Minneapolis: Fortress Press, 2008. Print.

Arditti, Joyce A., and Tiffaney Parkman. "Young Men's Reentry After Incarceration: A Development Paradox." *Family Relations* 60, no. 2 (April 2011): 205–20. Print.

Bogues, Anthony. *Black Heretics Black Prophets: Radical Political Intellectuals*. New York: Routledge, 2003. Print.

Bracher, Mark. *Lacan, Discourse, and Social Change: A Psychoanalytic Cultural Criticism*. Ithaca, NY: Cornell University Press, 1993. Print.

Brooks, Joanna, and John Saillant. *"Face Zion Forward": First Writers of the Black Atlantic, 1785–1798*. Boston: Northeastern University Press, 2002. Print.

Bruce Jr., Dickson D. *The Origins of African American Literature 1680–1865*. Charlottesville: University Press of Virginia, 2001. Print.

Butler, Judith. *Gender Trouble*. New York: Routledge, 1990. Print.

Calo, Mary Ann. "Alain Locke and American Art Criticism." *American Art* 18, no. 1 (Spring 2004): 88–97. Print.

Canon, Katie G. *Black Womanist Ethics*. Atlanta: Scholars Press, 1988.

Caster, Peter. *Prisons, Race, and Masculinity: In Twentieth-Century U.S. Literature and Film*. Columbus: The Ohio State University Press, 2008. Print.

Chao, Shun-liang. *Rethinking the Concept of the Grotesque: Crashaw, Baudelaire, Magritte*. Oxford: Legenda, 2010. Print.

Cixous, Hélène. "Sorties." In *New French Feminism: An Anthology*, edited by Elaine Marks and Isabelle de Courtivron, 90–98. New York: Harvester, 1980. Print.

Conaway, Carol B. "Mary Ann Shadd Cary: A Visionary of Black Press." In *Black Women's Intellectual Traditions: Speaking Their Minds*, edited by Kristin Waters and Carol B. Conaway, 216–45. Burlington: University of Vermont Press, 2007. Print.

Cone, James H. *A Black Theology of Liberation: 20th Anniversary Edition*. Ossining, NY: Orbis Books, 2005. Print.

———. *Martin & Malcolm & America: A Dream or a Nightmare*. Ossining, NY: Orbis Books, 2012.

———. *The Cross and the Lynching Tree*. Ossining, NY: Orbis Books, 2011.

Crane, Gregg D. *Race, Citizenship, and Law in American Literature*. Cambridge: Cambridge University Press, 2002.

Crouch, Stanley, and Playthell Benjamin. *Reconsidering the Souls of Black Folk: Thoughts on the Groundbreaking Classic Work of W.E.B. Du Bois*. Philadelphia: Running Press, 2002.

Davis, David Brion. *The Problem of Slavery in Western Culture*. New York: Oxford University Press, 1966.

Delany Martin R. *The Condition, Elevation, Emigration, and Destiny of the Colored People of the United States*. Bensenville, IL: Lushena Books, 2014.

———. *The Origins of Races and Color*. Baltimore: Black Classic Press, 1991.

Dewey, John. "Historical Roots and Reflections." In *The Philosophy of John Dewey*, 58–95. Chicago: The University of Chicago Press, 1973.

———. "The Search for the Great Community." In *The Later Works, 1925–1953*, vol. 2, 325–50. Carbondale: Southern Illinois University Press, 1984.

Douglass, Frederick. *My Bondage and My Freedom*. n.p.: Seven Treasures Publications, 2009. Print.

———. "What to the Slave is the Fourth of July?" http://teachingamericanhistory.org/library/document/what-to-the-slave-is-the-fourth-of- july/. Web.

Du Bois, W. E. B. "Criteria of Negro Art." *The Crisis* (October 1926): 993–1002.

———. *Darkwater: Voices from Within the Veil*. Mineola, NY: Dover Publications, Inc., 1999.

———. *Writing: The Suppression of the African Slave-Trade/ The Souls of Black Folk/ Dusk to Dawn Essays*. New York: Literary Classics of the United States, Inc., 1986.

———. *The Souls of Black Folk*. New York: Barnes and Noble Classics, 2003.

———. *The Philadelphia Negro: A Social Study*. Philadelphia: University of Pennsylvania Press, 1996.

———. *The Autobiography of Du Bois: A Soliloquy On Viewing My Life from the Last Decade of its First Century*. New York: International Publishers, 1968.

Eagleton, Terry. "The Ideology of the Aesthetic." *Poetics Today* 9, no. 2 (1988): 327–338.

Ernest, John. *Liberation Historiography: African American Writers and the Challenge of History 1794–1861*. Chapel Hill: The University of North Carolina Press, 2004.

Foucault, Michel. *Discipline & Punish: The Birth of the Prison*. New York: Vintage Books, 1977, 1995.

Gilroy, Paul. *The Black Atlantic: Modernity and Double Consciousness*. Cambridge, MA: Harvard University Press, 1993.

Glaude Jr., Eddie, and Cornel West, eds. *African American Religious Thought: An Anthology*. Louisville, KY: Westminster John Knox Press, 2003.

Glaze, Lauren E., and Laura M. Maruschak. "Parents in Prison and Their Minor Children." In *Bureau of Justice Statistics Special Report* (August 2008). http://www.bjs.gov/content/pub/pdf/pptmc.pdf.

Goff, Phillip Atiba, Matthew Christian Jackson, Brooke Allison Lewis Di Leone, Carmen Marie Culotta, and Natalie Ann DiTomasso. "The Essence of Innocence: Consequences of Dehumanizing Black Children." *Journal of Personality and Social Psychology* (February 24, 2014). http://www.apa.org/pubs/journals/releases/psp-a0035663.pdf.

Holmes, Eugene C. "Alain Locke and the New Negro Movement." *Negro American Literature Forum* 2, no. 3 (Autumn 1968): 60–68.

Hopkins, Dwight N. *Introducing Black Theology of Liberation*. Ossining, NY: Orbis Books, 1999.

Irigaray, Luce. "This Sex Which Is Not One." In *New French Feminism: An Anthology*, edited by Elaine Marks and Isabelle de Courtivron, 99–106. New York: Harvester, 1981.

Jackson, George. *Soledad Brother: The Prison Letters of George Jackson*. Chicago: Lawrence Hill Books, 1994.

———. "Interview with Karen Wald." In *The New Abolitionists (Neo) Slave Narrativesand Contemporary Prison Writings*, edited by Joy James, 227–34. New York: State University of New York Press, 2005.

James, Joy. *Transcending the Talented Tenth: Black Leaders and American Intellectuals*. New York: Routledge, 1997.

———. *Imprisoned Intellectuals: America's Political Prisoners Write on Life, Liberation, and Rebellion*. Lanham, MD: Rowman & Littlefield Publishers, 2003.

Jennings, Lyfe. "Made Up Mind." *Lyfe 268-192*. Columbia, 2004, compact disc.

———. "26 Years 17 Days." *Lyfe 268-192*. Columbia, 2004, compact disc.

King, Martin Luther. *A Testament of Hope: The Essential Writings and Speeches of Martin Luther King, Jr*. Edited by James M. Washington. New York: HarperCollins Publishers, 1986.

———. "Where Do We Go From Here: Chaos or Community?" In *A Testament of Hope: The Essential Writings and Speeches of Martin Luther King, Jr.*, edited by James M. Washington, 555–633. New York: HarperCollins, 1991.

———. "Remaining Awake Through a Great Revolution." In *A Testament of Hope: The Essential Writings and Speeches of Martin Luther King, Jr.*, edited by James M. Washington, 268–78. New York: HarperCollins, 1991.

Lacan, Jacques. *Feminine Sexuality*. New York: Pantheon Books, 1985.

Levine, Robert. *Martin Delany, Frederick Douglass, and the Politics of Representative Identity*. Chapel Hill: The University of North Carolina Press, 1997.

Lewis, David Levering. *W. E. B. Du Bois: A Biography*. New York: Henry Holt and Company, 2009.

Lincoln, C. Eric, and Lawrence H. Mimiya. *The Black Church in the African American Experience*. Durham, NC: Duke University Press, 1990.

Locke, Alain. "Pluralism and Intellectual Democracy." In *The Philosophy of Alain Locke: Harlem Renaissance and Beyond*, edited by Leonard Harris, 51–66. Philadelphia: Temple University Press, 1991.

———. "Value and Imperatives." In *The Philosophy of Alain Locke: Harlem Renaissance and Beyond*, edited by Leonard Harris, 31–50. Philadelphia: Temple University Press, 1991.

Long, Charles H. *Signification: Signs, Symbols and Images in the Interpretation of Religion*. Aurora, CO: The Davies Group Publishers, 1995.

Lumsden, Linda. "Good Mothers with Guns: Framing Black Womanhood in the Black Panther, 1968–1980." In *Journalism and Mass Communication Quarterly*, 900–922. Thousand Oaks, CA: Sage Publications, 2009.

Lynd, Staughton. *Intellectual Origins of American Radicalism*. New York: Cambridge University Press, 2009.

Malcolm X. *Malcolm X Speaks: Selected Speeches and Statements*. Edited by George Breitman. New York: Merit Publishers, 1965.

———. "The Ballot or the Bullet." In *Imprisoned Intellectuals: America's Political Prisoners Write on Life, Liberation, and Rebellion*, edited by Joy James, 48–61. Lanham, MD: Rowman & Littlefield Publishers, 2003.

Mannion, James. *The Essentials of Philosophy: The Basic Concepts of the World's Greatest Thinkers*. New York: Fall River Press, 2002.

Marable, Manning. "Black Studies and the Racial Mountain." *Souls: A Critical Journal of Black Politics, Culture, and Society* 2, no. 3 (June 5, 2009): 17–36.

———. *W.E.B. Du Bois: Black Radical Democrat*. Boston: Twayne Publishers, 1986.

Marrant, John. "The Sermon on the 24th Day of June 1789, Being the Festival of St. John the Baptist, at the Request of the Right Worshipful the Grand Master Prince Hall, and the Rest of the Brethren of the African Lodge of the Honorable Society of Free and Accepted Masons in Boston." In *"Face Zion Forward": First Writers of the Black Atlantic, 1785–1798*, edited by Joanna Brooks and John Saillant, 77–92. Boston: Northeastern University Press, 2002.

Mitchell, Beverly Eileen. *Black Abolitionism: A Quest for Human Dignity*. New York: Orbis Books, 2005.

Muhammad, Khalil Gibran. *The Condemnation of Blackness: Race, Crime, and the Making of Modern Urban America*. Cambridge, MA: Harvard University Press, 2010. Print.

Pager, Devah. "Black in American 2." Interview by Soledad O'Brien. *Soledad O'Brien Presents*, CNN, 2009. DVD, 35:25.

———. *Marked: Race, Crime and Finding Work in an Era of Mass Incarceration*. Chicago: The University of Chicago Press, 2007. Print.

Patterson, Orlando. *Slavery and Social Death: A Comparative Study*. Cambridge, MA: Harvard University Press, 1982.

Perkinson, Robert. *Texas Tough: The Rise of America's Prison Empire*. New York: Picador, 2010.

Pinn, Anthony B. "Black Bodies in Pain and Ecstasy: Terror, Subjectivity, and the Nature of Black Religion." In *Nova Religio* 7, no. 1 (2003): 76–89.

———. *Terror and Triumph: The Nature of Black Religion*. Minneapolis: Fortress Press, 2003.

Pratt, Geronimo. "Interview with Heiki Kleffner." In *The New Abolitionists (Neo) Slave Narratives and Contemporary Prison Writings*, edited by Joy James, 235–46. New York: State University of New York Press, 2005.

Price, Emmett G., ed. *The Black Church and Hip Hop Culture: Toward Bridging the Generational Divide*. Lanham, MD: Scarecrow Press, 2012.

Robinson, Cedric J. *Black Marxism: The Making of Black Radical Traditions*. London: Zed Books, 1983.

Rodríguez, Dylan. *Forced Passages: Imprisoned Radical Intellectuals and the U.S. Prison Regime*. Minneapolis: University of Minneapolis Press, 2006.

Rose, Tricia. *In The Hip Hop Wars: What We Talk About When We Talk About Hip Hop—And Why It Matters*. New York: Basic Books, 2008.

Rothstein, Richard. *Race and Public Housing: Revisiting the Federal Role*. Web. Economic Policy Institute, 17 December 2012. http://www.epi.org/publication/race-public-housing-revisiting-federal-role/.

Sankofa, Shaka. "An Interview with Shaka Sankofa (Gary Graham) 1996." In *The New Abolitionists(Neo) Slave Narratives and Contemporary Prison Writings*, edited by Joy James, 275–86. New York: State University of New York Press, 2005.

Shakur, Sanyika. *Monster: The Autobiography of an L.A. Gang Member*. New York: Penguin Books, 1993.

Shusterman, Richard. "Art in Action, Art Infraction: Goodman, Rap, Pragmatism." In *Practicing Philosophy: Pragmatism and the Philosophical Life*. New York: Routledge, 1997.

Stauffer, John. *The Black Hearts of Men: Radical Abolitionists and the Transformation of Race*. Cambridge, MA: Harvard University Press, 2001.

Thurman, Howard. *A Strange Fruit: The Best of Howard Thurman on Religious Experience and Public Life*. Edited by Walter Earl Fluker and Catherine Tumber. Boston: Beacon Press, 1998.

———. *The Search for Common Ground*. Richmond, IN: Friends United Press, 1986.

Trulear, Harold Dean. "Balancing Justice with Mercy: Creating a Healing Community." *Social Work and Christianity* 38, no. 1 (2011): 74–87.

Turner, Nat. *The Confessions of Nat Turner*. Baltimore: Thomas R. Gray, 1831.

Vesely-Flad, Rima. "The Social Covenant and Mass Incarceration: Theologies of Race and Punishment." *Anglican Theological Review* 93, no. 4 (2011): 541–62.

Walker, David. *David Walker's Appeal: The Coloured Citizens of the World, but in Particular, and Very Expressly, to Those of the United States of America*. New York: Hill and Wang, 1965.

Wallace, Maurice O. *Constructing the Black Masculine: Identity and Ideality in African American Men's Literature and Culture, 1775–1995*. Durham, NC: Duke University Press, 2002.

Washington, James M., ed. *A Testament of Hope: The Essential Writings and Speeches of Martin Luther King, Jr*. San Francisco: Harper San Francisco, 1991.

Washington, Mary Helen. "Anna Julia Cooper: A Voice from the South." In *Black Women's Intellectual Traditions: Speaking Their Minds*, edited Kristin Waters and Carol B. Conaway, 249–68. Burlington: University of Vermont Press, 2007.

West, Cornel. *Prophesy Deliverance!: An Afro-American Revolutionary Christianity*. Louisville, KY: Westminster John Knox Press, 2002.

Western, Bruce. *Punishment and Inequality in America*. New York: Russell Sage Foundation, 2006.

Willingham, Breea C. "Black Women's Prison Narratives and the Intersection of Race, Gender, and Sexuality in US Prisons." *Critical Survey* 23, no. 3 (2011): 55–56.

YouTube video. "The Cross and the Lynching Tree (James Hal Cone and Bill Moyers)." https://www.youtube.com/watch?v=BVyo5dzYs44. Published January 26, 2014. Web.

YouTube video. "Leadbelly and Lomax, 1940's—Film 429." https://www.youtube.com/watch?v=w-t9YlYa_S8. Published September 20, 2013.Web.

YouTube video. "The Story of American Folk Music 1." https://www.youtube.com/watch?v=F9ZNgpb_NkM. Published May 1, 2013. Web.

YouTube video. "Day of the Gun." https://www.youtube.com/watch?v=7XRuLlwx1sw. Published July 19, 2012. Web.

YouTube clip. "George Jackson Speaks! 1971 Interview." https://www.youtube.com/watch?v=P8Va-wxoJYQ. Published May 22, 2015. Web.

Index

About the Author

Dr. Marlon A. Smith is a scholar-activist who has over twenty years of experience working with community and faith-based organizations in the areas of community development and outreach. He is the founder of Black Greeks Speak Social Justice and Human Rights Council (BGS), an education and policy studies organization. BGS brings together academic and activist culture for the development of policy and social justice projects. He is also the senior manager of Policy and Engagement for Baker Ripley (formerly Neighborhood Centers Houston). Prior to working for Baker Ripley, Dr. Smith served as the Texas State reentry manager for the Innerchange Freedom Initiative (IFI). The IFI is one of the oldest and largest faith-based pre-release prison reentry programs in the country under Prison Fellowship Ministries. As the reentry manager, Dr. Smith developed partnerships with local, state, and national public officials, educators, and advocacy organizations to impact the rate of incarceration in communities of color, and developed programs and policy initiatives to address the challenges previously incarcerated men and women face when they leave prison and jails. While at IFI, Dr. Smith helped to reduce the recidivism rate of program graduates to 13 percent, and increased the number of men enrolled in a college degree program by over 65 percent.

Dr. Smith attended Texas Tech University and the University of Houston, earning a bachelor's in journalism with a minor in African American studies. He went on to earn his master's in theological studies from Brite Divinity School at Texas Christian University. He later earned his PhD in interdisciplinary studies, majoring in humanities and culture with a specialization in Martin Luther King, Jr. studies, from Union Institute & University. Dr. Smith continues to work with local, national, and international organizations to bridge academic, religious, and activist life for the development of concrete institutions and partnerships. He currently lectures in Africana studies at the University of Houston.